Dissertations
in
American Economic History

This is a volume in the Arno Press collection

Dissertations in American Economic History

Advisory Editor
Stuart Bruchey

Research Associate
Eleanor Bruchey

See last pages of this volume for a complete list of titles.

LONG TERM CAPITAL FLOWS AND THE GREAT DEPRESSION:
The Role of the United States, 1927-1933

Heywood W. Fleisig

ARNO PRESS
A New York Times Company
New York – 1975

First publication in book form, Arno Press, 1975

DISSERTATIONS IN AMERICAN ECONOMIC HISTORY
ISBN for complete set: 0-405-07252-X
See last pages of this volume for titles.

Manufactured in the United States of America

Publisher's Note: This dissertation was reproduced from the best available copy.

Library of Congress Cataloging in Publication Data

Fleisig, Heywood W
Long term capital flows and the great depression.

(Dissertations in American economic history)
Originally presented as the author's thesis, Yale, 1969.
Bibliography: p.
1. Investments, American--History. 2. Depressions--1929. I. Title. II. Series.
HG4910.F59 1975 332.6'0973 75-2580
ISBN 0-405-07200-7

FOREWORD

I. Introduction

Stripped of qualification, the following text argues that the world depression began in the United States: it was neither caused externally nor an unfortunate confluence of unhappy circumstances. Two major developments in the United States led to the world depression. The first was the decline in long term international lending in 1928 and 1929 that was largely a product of American prosperity; indeed, it is the conjunction of American prosperity with worsening conditions elsewhere in 1928 and 1929 that has misled many investigators into concluding that the depression spread from the world to the United States. The second step, largely independent of the first, was the decline in U.S. imports that occurred between 1930 and 1933.

Since the completion of this dissertation, I have had considerable opportunity to reconsider some of the issues raised in it.* In this new introduction I will try to describe how I now think the problem might be approached so that the reader, armed with this structure, might more easily approach the problems in the text.

The assertions made in the first paragraph may be decomposed into several distinct propositions that require independent evidence and argument. First, we must show that the decline in U.S. long term lending and U.S. imports had some adverse impact on world economic activity and that they were independent of each other. Then we must show that these effects

---

* H. Fleisig, "The United States and the Non-European Periphery during the Early Years of the Great Depression", H. Van der Wee, ed., The Great Depression Revisited (The Hague: Martinus Nyhoff, 1973).

were more important than the effects of other independent factors that might also be used to explain the world depression. Finally, we must show that international factors were not responsible for the original declines in U.S. long term lending and imports that set the chain of events in progress.

In unraveling these questions, several problems arise in deciding just what constitutes an "explanation" of the depression. Not wishing to add to the world's supply of jokes about methodology, let me only promise that an investment of a few pages in discussing some of these issues will repay us in time saved separating one explanation from another. Having done that, we can work through the stages of the discussion and conclude by placing the findings of the thesis in the context of the all-important qualifications that we stripped away at the opening.

II. "Explaining" the World Depression

Even a casual student is aware that there are a number of plausible explanations of the world depression, or, to put it another way, there are a number of apparently sensible answers to the question "Why was there a world depression?" We need clear and satisfactory grounds for accepting some explanations and dismissing others.

Part of the confusion over the "explanation" of the world depression is a semantic difficulty rather easily resolved: some explanations treat the origins of the depression while others treat the severity, the latter referring generally to its length, quantity of resources unemployed, and the number of countries and regions it affected. What might be a satisfactory explanation of the origins might not be a satisfactory explanation of the severity, yet together these explanations might comprise a coherent and plausible answer to a more precisely phrased question such as "Why did the world depression begin and why was it so severe?"

Less easily resolved is the confusion over the explanation of the world depression that rests on questions concerning the adequacy of economic theory and the logic of our notions of explanation. Let us look at a simple and well-behaved case first.

Usually what an economist means when he talks about an "explanation" is the invoking of a general rule of economic behavior, sometimes formally embodied in a model, to "cover" a particular event. For example, were there a year in which a peculiar combination of ideal weather conditions in the United States combined to produce an unusually large wheat crop, and we observed a decline in the price of wheat, an economist might "explain" the price decline with a story like "an outward shift in the supply curve for wheat 'caused' a decline in the price." Other economists would find this story reasonable because the conditions necessary for its plausibility -- upward sloping supply curves, downward sloping demand curves, and the relation between weather and crop growth -- can be shown to be broadly consistent with many other beliefs about economic and biological behavior, all of which, to one degree or another, are consistent with what we observe in the world. The belief of the typical economist in such a model is so strong that were we to observe a bumper crop accompanied by a <u>rise</u> in the price of wheat, we would normally still believe in the underlying view of the world and search for the factor not included in our explanation that reconciles the observation with the simple theory: for example, we would look for a failure of a wheat crop in some other market or a more-than-compensating outward shift in demand curves. Indeed, the degree of belief in such a model is so strong that were someone to claim that the occurrence of a price increase in the face of the bumper crop proves the underlying model false, proves perhaps that demand curves must slope upward and supply curves downward, his story would probably be rejected as implausible even if no-one had bothered to look for the offsetting exogenous factor.

This example should be sufficient to indicate two points: "explanation" of an event consists in subsuming the event under the appropriate economic model, whether in mathematical or verbal form; "cause" is not, as Hume observed long ago, discovered by looking at sequences in the world, but rather by examining changes in exogenous factors or parameters in the model--"cause" is <u>defined</u> by the model.

While this procedure may enable us to explain events like a fall in the price of wheat in a satisfactory way, several limitations emerge when we try to perform the same operation in explaining the world depression. These difficulties arise when the covering law (or generalization about economic behavior) is stated in probabilistic terms, when the event involves changes in economic magnitudes larger than those over which the law has been traditionally observed to operate, when there is disagreement over the appropriate covering law, when there is no appropriate covering law, and when explanations are couched in terms of events that did not occur. Let us look more closely at these problems.

When a unique covering law exists, it is customary in the social sciences to state it in probabilistic terms. The problem of subsuming a unique historical incident under a probabilistic law has not been solved entirely satisfactorily.

Our confidence in the empirical validity of the general rules of economic behavior is normally based on observing the rule operate over a large number of relatively normal periods during which changes in variables tend to be small. It is not obvious that the same rules accurately describe economic behavior when changes are relatively large, as they were during the depression. As a formal statistical procedure, the confidence intervals for our predictions grow larger as explanatory variables depart substantially from their usual values. But even that statistical procedure assumes that the underlying model remains true; however, we cannot be confident of that.

Lack of agreement over which is the appropriate covering law affects the explanation of the depression most seriously when "monetarist" and "Keynesian" views of how the economy functions lead to attaching different significance to particular events. In some cases, we may determine the appropriate view by examining the depression more closely and looking for the existence of phenomena predicted by one view but not by another. In other cases this is impossible, and determining which explanation is correct depends on resolution of the broader empirical question of which view of the world is ultimately proved most appropriate.

In some cases there is no covering law: phenomena may appear to merit notice but are not incorporated into the body of economic theory. There may then be no easy way to compare factors outside the model that appear important with factors that are important within the model's frame of reference. It is inappropriate, of course, to take this as evidence of the unimportance of the factors not included in the model. These difficulties are pronounced in dealing with explanations centering on the effect of the stock market on expectations, the burden of the war debts on the international capital markets, and the importance of a "center" for the smooth functioning of the gold standard.

Finally, some explanations are put forward in terms of the failure of certain variables or structures to change. For example, some explanations of the depression cite the failure of the Federal Reserve System to run a more expansionary monetary policy, the failure to institute a system of flexible exchange rates, or the failure of government policymakers to increase intergovernmental cooperation toward the solution of common problems. It has been objected that such "explanations" must be dismissed out of hand, since something that did occur cannot be caused by something that did not occur, or, alternatively, if we do choose to view something that did not occur as the "cause" of something that did occur, why do we not view that same non-occurring event as the cause of every other event when it did not occur. This objection is, I believe, an excessively formal objection to reasonable common usage. It is a simple semantic task to convert explanations phrased in terms of non-occurring events into explanations phrased in terms of occurring events: for example, we might speak instead of the Federal Reserve System passively permitting the money supply to decline, or the rigidity of a fixed exchange rate system, or factors that explain an inadequate level of intergovernmental cooperation.

The evaluation of explanations phrased in terms of non-occurring events and the comparison of the importance of those events with causal factors that did occur is a bit more complex. It is first necessary to determine what impact the event that did not occur would have had, were it to have occurred. For example, it would be necessary to demonstrate how the income path would have changed had the Federal Reserve System pursued a different monetary policy. Then it is necessary to make some historical judgment about the reasonableness or usualness of the course of action being proposed. This is presumably why a number of economists and historians have asked why Roosevelt did not pursue a more active fiscal policy, while that question has never been asked about Andrew Jackson. A similar procedure applies to market behavior. To assert, for example, that the failure of short term capital to flow in greater volume in response to arbitrage incentives caused greater income adjustment, one presumably would want to show that short term capital was flowing at historically low rates; one would be interested in deviations from customary market behavior.

III. The Decline in U.S. Long Term Lending and the World Depression

The stock market boom led to a reduction in net U.S. long-term lending in several ways. During the second half of 1928 and the first three quarters of 1929, foreign purchases of U.S. stocks rose and U.S. purchases of outstanding foreign securities fell. In the face of rising long-term interest rates, U.S. new long-term portfolio lending fell, a development consistent with an inward shift in U.S. demand for foreign bonds as U.S. investors shifted their funds to the U.S. stock market. We estimate that the decline in U.S. long-term lending during the stock market boom, compared with the preceding period of similar length, was \$1.4 - \$5.0 billion.*

The decline was sufficient to reduce net U.S. long-term lending below interest and amortization payments payable to the U.S. on outstanding long term debts. Such payments are only adjustable by default, a measure that countries were loathe to take until other measures had been tried: default was generally deferred until the period 1931-1933.

The brunt of adjustment in Europe, therefore, was borne by reserve losses and attempts to finance with short-term borrowing. In Germany and the United Kingdom, the two largest industrial countries outside the

---

* Charles Kindleberger takes issue with the breadth of this range of estimates and settles on a net change in lending of about \$2 billion, on the grounds that net flows in outstanding securities are typically less than 20% of gross flows (C.P. Kindleberger, The World in Depression. London: The Penguin Press, 1973). One difficulty with this solution is that the 1928-1929 boom was quite atypical. Some advance in current research concerning the determinants of international transactions in outstanding securities may enable us to speak with greater precision about the likely size of the flows.

United States, we observe rising short-term interest rates, declining new international lending, reduced rates of growth of industrial output, declining new issues for domestic financing purposes, and rising rates of unemployment.

Countries on the periphery, less able to finance deficits by borrowing in the short-term capital market, exhibit a mixture of deficit financing by reserve reduction, import restrictions, and in some cases abandonment of gold parity.

These reactions reinforced each other; attempts by the periphery to reduce imports contributed to slackening economic activity among European exporters, while the latter led to further declines in primary product prices, export revenues of primary producers, and thence to further attempts to restrict imports. Some of this is isolated in the text, but much of it is difficult to disentangle from the effects of the decline in U.S. imports that occurs between 1930 and 1933.

IV. The Decline in U.S. Imports and the World Depression

To discuss the substantial decline in U.S. imports between 1930 and 1933 as an independent cause of the world depression, it is necessary to establish that the decline in U.S. imports was not an indirect effect of the earlier decline in U.S. long-term lending. This may be shown with two complementary demonstrations. First, we may show that plausible connections between the decline in U.S. long-term lending and the decline in U.S. imports were not empirically important. Second, we may show that there is an alternative satisfactory explanation of the decline in U.S. imports; we will discuss this question later.

One possible link between the decline in U.S. long-term lending and the decline in U.S. imports might be that the same domestic tight monetary policy that contributed to the reduced long-term lending brought on the domestic depression. The text concedes some validity to this position but points to other independent domestic factors as well.

A second possible link might be from reduced world economic activity in 1929, through a reduction in U.S. exports and thence to a decline in U.S. income and imports. The decline in U.S. exports that we see in 1930, however, is not a substantial factor compared to other domestic factors.

A third possible link might be from reduced world economic activity, through a decline in the demand for primary products, to a decline in U.S. farm incomes, thereby reducing aggregate demand and income, either directly through the effects of the income redistribution, or indirectly through the effects on rural bank failures and thence on expectations and on the money supply. This possibility is difficult to handle analytically and has not received adequate attention.

It is, therefore, not possible to rule out all the possible connections between the decline in U.S. long-term lending and the subsequent decline in U.S. income and imports. We will see below that part of an explanation for the decline in U.S. income can be constructed from domestic factors, but that explanation does not suffice to explain the magnitude of the decline in U.S. income. The possibility cannot be dismissed that the observed decline in imports is the joint product of new domestic exogenous shocks and the secondary international effects of the earlier decline in U.S. long-term lending.

V. The Importance of the U.S. Role Compared with other Factors

Ideally, we could determine the relative importance of the U.S. role with an economic model of the world economy that incorporated, given vigorous prior examination, all behavior suggested as being important in explaining the origins and severity of the depression. With such a model, fully estimated, we could measure the contribution of each independent factor to the decline in total output. There is, however, little present agreement on what such a model would look like, and the first attempts to measure full-scale interactive international models are just now being made.

Therefore, we must settle for considerably less than the ideal. Explanations that center on factors other than the U.S. role can be broadly divided into those that may be assessed in the context of our current views of how the international economy works but which are incorrect or relatively unimportant, and those that cannot be assessed in the context of our current views.

A number of explanations do not withstand close examination. If the overproduction of primary products means shifts in producer supply curves that lead to price and total revenue reductions, there was no primary product overproduction in 1928 and 1929 save in a few commodities. We do observe reductions in prices and in quantities produced after 1930, but this observation is consistent with relative inward shifts of demand curves in industrial countries, not with outward shifts in supply curves in producer countries.

The view that the U.S. surplus on current account placed unbearable strain on countries desiring to pay off debts to the United States rests ultimately on an arbitrary view that United States was then a "mature creditor country". The U.S. surplus presented no problem as long as the United States continued long-term lending; attention should be focussed on the cessation of that lending, not on the current account surplus that permitted it.

A shift out of foreign exchange reserves and into gold did not precipitate a liquidity scramble. Reserves increased in 1928 and 1929 and declined thereafter in a manner consistent with the decline in international trade. Difficulties may have been caused by the distribution of international reserves, as proponents of the "maldistribution of gold" explanation argued, but their case would have been much stronger were there any demonstratable relation between the size of a country's international reserves and its willingness to lose them in order to pursue domestic expansionary policies. The United States held most of the world's international reserves, but officials consistently argued that reserves were barely adequate, and always took swift monetary actions when gold flowed out, irrespective of domestic economic conditions.

Finally, while the war-induced movement to autarchy among the traditional customers of European exporters may have caused some difficulty for Great Britain, there was a general increase in manufactured imports by countries on the periphery during this period.

A second set of explanations revolves around factors that can be incorporated to some degree in our existing views of how the world economy operates, but which do not appear to have been very important. Speculative short-term capital flows appear in 1931 in Germany and the United Kingdom and again in 1933 in the United States, but they appear at the very end of long periods of economic contraction and international difficulty. It is hard to see how the absence of speculative flows would have appreciably changed the nature of the steps ultimately taken, although the timing might have been altered marginally.

The failure of transport rates to decline represents the disappearance of a market phonomenon that had existed in the past, and a factor that had cushioned the decline in primary product prices at the producer level during past recessions. However, the decline in prices was so great that even previously experienced reductions in transport costs would not have substantially raised the income of primary product exporters and altered the redistributive effects of the price change.

It is undoubtedly true, in retrospect, that the absence of greater international cooperation was important in the sense that sufficient international cooperation coupled with appropriate domestic policies could have substantially reduced the severity of the depression. However, intergovernmental economic cooperation to solve financial difficulties appears to have been much greater than ever before undertaken. Moreover, intergovernmental cooperation was generally carried on with the understanding that borrowing governments would pursue "sound" monetary and fiscal policies, policies that our current economic understanding would say worsened the situation. As a historical assertion, international cooperation was remarkably great, not remarkably small; as a technical assertion, it may well be that the conditions attached to intergovernmental cooperation aggravated, not mitigated, the depression.

The failure to create international commodity price stabilization agreements cannot be regarded as very important because commodity cartels are extremely difficult to maintain during periods of slack demand, when the incentive and ability of members to cheat on quotas is great: most members have many possible expenditures with high social returns and surplus output to ship outside of their quotas. We should expect to see cartels collapse during periods like the great depression, which they did; we should not consider the failure to create new ones in any way remarkable. There is also an unresolved technical difficulty in the proposal: primary product cartels would have arrested the redistribution of income, but would have done so by sharply reducing the output of commodities. It is not obvious how a reduction in real output in a depression contributes to getting out of the depression, and the net effect of the redistribution of income and the absolute decline in output is not obvious.

A similar problem exists with explanations phrased in term of the failure to adopt flexible exchange rates. Waiving the technical merits of the proposal, most important countries were adamant in opposition to the institution of flexible rates, had been so before the depression, and continued to be so after the Second World War. There is nothing unusual in the rejection of this option during the early years of the depression. It might be recalled in this context that even after the turbulent period from 1930 to 1933, one of Britain's major aims at the 1933 World Economic Conference was the reinstitution of de jure fixed rates. What is perhaps most curious about the fixed-versus-flexible rate question in the inter-war period is the number of recent academic examinations that judge as successful Europe's brief experience with floating during the 1920's, without explaining in a very satisfactory way why these same countries hastened to abandon the system by the late 1920's.

Finally, there are a number of explanations that involve factors that appeared then and appear now to have been important but that are difficult to incorporate into our current understanding of how the international economy works. We have no complete view on the effect of the collection of exchange rate and tariff policies then termed "beggar-thy-neighbor" policies. War debts and reparations payments were thought to have dislocating effects on the world economy, but the flows associated with these debts, which are relatively easy to examine in the context of our current models, were quite small, whereas changes in the capitalized value of these debts through interest rate and price changes were enormous, but difficult to capture in our current theories. The notion that Britain served a stabilizing function at the center of the gold standard that was only imperfectly served by the United States at the center of a gold exchange standard has no analogue in the models of the international economy with which we are accustomed to dealing. Last, we have no satisfactory way of determining the effects of international debt-default, banking failures, and other abnormalities, on expectations and thence on consumption and investment decisions.

VI. International Factors and the Origins and Severity of the U.S. Depression

In the absence of our ideal model, we may show that the U.S. depression originated independently of the world depression by finding a plausible explanation of the domestic depression independent of the international economy and by showing that proposed connections between the world economy and the origins of the U.S. depression do not appear important.

The thesis presents no new conclusions concerning the domestic origins of the U.S. depression, except to apply the findings of Arena and of Modigliani and Brumberg on the size of the wealth effect to confirm the importance of the collapse of stock prices in reducing consumption and, thereby, aggregate demand. Recent studies of the effects of stock values on aggregate income indicate that the thesis probably understates the importance of the stock market collapse. Thereafter, the thesis relies on the traditionally accepted elements: a decline in the demand for housing because of demographic changes, the general effects of a tight money policy aimed at curbing speculation, and possible saturation of the automobile market.

None of these factors has anything to do with international developments, save the suggestion that the stock market collapse was triggered by foreign selling. The text explores this possibility and finds it quite unlikely. I offer no independent explanation of the stock market crash, but elements of the traditional story about the stock market crash could be put together to form a convincing explanation: a once-and-for-all increase in price-earnings ratios because of "New Era" confidence that the trade cycle was extinct, a heavily margined market that meant that new levels of price-earnings ratios had to be approached carefully, and substantial increases in call money rates toward the end of 1929.

The case that the severity of the U.S. depression was independent of international factors is considerably weaker. We have discussed the possible connection between the decline in primary product prices and massive internal redistributions of income away from primary product producers, leading to reductions in aggregate demand and to the failure of the rural banking system, and contributing thence to declines in confidence and contraction of the money supply.

Another type of feedback was Federal Reserve increases in interest rates and contractions of the money supply in 1931, around the time of the Sterling devaluation, and again in 1933 when gold flowed out in response to rumors that the United States was about to devalue. In assessing the role of the Federal Reserve in those episodes, it should be observed that tightening in response to reserve losses was typical central bank behavior then. What is curious about Federal Reserve behavior during this period is that tightening took place in the face of massive banking failures: yet, the prevention of bank failures lies closer to the heart of the Federal Reserve Act than macroeconomic objectives or "defense" of the nation's gold stock. How the Federal Reserve System chose among those objectives, and why it permitted massive failure of the banking system, is an interesting historical question that has received insufficient attention, despite the recent abundance of excellent work on the Federal Reserve System during that period.

VII. Conclusion

The explanation presented here of the world depression posits its origins in the domestically generated decline in U.S. international lending, with a subsequent decline in U.S. income and imports that can also be traced to internal developments in the United States. In the process of constructing this explanation, some alternatives have been cast aside as incorrect or unimportant. Other alternatives have been set aside, because while they appear important, they have not been posed in a way that permits their incorporation into our current views of how the international economy works. In the process of analyzing those uneasy cases, we will discover information about economic behavior that will lead to modifications of our current understanding of economic behavior, certainly when the economic system is subject to large stresses, and perhaps for normal periods as well. Modification of our views of how the economy works will lead, in turn, to a re-examination of the factors here judged incorrect or not important, since such judgments can only be made in the context of a particular model or view of the world. Those who suspect that such a process is endless and that the "ideal model" is not attainable are correct: Gödel has proved it.

Finally, I would like once again to thank my thesis advisers, Robert Triffin, William Parker, and the late Stephen Hymer, all of whom read my drafts carefully and returned them promptly, with copious remarks--exertions I have come to appreciate more, having since supervised some theses myself.

Heywood Fleisig

Washington, D.C.
March 1975

Division of International Finance,
Federal Reserve Board and
Department of Economics,
University of Maryland

LONG TERM CAPITAL FLOWS AND THE GREAT DEPRESSION:

THE ROLE OF THE UNITED STATES, 1927-1933

Heywood W. Fleisig
1969

A Dissertation Presented to the Faculty of the
Graduate School of Yale University in
Candidacy for the Degree of Doctor of Philosophy

SUMMARY

Although the world depression of the nineteen-thirties has been studied extensively, attention has been accorded primarily to the general problems facing the world economy prior to the depression and to the series of dramatic events which occurred once the depression had begun. However, relatively little attention has been paid to the manner in which these potential economic dangers were transformed throughout the world into the actuality of economic depression. In this dissertation, we argue that this transition from prosperity to depression is best explained by the sharp decline in American long term international lending during 1928 and 1929.

The decline in American lending during these years led to tightened money markets and balance of payments problems in many important foreign countries and regions. Their response to these problems was generally a combination of reduced international lending, reduced domestic lending, or reduced imports. These responses produced a decline in the rate of foreign economic growth during the years of greatest American prosperity.

These foreign economic conditions, together with the beginning of recession in the United States, led to sharp declines in the prices of primary products in 1930 despite the decline in the rate of growth of primary production. The decline in raw material prices reflected back on the industrial countries through reduced exports to primary-product producing areas and through the reduced value of their domestic primary-product output. In this way, domestic as well as foreign demand for industrial products declined further.

The decline in American long term lending during 1928 and 1929 thus led to the declines in industrial output and raw material prices which appeared in 1930 and which, together with the continued decline in long term lending, dominated the world depression in the years which followed.

ACKNOWLEDGEMENT

I am indebted to Professor Robert Triffin for the deeper appreciation of the subtleties of the international financial system which his course and conversations with him afforded me. Professors Stephen Hymer and William Parker were generous with useful advice and criticism.

Professor Hajo Holborn of the Yale History Department was uncommonly kind in discussing source materials and interpretations of the political developments during the interwar period. I owe my original interest in the relation between international politics and economics to the stimulating seminars and discussions at Swarthmore with Professor Kenneth Waltz, now at Brandeis. Mr. Ralph Bryant of the Federal Reserve Board graciously obtained some important unpublished data for me.

My wife, Susan, performed much of the statistical tabulation and was a constant sounding board for the ideas which are developed below, accepting without complaint the addition of the crises of the interwar years to the daily routing of domestic dislocations. I need only add that any errors in fact, interpretation, or style are my own.

Chapter 1

Introduction

Many writers have given the United States the central role in the world depression. They have cited the war debts and America's unyielding attitude concerning their repayment, the decline in American imports during the 1930 recession which they attributed to an excessively permissive monetary policy during the late twenties, the failure of the United States to run a current account deficit as a proper creditor country should, America's excessive share of the world's monetary gold, her failure to abide by the rules of the game, and her failure to control the stock market boom.

Other writers have constructed explanations of the world depression which give the United States a less central role. Some have cited the decline in population growth, the decline in international migration, the growth of autarchy, the detrimental effect of technological progress on some countries' international competitiveness, the strain of postwar reconstruction, the inherent instability of the gold exchange standard, the rigid links of fixed exchange rates, the failure of transport rates to decline, and the overproduction of primary products. Others have fixed the blame on countries other than the United States, citing the overvaluation of sterling, the undervaluation of the French franc, the shift by France from foreign exchange to gold, and reckless German borrowing.

If we are to determine the role of American net long term capital exports in an event already possessing such a broad range of explanations, we must discover whether these capital exports behaved differently from other elements of the American balance of payments, why they behaved in this way, how they contributed to the world depression, and how their behavior relates to these other views of the world depression.

In the next chapter we have found that United States net long term capital exports alone changed consistently in such a way that made it more difficult for foreigners to make payments to the United States. Moreover, the decline in net American long term capital exports probably began as early as mid-1928 indicating that they might better explain the later downward adjustment of world economic activity.

In chapter 3 we have considered the causes of this decline in long term capital exports and have found that the large inflow of foreign funds to the New York stock markets was probably based on the stock market boom while the decline in new portfolio lending seems to have been due to the tightening of the New York money market, accentuated by a Federal Reserve policy which aimed at further restricting credit. Later in chapter 3 we have considered the effects on the world economy of the decline in lending and the changes in various dimensions of the long term portfolio. We have found that these exerted deflationary pressures on the world economy in a variety of ways. The initial deflationary effect of the decline in net foreign investment by the United States was reinforced by tight money policies initiated in many foreign countries in order to maintain their balances of payments. This tended to reduce their domestic investment and their foreign lending. In developing countries, exporting primary products, domestic investment and monetary policy tended to be relatively unimportant determinants of domestic economic activity. Since exports could not be expanded in the short run, policies of import restriction were introduced in an attempt to maintain external balance. Thus, the initial effects of the constriction of investible funds were reinforced by the subsequent deflationary effect of a declining rate of growth of exports from the industrial countries.

Absolute reductions in and the declining rates of growth of investment and exports contributed to the decline in the rate of growth of aggregate demand. These led to the sharp decline in primary product prices during 1930, to the sharp reduction in imports by primary commodity exporters, and to the reduction in the value of raw material production within the industrial countries. These reactions contributed to further reduction in investment, thereby forming the major elements of the decline in world output.

Long term capital flows and the long term portfolio continued to exert deflationary pressure on the world economy between 1930 and 1933 in a variety of ways. Following an upward spurt in portfolio lending by the United States in 1930, portfolio lending declined until 1933. Similarly, United States direct investment declined sharply between 1930 and 1933. Relatively inflexible debtors' payments of interest and amortization, and their repatriation of outstanding bonds from the United States, in conjunction with falling export proceeds, increased the adjustment problem of deficit-ridden debtor countries. Any tendency to increase consumption, as the real value of debt increased in the face of declining prices, was dampened or reversed: government defaults offset the increase in the real value of private holdings of official debt while creditors' and debtors' apparently inconsistent expectations of repayment implied that the increase in the expected real value of private debt was greater than the increase in the expected real value of private assets.

On the basis of these observations we have concluded that the decline in American net long term lending and changes in certain aspects of the American long term portfolio were the earliest and most important American contributions to the depression. Furthermore, changes in American lending and in the American portfolio maintained their deflationary pressure on the world economy as the depression wore on.

This argument is not without precedent. In 1931, in The Course and Phases of the World Economic Depression,[1] Bertil Ohlin repeatedly emphasized the importance of the decline in long term lending which began in 1928. The League of Nations, in its 1935 report on World Production and Prices,[2] indicated that the decline in industrial demand caused the decline in commodity prices and the growth of stocks. We have discussed the other explanations of the world depression in chapter 4 and have attempted to relate them to an explanation of the world depression in which the decline in American lending plays a leading role. We have found that the decline in American lending was not only the most deflationary act undertaken by the United States, but probably the most critical deflationary occurrence in the world during the years 1927 to 1930. A number of events which occurred during the period 1930 to 1933 were of an equal or greater order of magnitude, but many of these events followed from the decline in lending.

---

[1] Bertil Ohlin, The Course and Phases of the World Economic Depression, pp. 35, 200-214.

[2] League of Nations, World Production and Prices, p. 7 and passim.

Chapter 6 contains a summary and several conclusions. Among these conclusions, the most important are that long term international investment was sufficiently large and unstable to initiate severe disturbances in the world economy; and, moreover, that nations did not cooperate in solving their mutual economic problems largely because of apparently irreconciliable differences in political and economic interest. We economists might profitably ponder the significance of such differences for the policies, plans, and expectations of today.

We may note, finally, that the discussion of data and estimating problems has generally been confined to appendices in order to avoid further complicating an already intricate narrative. A detailed table of contents for the appendices follows the list of charts in the front of the book and the interested reader might also browse through the appendices themselves inasmuch as they contain a considerable amount of additional information about the period. Since they contain a number of estimates dealing with extremely broad questions, they may be of value to future students who, hopefully, will continue to probe the dimensions of the Great Depression, an event which has marked all of us in innumerable ways.

Chapter 2

United States Net Exports of Long Term Capital: Background and Description

Introduction

Changes in the pattern and the size of long term capital flows were among the most important causes of the world depression. In the following discussion, we will first place these capital flows in the broad context of regional international payments during the period 1927 to 1933. Subsequently, we will consider the behavior of the major components of the American balance of payments and the main elements of American long term international lending.

Regional Patterns of International Payments

In general, Europe tended toward overall balance of payments surplus during the years 1927 to 1933, the United States tended toward neutrality, while the rest of the world tended to be in deficit (chart 1). However, Europe generally had a deficit on merchandise account, in contrast to the merchandise surpluses of the United States and the rest of the world. Thus, the overall balances of these regions tended to be quite different from the balances on their merchandise accounts.[1] This difference may be explained largely by the behavior of long term capital flows and the flows associated with the long term portfolio. This can be seen quite clearly in the regional balance of payments of the United States. The United States had an overall deficit against Europe, since the American current account surplus with respect to Europe was more than offset by substantial long term lending. On the other hand, the United States was in overall surplus

---

[1]Data for the United States merchandise account taken from Hal. B. Lary, The United States in the World Economy, table I. Data for other merchandise accounts calculated from the League of Nations Monthly Bulletin of Statistics, Vol. 11, 1930, p. 447 (1927 data); the League of Nations, Statistical Yearbook 1933/1934, pp. 194-195 (1928-1930 data); and the League of Nations, Statistical Yearbook, 1934-1935, pp. 208-209 (1931-1933 data).

Chart 1

Gold and Official Foreign Exchange Assets by Region

1926 - 1933

(end of year data; $000,000)

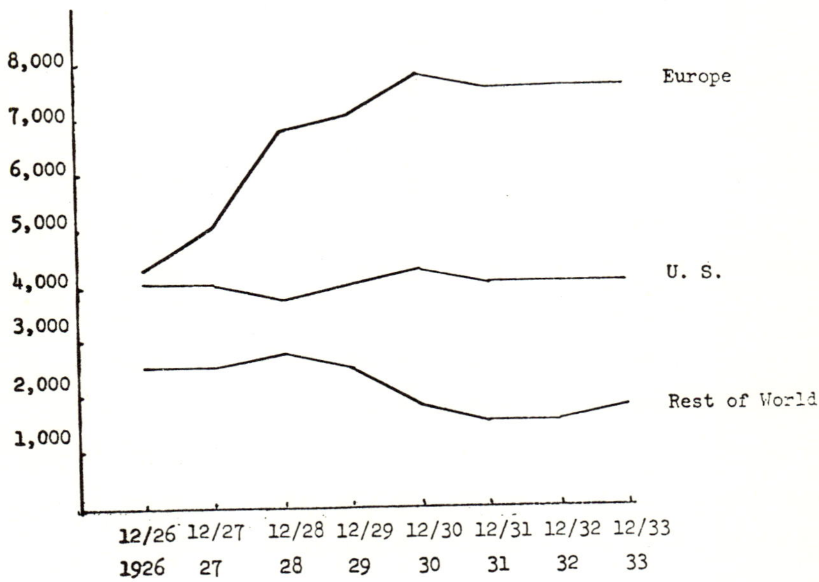

Source: Estimates of gold reserves were taken from the Federal Reserve Board, Banking and Monetary Statistics (1943 ed.), pp. 544-545, 550-551. Estimates of official foreign exchange assets were taken from the League of Nations Statistical Yearbook 1933 - 1934, pp. 210-212.

Chart 2

U. S. Gold Imports and Exports

1927 - 1933

($000,000)

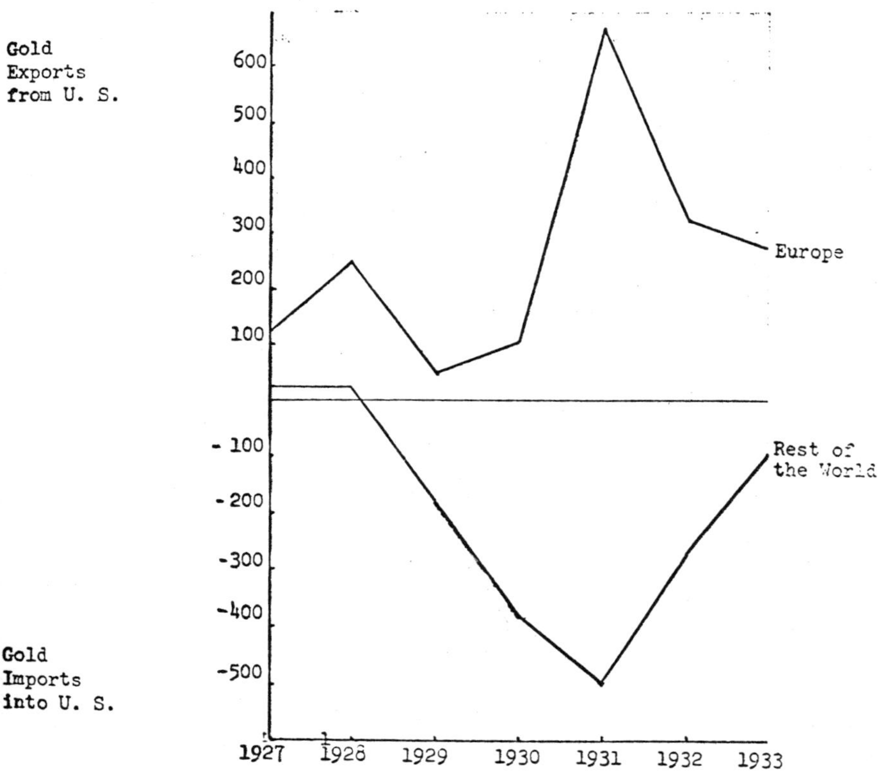

Source: Gold shipments by country taken from Federal Reserve Board, Annual Report for 1929, p. 82 (1927-1929 data); Annual Report of 1933, p. 139 (1930-1933 data). Gold earmarks by region are calculated from data supplied by the Federal Reserve Board (see appendix 1, note 3).

against the rest of the world, her current and capital account deficits more than offset by the inflow of interest, dividend, and amortization payments.[1]

Thus, the sign and size of the balances of payments of the various regions of the world depended critically on the size and pattern of long term capital flows and the flows associated with the long term portfolio: interest, amortization, and dividend payments.

Long Term Capital Flows and the American Balance of Payments

Net long term capital exports from the United States declined from $1 billion in 1927 to $250 million in 1930 and ceased completely between 1931 and 1933 (chart 3). Some idea of the importance of the net long term capital exports of the United States may be gained from the following comparisons. The net outflow of one billion dollars from the United States in 1927 was greater than the combined new long term foreign lending of all other major lending countries.[2] It exceeded 15% of the total domestic new issues in the United States[3], 30% of the total domestic new issues for Europe[4], and, no doubt, was an even larger proportion of new investments in those developing areas of the world in the sphere of influence of the United States, particularly Latin America.

The long term capital account was the only major account to change in a way which steadily increased the difficulty with which the world could make

---

[1]See chart 2 and appendix 1, note 7 and note 8.

[2]See appendix 1, note 4.

[3]See appendix 1, note 5.

[4]See appendix 1, note 6.

Chart 3

U. S. Balance of Payments

1927 - 1933

($000,000)

Source: Hal B. Lary, The United States in the World Economy, table III.

payments to the United States. In contrast, the surplus on goods and services became a deficit, the inflow of interest and dividend payments declined, and the inflow of short term funds became an erratically increasing outflow (chart 3).

American long term capital exports declined by 1928 to the point where they no longer covered the payment of interest, dividends, and amortization by countries in debt to the United States (chart 4). This pressure was exerted on all regions by 1929 (chart 5). It is customary to place interest payments in the current account and amortization payments in the capital account since the former represent payment for the use of the capital while the latter represent the return of the capital itself. On these grounds, the separation is conceptually appealing. Yet insofar as interest payments on portfolio investment and war debts are scheduled far in advance of the date paid, and may be adjusted only through negotiation, default, or repudiation, they represent charges on past investment which are as inflexible as amortization payments. The comparison of current long term investment with interest and amortization payments on past investments, therefore, gives us an idea of the quantitative impact of past and current long term capital transactions on the international economic relations of the United States.

The Components of United States Long Term International Capital Exports and Imports

The sharp decline in net long term capital exports appears to be most clearly related to the sharp decline in new portfolio and direct investment; net transactions in outstanding securities show no clear trend according to the calendar year official estimates (chart 6). During the critical years from 1927 to 1929, $500 million of a total decline of about $800 million in

Chart 4

Long Term Capital Flows and Debt Charges

1927 - 1933

($000,000)

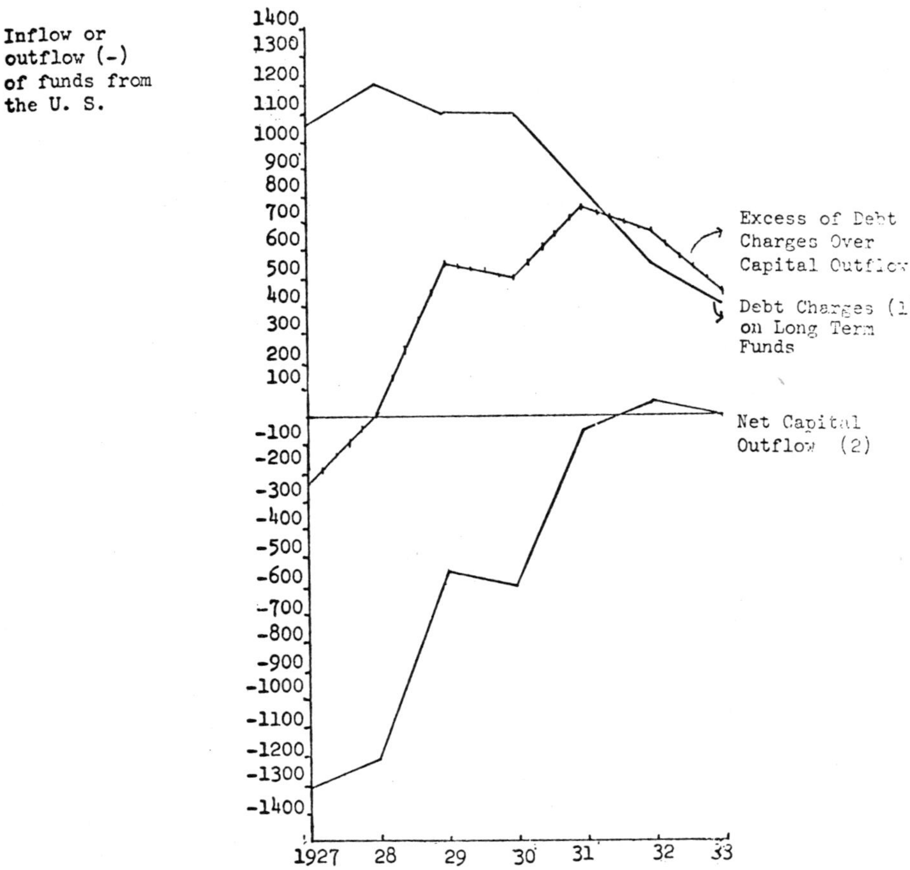

Source: Appendix 1, note 7.

Notes: (1) "Debt charges" comprise interest and dividend payments on U.S. long term private investment overseas, interest and amortization payments on war debt, and private amortization payments on long term debt.

(2) "Net capital outflow" comprises the outflow of capital due to portfolio investment, direct investment, and transactions in outstanding securities minus the inflow attributable to these transactions. Amortization payments are included in debt charges.

Chart 5

Long Term Capital Flows and Debt Charges:
the U.S. Accounts by Region

1927-1933 ($000,000)

a. Europe

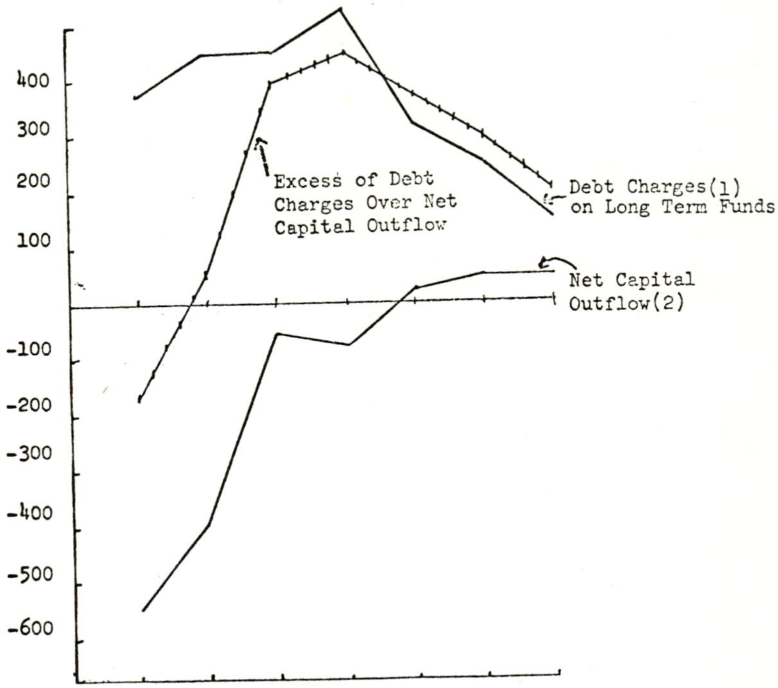

b. North America

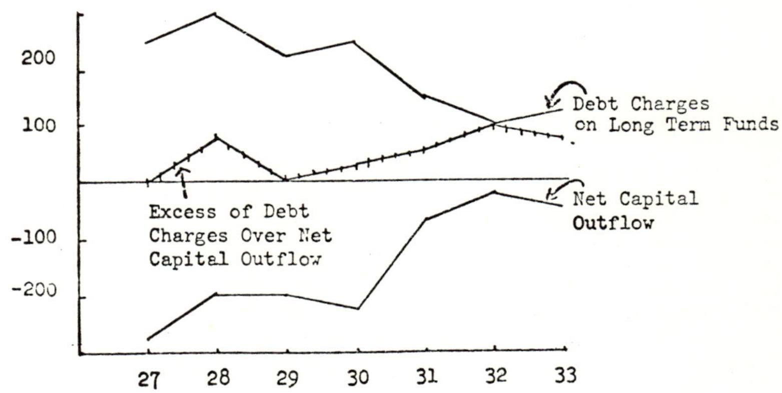

Chart 5 - Continued

c. South America

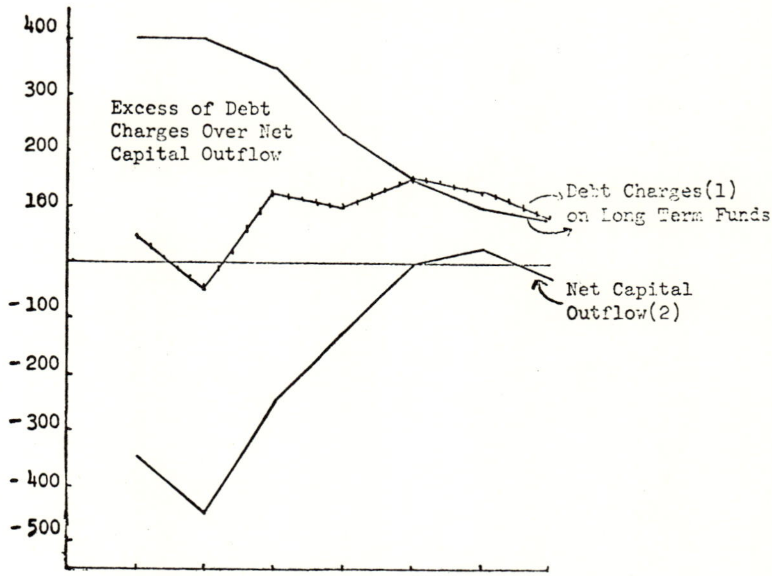

d. Asia-Oceania-Africa

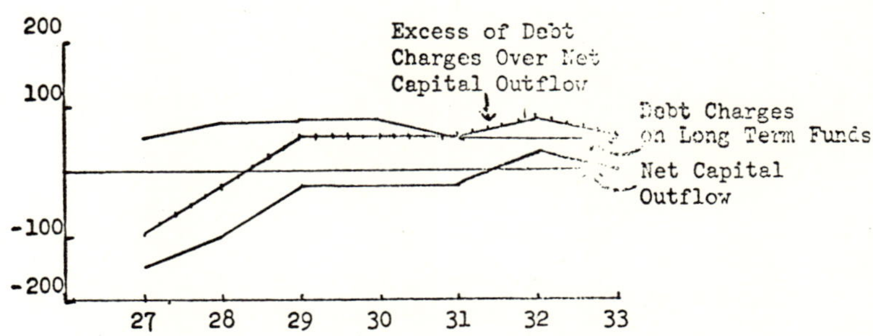

Source: Appendix 1, note 7.

Notes: (1) "Debt charges" comprise interest and dividend payments on U.S. long term private investment overseas, interest and amortization payments on war debt, and private amortization payments on long term debt.

(2) "Net capital outflow" comprises the outflow of capital due to portfolio investment, direct investment, and transactions in outstanding securities minus the inflow attributable to these transactions. Amortization payments are included in debt charges.

Chart 6

Elements of the U. S. Capital Account

1927 - 1933

($000,000)

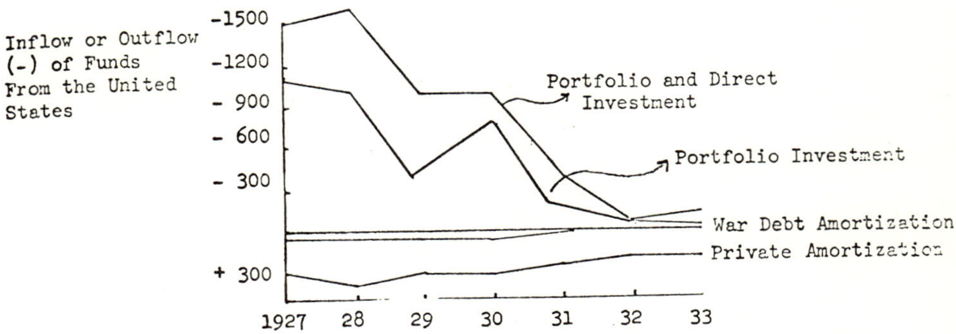

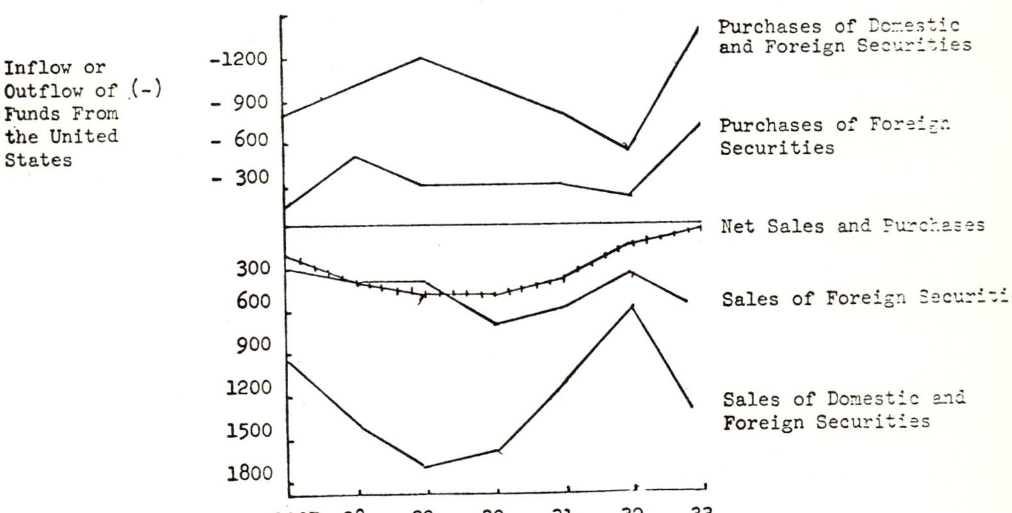

Source: Hal B. Lary, The United States in the World Economy, table III.

long term capital exports from the United States is attributable to the decline in new long term lending while $300 million is attributable to an increased inflow of funds due to transactions in outstanding securities. However, the use of calendar year estimates of the capital flows may understate the importance of the decline in lending and may also misrepresent the relative sizes of the decline in portfolio lending and the increased inflow of funds due to outstanding security transactions. The most serious period of monetary tightness seems to have occurred between June 1928 and September 1929. The bulk of the bull swing of the New York stock markets occurred during the same period. Thus, during this period we would expect to find the largest negative impact on new portfolio lending combined with the largest inflow due to transactions in outstanding securities.

We can briefly summarize the findings of the following chapter. New portfolio lending by the United States during the period of relative monetary ease (January 1927 to June 1928) was $1.9 billion. However, during the period of relative monetary tightness (July 1928 to September 1929) new portfolio lending declined to $.6 billion, a decline in new portfolio lending of $1.3 billion.[1]

There are few data on securities transactions within the calendar year. However, we estimate that the inflow of funds due to transactions in

---

[1]See appendix 2, note 1. The observant reader may note that a period of eighteen months (January 1927 to June 1928) is being compared to a period of fifteen months (July 1928 to September 1929) and, thus, that even were these flows perfectly uniform, the second period would have a smaller total of lending than the first. Unfortunately, the statistical difficulties of removing the first three months from the first period were too great. However, the reader might observe that the monthly rate of lending in the first period was $105.6 million while the monthly rate of lending in the second period was only $40.0 million. Thus, the change noted in the text does reflect a substantial change in the rate of lending.

outstanding securities during the main bull swing of the New York exchanges (July 1928 to September 1929) was between $100 million and $3900 million greater than the inflow during the period of relative stock exchange calm (January 1927 to June 1928).

Because of the range of the above estimates of transactions in outstanding securities, it is difficult to compare the decline in portfolio lending with the increased inflow of funds for outstanding securities transactions. What is clear however, is that the use of calendar year measures tends to underestimate the decline in net American long term lending between 1927 and 1929.[1]

During the years 1930 to 1933 American portfolio and direct investment ceased to be an important factor in international payments. We will concentrate instead on the continued inflows of interest, dividend and amortization payments and the repatriation and speculative movements of funds which seem to be present in transactions in outstanding securities.

Summary

Capital flows and flows of funds associated with the long term portfolio were everywhere of crucial importance in determining the sign and size of the balances of payments of the various regions of the world. The United States was the major source of long term capital. Nonetheless, for at

---

[1]To illustrate this, we may convert our intra-calendar year estimates to twelve month estimates by calculating monthly rates of portfolio lending and outstanding securities transactions. On this basis, portfolio lending in hypothetical calendar year 1 would have been $1.3 billion while portfolio lending in hypothetical calendar year 2 would have been $.5 billion, a decline of $.8 billion. This is substantially greater than the actual calendar year decline of $.5 billion which was captured by the change in the estimates for 1928 and 1929. Transactions in outstanding securities would have ranged between an inflow of $.3 billion and an outflow of $.6 billion in hypothetical calendar year 1 and between inflows of $.4 billion to $2.5 billion in calendar year 2, for an estimated increase in net inflow of $.1-$3.1 billion. This might then have been greater than the recorded calendar year increase in inflow of $.3 billion.

least fifteen months prior to the American stock market crash the net outflow of funds from the United States was declining. The reasons for that decline in lending and the effects of that decline on the world economy will be discussed in the following chapter.

Chapter 3

The Decline in Net American Long Term Capital Exports: Its Causes and Its Effects on the World Economy, 1927-1933

Introduction

In this chapter we will discuss the causes of the decline in United States net long term capital exports and the effects of this decline on the world economy. In the first section we will consider the various factors which led to the decline in new portfolio lending, to the decline in direct investment, to the increased inflow of funds to the United States due to transactions in outstanding securities, and to the relative constancy of the inflow of interest and amortization payments. We will consider the effects on the world economy of this decline in net lending in two sections: the first dealing with the years between 1927 and 1929, the second dealing with the years between 1930 and 1933. Finally we will discuss the effect on the world economy of changes in various dimensions of the long term portfolio: changes in the real value of the portfolio, the real value of flows associated with the portfolio, and changes in the probability of debt repayment.

a/ Causes of the Decline in United States Net Long Term Lending

The attrition in net long term lending by the United States was based on a variety of factors, depending on the type of flow and the changing influences of different years. We will consider, in turn, new issues, direct investment, transactions in outstanding securities, and private and public amortization payments.

a-1/ New Capital Issues

New capital issues of most major lending countries declined sharply in 1929.[1] It is generally believed that this decline in new lending was a reflection of the increased cost of long term borrowing in major financial centers. That this was the problem, rather than lenders unwillingness to lend, seems to be confirmed by the increase in new lending in 1930 when lenders, at lower rates and with borrowers in considerably more unsound condition, increased their loans. In short, it seems that in 1929 had borrowers been willing to pay the price, funds might have been raised at most financial centers.

The increase in the price of money in the United States is attributable to the increased demand for short term funds due to stock market investment and speculation and to the tight money policies of United States economic authorities interested in curbing that speculation. In contrast, the tight money policies of other financial centers during 1929 can be interpreted only as policies aimed at defending their external positions against the drains of long and short term capital which were, as we have discussed, the

---

[1]See table 4, p. 41 and chapter 2, chart 6, p. 16.

combined result of the decline in new lending and the movement of funds to the New York stock markets.[1]

During the period 1930 to 1933 the importance of risk in long term foreign lending increased sharply. This was due primarily to the series of defaults which punctuated the period. Devaluation was not a serious problem from the point of view of creditor countries since most bonds during these years were denominated in the currency of the lender.

The increased risk of foreign lending, coupled with the concern in the lending countries about the soundness of their own banks and investment houses, implies that considerably more of the decline in new lending during this period was due to the reluctance of lenders to finance new issues at any but the most prohibitive rates except to the most highly qualified borrowers. The international situation was quite similar to that of the domestic economy where published rates were extremely low but quantity restrictions were rapidly tightened.

a-2/ Direct Investment

American direct investment increased until 1929 and decreased thereafter.

---

[1]There is some evidence that the U. S. tight money policies of early 1929 were conceived with at least some attention to the U. S. gold stock. Independent of the stock market boom, some authorities seem to have been concerned over the outflow of gold from the U. S. (See e.g. W. Randolph Burgess, "The Money Market in 1928", Review of Economics and Statistics, Feb. 1929). I am unsure about the relative weights placed on speculation and the declining gold stock by the authorities of the period. Of the two most recent writers on the period, Stephen Clarke, in Central Bank Cooperation, 1924-1931, pays scant attention to the events of early 1928; Elmus Wicker, whose Federal Reserve Monetary Policy, 1917-1933 includes a hitherto unexcelled discussion of the role of international factors in determining Federal Reserve policy, appears to consider the causes of the early 1928 increases in rates as entirely domestic. In correspondence with him, he has confirmed this position and suggested that while the New York Federal Reserve Bank might have been attuned to international considerations, the System's policy in early 1928 was determined by the behavior of the stock market. Nonetheless, I am still unconvinced and feel that this question might profitably be investigated further.

It is likely that the primary explanation for the decline in direct investment is similar to the explanation of the decline in domestic investment: the decline in the rate of growth of demand and hesitance over committing funds to long term projects in light of the chaotic economic condition of the world. There are, however, criteria which intrude on the decision to make a foreign direct investment which are normally absent from a thoroughly domestic business investment decision.

First, given the condition of the banking system after 1929 and the extremely variable supply of short term funds, it is reasonable to expect that preservation of the home plant would precede expansion of the foreign plant. Thus, funds which might normally have been invested abroad might remain home due to the increased desire for liquidity in the face of the periodically collapsing banking system.

The prospect of devaluation also affects the profitability of the investment decision. In the case of a person making an investment in the production of raw materials in a foreign country with a small home market for the commodity (e.g. a copper mine in Chile), the devaluation of that country's currency will tend to have little effect on the price of the world traded product. Nonetheless, a devaluation will tend to reduce the price, in terms of dollars, of untraded resources associated with the investment. Thus, in terms of dollars the cost of labor and construction materials in the devaluing country will tend to be lower after devaluation than before. Therefore, it may be profitable to wait until after an expected devaluation to invest in that country. It is likely, though, that in cases such as these it was the bleak outlook for commodity prices due to the decline in industrial activity that tended to retard investment in primary producing countries.

If the direct investment is made in a country with a large internal market, in order to produce for that market, prospective foreign investors could gain a great deal by waiting until after a devaluation. Investments made prior to devaluation will decline in value in terms of dollars and will have to be written down on the books of the parent companies; this loss can be avoided by waiting until the devaluation has occurred. It is possible for companies to hedge against this risk by maintaining a forward short position equal to their investment. However, as Einzig points out, such hedging is expensive and it is virtually impossible to offset all of the risk: there is no guarantee that internal prices and property values will change by the same amount as the devaluation.[1]

Finally, waiting until a devaluation has occurred will also increase the profits from a direct investment in a foreign plant producing for the export market. Suppose a United States investor should construct a plant in a foreign country despite the threat of a devaluation which does shortly take place. In terms of dollars the value of that plant declines. However, if the devaluation is successful, then his profits should rise and with it the capitalized value of his plant in terms of both the domestic currency and dollars. However, the post-devaluation value of the plant may or may not equal the value of the plant, in terms of dollars, prior to the devaluation. In such a case the potential investor can avoid the initial capital loss and capture all of the gain by waiting until the devaluation has occurred. As before, he can only hedge imperfectly against the devaluation.

In conclusion, the main determinant of direct investment was probably

---

[1]Paul Einzig, A Dynamic Theory of Foreign Exchange, p. 90.

the generally worsened economic outlook. However, the prospect of devaluation in borrowing countries, amply fulfilled during this period, would also point toward a decline in direct investment.

a-3/ Transactions in Outstanding Securities

There are four movements of major importance in transactions in outstanding securities: the movement of funds to the New York stock markets from mid-1928 to late 1929; the withdrawal of funds from New York following the stock market crash; the repatriation of securities by debtor countries; and the purchase of Gold Bloc[1] bonds prior to the United States devaluation.

The movement of long term funds to the United States during the long bull swing of the New York stock market from June 1928 to October 1929 was based primarily on the opportunities for capital appreciation which that move offered. Yields on common stocks, as is common during bull swings, fell to about one-half of the yield on United States high grade securities and was even less than one-half of the average yield on foreign bonds.

With the exception of the Canadian and French stock markets, only the New York stock market offered such opportunities for capital appreciation. The steadiness of the British stock market and the slow downward drift of the German stock market during this same period, combined with generally declining investment prospects in those countries, made investment in United States equities extremely attractive in comparison. The withdrawal of funds from New York after the crash presumably reflected the apparent cessation of such opportunities for capital appreciation.

---

[1]The Gold Bloc comprised France, Switzerland, Belgium, the Netherlands, Luxembourg, and Italy.

There is no evidence that either the purchase of United States equities or their subsequent liquidation was based on the lack of soundness of any currency. In particular, there is no evidence that purchases of United States equities reflected lack of confidence on the part of German or British investors in the mark or the pound respectively; nor is there any indication that liquidation was based on fears that the dollar might be devalued. Any suspicions of this sort are completely absent from the leading financial journals of 1929.

We have already discussed the repatriation of outstanding securities by debtor countries. While it may seem prima facie obvious why foreign governments and firms would be interested in settling their outstanding debts for, in some cases, as little as 15¢ on the dollar (see chart 1), the explanation is actually quite complex.

The real value of a fixed money asset depends on the price, the coupon rate of interest, the market rate of interest, the face value of the bond, and the probability that interest and amortization payments will be made. Given the coupon rate of interest of most foreign bonds and the market rate of interest during the period 1930 to 1933, the prices of foreign bonds should have risen. Instead prices fell, because of widespread defaults on either or both interest and sinking fund payments. During this period of low foreign bond prices, extensive repatriation took place.

This implies that, given the price of the bond, residents of the debtor countries considered them more attractive than residents of the creditor country[1]: that is, that

$$\frac{E(W)}{P} \text{ (debtor)} > \frac{E(W)}{P} \text{ (creditor)},$$

[1]If the market price were viewed equally by residents of both the debtor and creditor country, one would not expect to see net purchases by debtors and net sales by creditors.

Chart 1

Selected Monthly Average Bond Prices
as a Percentage of Par Value

January 1929-December 1933

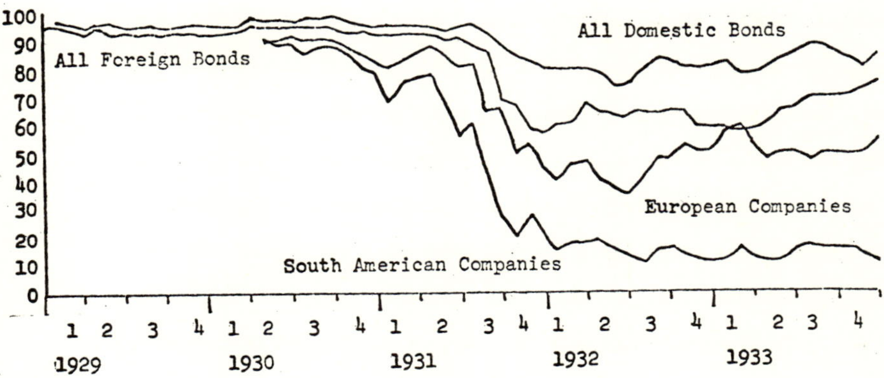

Source:
1. Monthly average prices of all listed foreign and domestic bonds on the New York Stock Exchange: 1929-1931 data from Survey of Current Business Annual Supplement 1932 p. 97; 1932-1933 data from Annual Supplement 1936, p. 60.

2. March 1930-December 1933 monthly average prices of bonds of European and South American companies: data from New York Stock Exchange Bulletin March 1930, vol. 1, no. 1 - December 1933, vol. IV, no. 12.

where W indicates the face value of the bond; p, the general price level; and E, the expected value.

The price level in the United States declined by as much or more than the price level within any country. Thus, ceteris paribus, movements in the price level fail to explain why the expected real value of the bond should increase less in the United States.

Another possible explanation of this phenomena is that debtors in foreign countries thought repayment was more likely than did creditors in the United States. Some observers have claimed that foreign countries deliberately went into default in order to repatriate their bonds at low prices, resume payments on the smaller remaining balance, and then qualify for the resumption of new lending by the United States.[1] This of course does not contradict the previous argument but may explain why foreign debtors thought the probability of repayment was greater than did American creditors. Another possible explanation might be a sort of "debtor's myopia": a persistent tendency on the part of debtors to overestimate their future prospects compared to creditor's evaluation of the debtor's prospects.

Activity in transactions in outstanding securities tended to decline between 1930 and 1932. There was an eruption in trading activity during 1933, however, when American purchases of foreign securities rose by $500 million[2], but this activity appears to have been concentrated largely in the gold bonds of the Gold Bloc.[3] The most plausible explanation for this flow of funds is that American citizens were hedging against an increase in the price of gold, or equivalently, hoping to gain from a devaluation of the dollar relative to gold.

---

[1]Private investors were understandably uneasy about new lending to countries in default; the State Department discouraged private lending to countries in default on private debt; and foreign governments in default to the United States could not resume borrowing in the U.S. market until they had settled their outstanding debts according to the Johnson Debt Default Act of 1934.

[2]Hal B. Lary, The United States in the World Economy, p. 107.

[3]A considerable amount of qualitative evidence to this effect is cited in "The Balance of International Payments of the United States in 1933", U.S. Department of Commerce, Trade Information Bulletin No. 819, pp. 84-89 passim.

Foreign purchases of American domestic securities also rose by about $500 million in 1933.[1] Stock prices on the New York Stock Exchange rose by about 50% between January and December 1933.[2] This might itself have been attractive enough to draw in foreign funds. However, even in the absence of rising stock prices, the depreciation of the dollar would have increased the attractiveness of American equities. There would at least have been arbitrage purchases of equities traded in international markets since the dollar depreciated (quite steadily) relative to the pound and the French franc during 1933.[3] Since the prices of American equities in terms of sterling or French francs would decline with depreciation, there would be incentive for foreigners to purchase these equities in New York while selling them in their domestic markets. Moreover, investors might consider American equities (becoming lower priced in terms of their home currencies,) more attractive relative to their domestic equity investment opportunities and purchase them outright. Finally, it is possible that the purchase of equities by foreigners represented only speculation in favor of a rise in the dollar relative to their home currencies.

a-4/ Private and Public Amortization, Interest, and Dividend Payments

The amount and scheduling of amortization and interest payments on outstanding bonds are fixed at the time the bond is issued. They do not vary with the economic condition of either the debtor or the creditor country. Any change in the terms of payment may be gained only through negotiation between debtor and creditor or through default, complete or partial, on either or both interest and amortization payments.

---

[1] Lary, op. cit., p. 107.

[2] Standard and Poors Index, cited in Banking and Monetary Statistics, 1943 ed., p. 481.

[3] ibid, pp. 670-681.

Direct investment generally is less of a burden since remissions depend to some degree on the condition of the foreign firm which often parallels the condition of the country in which the firm is located. For example, if the price of copper drops, the Chilean balance of payments worsens but the remission of profits by foreign-owned firms in Chile will presumably decline as well. However, whatever the price of copper, interest and amortization payments on Chilean bonds do not vary automatically.

b/ The Effect of American Long Term Capital Exports and Imports on the World Economy (1927-1929)

United States net long term capital exports[1] during the period of relative monetary ease, from January 1927 to June 1928, were substantially greater than the net outflow of long term funds during the period of relative monetary tightness, from July 1928 to September 1929. We estimate, based on different assumptions about the quarterly flows of transactions in outstanding securities, that the decline in the net outflow of funds during the second period was between $1.3 billion and $5.0 billion (table 1).

The decline in American net long term lending had several deflationary effects of varying directness. The reduction in the quantity of new lending at the going interest rates was itself deflationary to borrowing countries. The reduction in American lending contributed in a number of ways to the balance of payments problems of other creditor countries, leading authorities in these countries to take measures to tighten money and, thereby, further constricting the supply of funds available to borrowers. Finally, many of the borrowers themselves were forced to take independent measures to tighten their domestic money markets to attempt to offset the adverse balance of payments effect of the decline in world lending. In the less developed areas, interest rate manipulations tended to be comparatively ineffective because of the absence of important domestic money markets and the relatively great importance of exports and imports in determining the level of domestic economic activity. Therefore, the measures chosen by these countries frequently involved attempts to improve the balance of trade by reducing imports, policies which were likely to be globally deflating.

---

[1]Excluding amortization payments.

b-1/ The Primary Deflationary Effects on the World Economy of the Decline in United States Lending

It is axiomatic in economics that a decline in investment, ceteris paribus, reduces the level of economic activity. What is particularly interesting, however, is the largeness of the decline in American net[1] capital exports relative to world investment. We estimate that United States net capital exports declined by $1.3-$5.0 billion in the tight money period during July 1928 to September 1929, from a level of $2.1-$3.3 billion during the relatively easy money period between January 1927 and June 1928 (table 1). This decline of $1.3-$5.0 billion was equivalent to something between 8% and 37% of net capital formation outside the United States.[2]

Considering only American lending to Europe we find, upon comparing the same two periods, that net capital exports to Europe declined by $.9-$3.2 billion (table 2). This was the equivalent of 8%-33% of European net capital formation.[3]

---

[1]Net capital exports are here defined as gross capital exports less gross capital imports, excluding amortization.

[2]See appendix 2, note 7 for the method of estimating world (excluding the United States) net national capital formation and the percentage share of American net capital exports. We have taken account of the fact that we are contrasting periods of different lengths of time.

[3]See appendix 2, note 4 for the method of estimating European net national capital formation and the percentage share of American net capital exports. We have taken account of the fact that we are contrasting periods of different lengths of time.

Table 1*

A Comparison of United States Long Term Lending Between January 1927 and June 1928 with United States Long Term Lending Between July 1928 and September 1929[1]

($000,000)

		[a] January 1927 to June 1928[2]	[b] July 1928 to September 1929[2]	[b]-[a] Change[3]
I.	Portfolio	-1874	- 605	+1269
II.	Direct	- 630	- 730	- 100
	I + II ...	-2504	-1335	+1169
III.	Transactions in Outstanding Securities[4]			
	Estimate 1	357	557	+ 200
	Estimate 2	62	1478	+1416
	Estimate 3	- 810	3069	+3879
Total:[5]				
	I+II+III (Est. 1)	-2147	- 778	+1369
	I+II+III (Est. 2)	-2442	+ 143	+2585
	I+II+III (Est. 3)	-3314	1734	+5048

Source: Calculated from appendix 2, note 1, table 10; this note contains a detailed description of estimating procedures.

*Revised, 1975

Estimate 1: Assumes that all transactions in outstanding securities are undertaken at a uniform rate over time.

Estimate 2: Assumes that foreigners and Americans sell each other securities when the U. S. stock market is steady or declining but purchase each others securities when the U. S. stock market is rising.

Estimate 3: Assumes that when the U. S. stock market is steady or declining foreigners will reduce their holdings of American securities while Americans increase their holdings of foreign securities; conversely, when the American stock market is rising, foreigners increase their holdings of U. S. securities while Americans reduce their holdings of foreign securities.

[1]We have taken account of the problems involved in comparing flows over a period of 18 months with flows over a period of 15 months. See chapter 2, page 17 and appendix 2, note 2 and note 3.

[2](-) indicates outflow of funds from the United States.

[3](+) indicates decline in the outflow of funds from the United States.

[4]These estimates are based on the following assumptions.

[5]Excludes amortization payments.

Table 2

A Comparison of United States Long Term Lending to Europe Between January 1927 and June 1928 with United States Long Term Lending Between July 1928 and September 1929[1]

($000,000)

		[a] January 1927 to June 1928[2]	[b] July 1928 to September 1929[2]	[b]-[a] Change[3]
I.	Direct Investment	- 241	- 250	- 9
II.	Portfolio Investment	- 858	- 190	+ 668
	I + II ...	-1099	- 440	+ 659
III.	Transactions in Outstanding Securities[4]			
	Estimate 1	+ 221	+ 413	+ 192
	Estimate 2	- 156	+1399	+1555
	Estimate 3	- 514	+1883	+2397
Total:[5]				
	I+II+III (Est. 1)	- 878	- 27	+ 851
	I+II+III (Est. 2)	-1255	+ 959	+2214
	I+II+III (Est. 3)	-1613	+1443	+3056

Source: Calculated in appendix 2, note 3.

[1]We have taken account of the problems involved in comparing flows over a period of 18 months with flows over a period of 15 months. See chapter 2, page 17 and appendix 2, note 2 and note 3.

[2](-) indicates an outflow of funds from the United States.

[3](+) indicates a decline in the outflow of funds from the United States.

[4]The assumptions behind these estimates are described briefly in table 1 note 3 and in detail in appendix 2, note 3.

[5]Gross outflow minus gross inflow excluding amortization payments.

Germany and Great Britain probably felt the most severe effects of the decline in American lending to Europe. The 1929 decline in United States portfolio lending (chart 2) alone amounted to about 10% of German domestic net capital formation.[1] Since it is likely that Germany participated in the New York stock market boom, this estimate would tend to be a minimum estimate of the actual net decline in American capital exports to Germany relative to German net capital formation.

Chart 2

U.S. New Portfolio Lending to Germany, 1927-1933

($000,000)

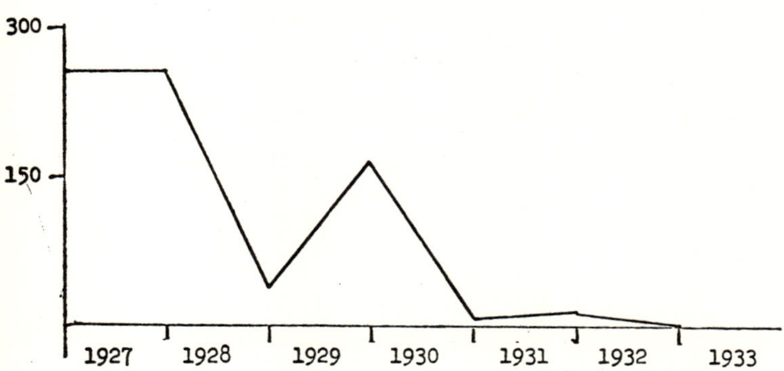

Source: Cleona Lewis, America's Stake in International Investment, pp. 619-629.

---

[1]See appendix 2, note 5 for the method of estimating German net capital formation.

Great Britain possessed one of the largest pools of liquid investible capital in the world. However, the British stock market was steady rather than strongly bullish.[1] To the extent that foreign participation in the New York stock markets was a function of the size of the foreigner's liquid assets and his alternative domestic investment opportunities, it is likely that a considerable portion of foreign transactions in outstanding securities originated in Britain.

The decline in the net outflow of American capital contributed to the rising interest rates in these countries (chart 3) and to the constriction of their domestic capital markets: domestic new issues in both countries declined sharply in 1929 (chart 4). Central Banks accentuated this tight money situation, despite the indications of the onsetting recession (chart 5). Unemployment in Britain declined slightly, but remained at relatively high levels. Unemployment and imports declined in Germany (table 3). It is important to note that conditions in the United States, by the same measures, remained relatively prosperous through the third quarter of 1929[2] (chart 3). Thus, the initial deflationary impact of the United States on

---

[1]Stock market price indices are taken from The League of Nations, Statistical Yearbook 1930-1931, p. 255.

[2]All unemployment statistics for these years are taken from the League of Nations, Statistical Yearbook, 1930-1931, pp. 56-57.

Chart 3

Private Short Term Interest and Discount
Rates: U.S., U.K., Germany
1927-1930
Per Cent Per Annum

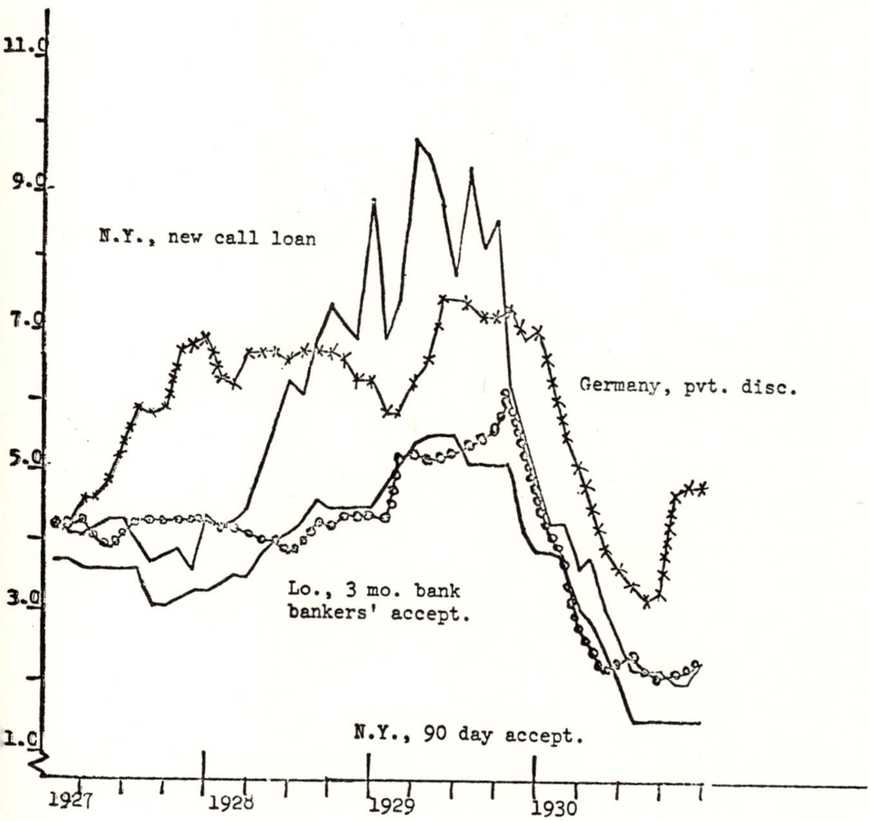

Source: Banking and Monetary Statistics 1943 ed.: British and German rates, pp. 656-658; New York money market rates, pp. 450-451.

Chart 4

Index of New Issues for Domestic Purposes: U.S., U.K., and Germany 1927-1930

(1927 = 100)

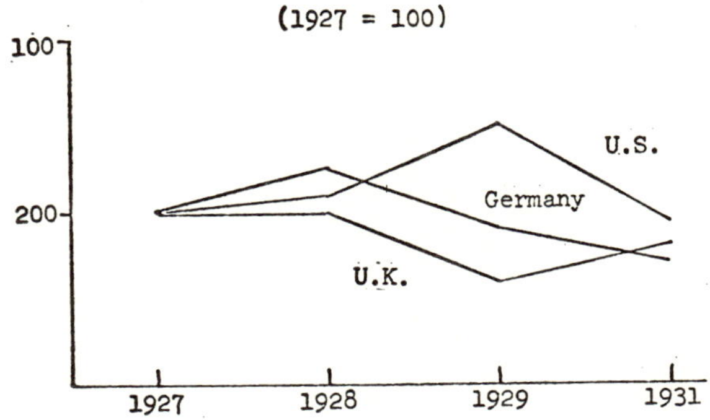

Source: Calculated from the League of Nations Statistical Yearbook 1933/34, p. 26.

Germany and Britain[1] was a product of the decline in net capital exports during the American boom, not of the later decline in American imports.

---

[1]Germany and Great Britain, accounting for 12% and 9% of world industrial output respectively, were the largest European industrial countries. Their industrial output was exceeded only by the United States, with her 45% of world industrial output. (Shares cited are the weights used in the League of Nations index of world industrial activity, League of Nations, World Production and Prices, p. 23.) It is interesting that among the less important European industrial countries, central bank discount rates were increased in 1928 or 1929 by the Netherlands, Switzerland, Belgium, Italy, Hungary, and Sweden, and were unchanged in France. In no country did the central banks ease domestic monetary conditions in order to offset the effects of the decline in new American lending and the increased flow of long and short term funds to the American stock market. (Discount rate data are taken from Banking and Monetary Statistics, 1943 ed., pp. 656-657.)

Chart 5

Central Bank Discount
Rates, 1927-1930

(Percent per Annum)

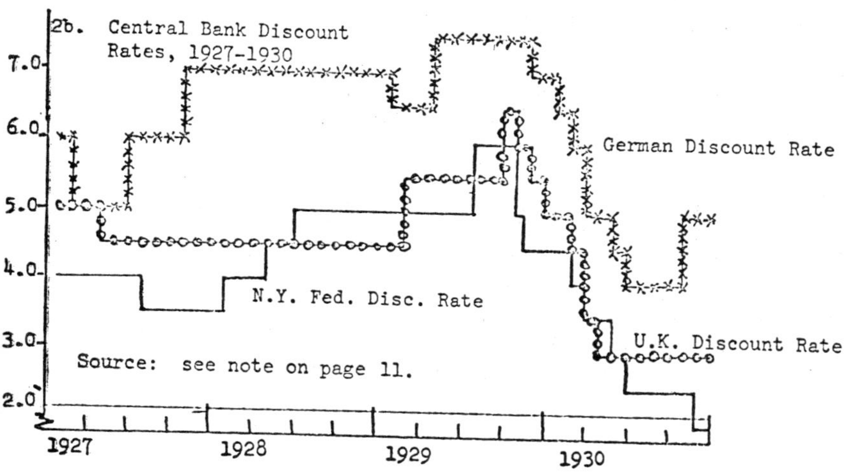

Source: Banking and Monetary Statistics, 1943 ed.: New York Federal Reserve Bank Discount Rate, pp. 440-441; British and German rates, pp. 656-658.

New Long Term Lending From Other Sources.

Since net American Capital exports declined, and foreign countries reacted by increased tightening of their own money markets, foreign lending by other major lending countries was the only remaining source of funds. However, the tight money of the period affected most international money markets and new long term lending from countries other than the United

Table 3

Merchandise Imports and Exports
U. S., U. K., and Germany
1927-1930

($000,000)

	1927	1928	1929	1930
Exports...				
U. S.	2,310	2,375	2,341	1,838
Germany	2,566	2,929	3,210	2,867
Great Britain	4,049	4,107	4,083	3,200
Imports...				
U. S.	1,264	1,249	1,333	909
Germany	3,381	3,341	3,202	2,476
Great Britain	5,929	5,818	5,941	5,081
Exports-Imports				
U. S.	1,046	1,126	1,008	929
Germany	- 814	- 412	+ 9	+ 391
Great Britain	-1,880	-1,712	-1,858	-1,880

Source: Calculated from U. S. Department of Commerce, Commerce Yearbook, Vol. II, 1931, pp. 724-726, and 1935, pp. 372-375; U. S. figures from Hal B. Lary, The United States in the World Economy, table I.

States declined in 1929 by about $250 million (table 4).

It is difficult to tell whether this decline was due to reticence of borrowers or suppliers. The increase in American and foreign lending in 1930,[1] at lower rates and with borrowers generally in worse condition, implies that borrowers reluctance to float new bonds during late 1928 and most of 1929 was part of the problem. Whichever was the most important factor, however, it is clear that the tight money policies and reduced capital exports of the United States acted to constrict the foreign and domestic capital markets of other countries.

---

[1]See table 4 and chapter 2, chart 6.

Table 4

New Long Term Lending by
Major Lenders Other Than the U. S.

1927-1933

($000,000)

	27	28	29	30	31	32	33
U. K.	674	696	461	529	209	102	125
Netherlands	145[a]	107[a]	45[c]	103[c]	16[c]	10[c]	---[b]
Sweden	38[a]	18[a]	21[c]	60[c]	20[c]	30[c]	---[b]
France	N/A	N/A	43[c]	55[c]	146[c]	65[c]	16[b]
Total	857	821	570	747	391	207	141

Sources:

a/ League of Nations *Balance of Payments Yearbook*, 1927-29, p. 26.
b/ League of Nations *Balance of Payments Yearbook*, 1933, p. 17.
c/ League of Nations *Balance of Payments Yearbook*, 1931-32, p. 14.

U. K. 1927-1932 data League of Nations *Balance of Payments Yearbook*, 1931-32, p. 16; 1933 data League of Nations *Balance of Payments Yearbook*, 1933, p. 169.

b-3/ The Effects of the Decline in United States Capital Exports on World Merchandise Trade

Britain faced not only the immediate effects of the increased outflow of long term funds to the United States, but the indirect effects of the decline in new American portfolio lending to British export customers as well. American new portfolio lending to Germany, Australia, Argentina, Brazil, and Japan declined sharply in 1929 (table 5). British exports to these countries declined by 7% in 1929, while British exports to others

Table 5

U. S. New Lending to Argentina, Brazil, Australia and Japan

1927-1930

($000,000)

	1927	1928	1929	1930
Argentina	108.9	49.8	1.5	145.3
Brazil	62.0	78.5	10.9	30.0
Australia	92.7	56.5	----	22.5
Japan	27.6	97.9	11.4	69.7

Source: Cleona Lewis, America's Stake in International Investment, pp. 619-629.

increased by 1% in the same period[1] (table 6). America's part in this problem again centered on the decline in net long term capital exports rather than on the merchandise account: total American imports from these countries increased in 1929 (table 7)[2].

The first foreign exchange crises occurred in late 1929: Argentina went off the gold standard while Australia finally ceased making payments in gold in early 1930. The $47 million decline in new American lending, alone,

---

[1]Assuming that the decline in U. S. new lending was the major problem facing these five countries, continuation of U. S. capital exports might have led to an increase of about 2% in total U. K. exports during 1929 (see note 6).

[2]The reader should note that even in those countries where exports to the United States declined, the decline was less than the decline in U. S. lending.

Table 6

United Kingdom Exports by
Country of Destination, 1927-1930

($000,000)

U. K. Exports to:	1927	1928	1929	1930
Germany	204	199	180	131
Argentina	131	152	142	123
Brazil	70	78	65	39
Australia	298	271	264	154
Japan	74	71	65	40
Subtotal	777	771	716	487
Changes as percentage of preceding year	----	-.8%	-7.1%	-32.1%
Total U. K. Exports	4,049	4,107	4,083	3,200
less exports to above countries	3,272	3,336	3,367	2,713
change as percentage of preceding year		+1.9%	+.9%	-19.4%

Source: 1928-1930 U. K. exports from U. S. Department of Commerce, Commerce Yearbook 1931, vol. II, p. 295; 1927 data from Commerce Yearbook 1929, vol. II, pp. 658-659.

Table 7

Exports of Germany, Argentina, Brazil, Australia and Japan to the U. S.

1927-1930

($000,000)

Exports to U. S. by:	1927	1928	1929	1930
Germany	184	190	236	163
Argentina	81	84	89	50
Brazil	199	216	193	126
Australia	89	43	27	25
Japan	395	383	421	250
Total	948	916	966	614

Source: U. S. Department of Commerce, Commerce Yearbook, 1931, Vol. II, p. 729; 1933, p. 350.

was equivalent to about 33% of the $133 million decline in the Argentine merchandise surplus, while the $57 million decline in new American lending to Australia during 1929 was equivalent to more than 50% of the $98 million increase in the Australian merchandise deficit.[1] The resulting exchange problems led each of these countries to introduce trade restrictions. The very fact that such measures were necessary indicate that the decline in imports would have been less had the inflow of long term funds continued[2].

---

[1]Merchandise trade data from the Commerce Yearbook 1931, vol. II, pp. 724-727.

[2]The tendency of developing countries to finance imports by lending would have had a stabilizing effect on the world, although in the short run it would have aggravated the payments problems of Australia and Argentina. We customarily treat imports as a function of income (given price) in the short run in the following way: $M=c + mY$ where M = imports, c = constant, m = marginal propensity to import, and Y = income. A worsening of the balance of payments due to a decline in exports is likely to reflect a decline in domestic income in countries with large export sectors such as Argentina and Australia; thus imports would also decline. However, in primary exporting, relatively unindustrialized countries it is likely that given the level of income the demand for imports will be greater -- perhaps because there is no possibility of producing them at home in the short run or because they represent necessities of life or of production. In such countries manufactured imports will tend to fall less than proportionately with export proceeds or income: people are more likely to dissave (or borrow) to purchase imports (i.e., "c" is greater).'

This would tend to have a stabilizing effect on the developed manufacturing countries which depend on these countries for an export market. However, if the balance of payments, rather than income, becomes the relevant constraint, authorities of the importing countries may nullify this effect through restrictive exchange and trade policies. Thus continued lending by the manufacturing countries to these countries could lead to an immediate increase (or prevention of a decrease) in imports by these countries. This is in contrast to the more customary longer range effects of long term lending which may affect the lenders exports by the multiplier effect on income in the borrowing importer's country.

c/ The Effects of American Long Term Capital Exports and Imports on the World Economy (1930-1933).

Insofar as we have correctly represented the decline in American net capital exports as a critical factor in the decline in world investment during 1928 and 1929, it was also indirectly responsible for the dramatic universal decline of primary product prices which was one of the most serious deflating elements in the world economy between 1930 and 1933. Other than this, the major effect of long term capital flows from the United States was their failure to return to the high levels of 1927. The United States exported only $300 million in long term funds in 1930 and was a net importer of long term funds between 1931 and 1933.[1,2]

While the major effects of the American capital exports on the world economy between 1930 and 1933 were their continued decline and the induced decline in commodity prices, a number of less important but nonetheless deflating long term capital flows were present. Most important of these were the flow of funds from debtor countries to the United States for the purpose of repatriating their outstanding bonds, the flow of long term funds from the United States to Europe prior to the devaluation of the

---

[1]See chapter 2, chart 3, p. 11.

[2]New portfolio lending by other major lending nations declined in a similar way. Average portfolio lending by these nations was more than $800 million in 1927 and 1928. A brief upward spurt of about $150 million in their lending in 1930 was more than offset by the decline in the net outflow of long term capital from the United States during the same year. Average annual new portfolio lending by these countries between 1931 and 1933 was $250 million. (Calculated from data in table 4).

dollar, and the flow of funds from Europe to the United States shortly following the devaluation.

The Decline in Primary Commodity Prices

The decline in world investment in 1928 and 1929, due in part to the decline in American net capital exports, contributed to the decline in world industrial demand which caused, in turn, the decline in primary commodity prices.[1] Because of the low price elasticities of demand for most of these products, the average decline in export revenues of Asia, Africa, Oceania, South America and Canada in 1930 was 25%[2]. Any advantage accruing

---

[1]The question of whether the decline in primary commodity prices was due to a decrease in industrial demand or an increase in supply will be discussed in detail in chapter 4. However, we may note tentatively that the quantum index of non-agricultural production declined in 1930 while the quantum index of agricultural production was steady. (League of Nations, World Production and Prices, p. 7). In short, there is no evidence of a general increase in supply. Moreover, in light of declining short term interest rates and generally declining prices in industrial countries, there is no reason to believe that storage costs rose. Thus, the decline in primary prices was probably due to a decreased willingness to hold or increase inventories in light of expectations of declining aggregate industrial demand.

[2]The weighted average of the decline in the exports from Asia-Oceania-Africa (-23.5%), South America (-28.4%), and Canada (-25.0%) calculated from the League of Nations Statistical Yearbook 1933-1934, pp. 194, 195.

to the industrial nations in terms of reduced import prices was countered by the decline in exports from these countries: exports from Europe declined by 14.6%.[1] The decline in the value of world exports in 1930 was $5.4 billion.[2] Greater than our $5.0 billion maximum estimate of the decline in American net capital exports, the decline in world exports in 1930 was, by similar reasoning, large enough to have had substantial impact on world economic activity. Furthermore, each industrial country had domestic primary commodity sectors[3] which also faced the reduction in the value of their output. Thus, the initial deflationary effects on the world economy of the decline in industrial demand were quickly reflected and amplified in these countries by further deflation due to the decline in their exports and the value of their domestic primary product production.[4]

---

[1]ibid. While Europe's commodity terms of trade improved, this cannot be taken as an unambiguous indicator of an increase in welfare because of the decline in the amount of trade. The improvement in the European income terms of trade is not an unambiguous indicator of an increase in welfare because it assumes that resources devoted to producing goods for export by Europe can now be shifted to the production of goods for domestic consumption. Such a transfer cannot be perfected in the short run in most cases and, thus, while potential European welfare rose, actual European welfare declined.

[2]Calculated from the League of Nations, Statistical Yearbook, 1933-1934, pp. 194-195.

[3]In the United States, for example, the average share of agriculture and mining was, on average, 13.0% to 15.3% of national income between 1919 and 1928. (Historical Statistics, 1961 ed., p. 140).

[4]In the United States, for example, both gross and net realized farm income declined by $2.0 billion (Historical Statistics, 1961 ed., p. 283). This decline was largely attributable to the decline in prices. It is equivalent to about 15% of the total decline in gross national product during 1930. (Calculated from data in Historical Statistics, 1961 ed., p. 139).

Repatriations

Foreign bond prices in New York began to sag badly early in 1931 under the pressure of extensive foreign defaults (chart 4). Many debtor countries responded to these price movements by repatriating their bonds. Repatriation complicated the balance of payments problems of debtor countries, most of whom, like Germany, already had deficits. We estimate that the flow of funds to the United States for purposes of bond repatriation was about $500 million between 1930 and 1933.[1]

Speculation in Outstanding Securities During 1933

American purchases of foreign securities rose by almost $500 million in 1933[2]. There is considerable qualitative evidence that much of this increase represented the purchase of gold bonds[3] of the Gold Bloc countries.[4] It is difficult to interpret this as anything other than speculation against the dollar by American citizens. As such, it contributed to the precipitous decline in the dollar rate after the American gold embargo of March 1933.

Foreign purchases of outstanding American domestic securities also increased by $500 million during 1933.[5] This flow was constructive from the

---

[1]Estimating procedures and estimates of repatriation, total and by region, are given in appendix 1, note 7/3-c.

[2]Hal. B. Lary, The United States in the World Economy, p. 107.

[3]Bonds payable in some quantity of gold and therefore not subject to devaluation relative to gold.

[4]See, for example, U. S. Department of Commerce, "The Balance of International Payments of the United States in 1933", Trade Information Bulletin No. 819, pp. 84-89 passim.

[5]It is difficult to tell whether this was based on a different foreign evaluation of the outlook for the dollar rate on the rise in equity prices in New York, or on both. We discussed this question in greater detail in this chapter, section a.

point of view of the United States insofar as it helped buoy the dollar exchange rate, which dropped steadily in 1933 relative to most major European currencies. However, inasmuch as we do not know what was the national origin of these funds, it is difficult to evaluate this flow from a global point of view.

d/ The Effects on the World Economy of Various Changes in the Real Value of American Long Term Assets and Liabilities and in the Relative Value of Flows Associated with these Assets and Liabilities (1927-1933).

Changes in various dimensions of American long term assets and liabilities and in the flows associated with them had a number of deflating effects on the world economy. Payments of interest, amortization, and dividends increasingly burdened the debtor countries as their long term borrowing and export revenues declined. The decline in the value of American equities reduced the real value of foreigners' wealth and probably had some negative effect on their consumption. Finally, the effect of falling prices in increasing the real value of money and government bonds and, thereby, consumption, was reduced by default and changing relative expectations about the likelihood of debt repayment.

Interest and Amortization Payments

Net interest and amortization payments to the United States exceeded net long term lending by the United States during every year from 1928 to 1933. These charges were fixed by the terms of the original loans, could not vary with economic conditions and represented an increasing burden to debtor countries as their borrowing and exports declined. Interest and amortization charges could be altered only by default or renegotiation of the loan. Renegotiation was a lengthy and possibly fruitless process; default was a serious breach of international financial ethics. Each measure tended to make creditors uneasy about additional long term loans.

Four options remained for a debtor country: short term borrowing, increasing exports, reducing imports, or expending reserves. Short term loans do not seem to have been generally available to debtors in an amount sufficient to finance their deficits. When they were, as in the case of Germany, their withdrawal at critical times was perhaps as damaging as the deficit which they financed. It is quite impossible for most primary commodity producers to increase the value of their exports in the short run. In many cases lengthy periods are required to increase production and in most cases increased output would lead to lower total export proceeds because of the price-inelastic demand for most primary commodities. Most primary exporting debtor countries could finance deficits for only a limited period of time with their relatively small holdings of international reserves. The only remotely feasible form of adjustment, then, was import reduction. This was very deflating with respect to the world since most of these countries lacked extensive domestic import-competing industries, and thus the compensating increase in the level of domestic economic activity would tend to be small.

In short, most of the policy options which were satisfactory from a global point of view were not open to primary exporting debtor countries; the feasible policy options tended to be deflationary. When these options failed, default resulted. Even default, however, did not completely free the debtor country from the deflationary effects which were linked with the portfolio:

> "In a number of cases (of default), the bankers have sent representatives at their own expense to the respective countries, and at all times have maintained close contact with the governments concerned... As long as a country reiterates

publicly its willingness to meet its external obligations and merely claims inability to pay, the only question to be considered is whether the right steps have been taken by the debtor to remedy the situation. If a country is making every effort to balance its budget, to confine expenditures to indispensible administrative functions, and to improve its balance of international payments...[1]

"As a matter of fact, two of the above countries have not included their debt service in their budgets and one has made provisions for only a small amount. This, in part, is due to decreased revenues resulting from difficult economic conditions, and in part, to public opinion which will not support the governments in the reduction of expenditure necessary to provide for debt-service payments. Unfamiliar with American conditions, the popular opinion prevailing in many South American countries is that their bonds are held by the bankers who purchased the issues and that it is easier for wealthy bankers to bear the losses resulting from their deficits than to impose new burdens on their own peoples."[2] (Emphasis mine)

Foreign Losses in the U. S. Stock Market

There is no reason to believe that the value of foreign holdings of American stocks did not decline in the same proportion as all American equities. Studies by Ando, Modigliani, and Arena indicate that changes in wealth and changes in consumption are positively correlated.[3] Therefore, the stock market decline probably reduced the level of foreign consumption.

The Real Balance Effect

In principle, the sharp decline in the general price levels in most countries should have increased the real value of outstanding government debt. This increase in "real balances" would lead people to save less, consume

---

[1] Institute of International Finance Bulletin, No. 51, April 14, 1932, p. 2.

[2] ibid, p. 3. The writer did not explain how popular opinion in South America misrepresented conditions in the United States.

[3] John J. Arena, "The Wealth Effect and Consumption: A Statistical Inquiry", Economic Essays, Fall 1963, pp. 274-276, 282; Albert Ando and Franco Modigliani, "The 'Life Cycle' Hypothesis of Saving: Aggregate Implications and Tests", American Economic Association, Readings in Business Cycle Theory, vol. X, p. 423.

more, and thus implies that the long term portfolio would have had, in this respect at least, an inflating effect on the world economy. The real balance effect rests on two assumptions which are critical for our purposes: 1/ governments do not default on outstanding debt; 2/ private debts and assets have no effect since the increase in the real value of private liabilities is offset by counterpart increases in the real value of private assets and debtors and creditors have equal marginal propensities to consume from changes in wealth. The failure to satisfy these assumptions during the period 1930 to 1933 suggests that the real balance was reduced, and possibly negative.

The failure to meet the assumption that governments do not default implies that any increase in the real value of debt due to falling prices would have been offset to some extent by the reduced probability that the debt would be paid. Furthermore, as we have said above, the effect of private debt was probably negative rather than neutral. We have stated why repatriation of bonds by debtors implies that debtors believe that repayment is more likely than do creditors. Given equal changes in the real value of the debt for both the creditor and debtor, if the debtor believes the probability of repayment is greater than does the creditor, the <u>expected</u> value of the increased value of the debtor's debt is larger than the expected value of the increase in the creditor's asset. Given equal marginal propensities to consume from changes in wealth for both debtor and creditor, the decline in the debtor's consumption will exceed the increase in the creditors consumption, and the net effect will be deflationary.

Summary

The decline in new American lending, the increased inflow of funds to New York for outstanding security purchases, and the Federal Reserve's tight money policy led to a worldwide tightening of monetary conditions which reduced domestic investment and foreign lending by other countries. The deflationary impact of this decline in investment was soon combined with the initial decline of the rate of growth of exports, particularly in Great Britain, as many countries reduced imports in an attempt to compensate for their rising balance of payments deficits, due largely to the decline in new lending.

The decline in aggregate industrial demand, caused by the worldwide tight money policy and declining investment, best explains the sharp declines in primary product prices which added to the deflationary problems facing industrial countries by reducing their exports to primary commodity exporting areas and reducing the value of their domestic primary material production. The basic forces which determined the decline in world economic activity had taken shape by 1930.

Long term capital flows and the long term portfolio continued to exert deflationary pressure on the world economy in a variety of ways after 1930. Direct investment by the United States continued to decline, while portfolio investment also declined following a brief increase in 1930. The relatively inflexible interest and amortization payment contributed to the payments problems of debtor countries which, after abortively attempting to adjust their balances of payments by import restriction, were forced to default on their debts and thus contributed to the atmosphere of crisis which further undermined creditor confidence and constricted long term lending. Repatriation of bonds led to flows of funds from debtor countries with deficits, further complicating their balance of payments problems. In 1933 Americans used outstanding long term securities as a vehicle to speculate against the dollar. Finally, any real balance effect, through which falling prices might have increased the real value of the government portfolio and thereby consumption, was dampened or eliminated by government defaults and by apparently inconsistent views by creditors and debtors about the likelihood of repayment which implied that the increase in the real value of private assets was less than the increase in the real expected value of private liabilities.

For these reasons, American long term lending was a critical contribution by the United States to the world depression. Not only did the American long term lending decline well before the 1930 decline in American imports in 1930 but the capital account was the only account which changed in a way which increased the difficulty with which foreigners could make payments to the United States. Therefore, America's tight money policy and the decline in her long term capital exports represented the major deflationary impact of the United States on the world economy and the major role of the United States in initiating the world depression.

The question still remains, however, as to the importance of the decline in United States long term lending relative to other deflationary problems in the world. We address that question in the following chapter.

Chapter 4

Alternative and Complementary Explanations of the Depression

Introduction

Allan Nevins has observed, quite reasonably, that "great and complex events have great and complex causes".[1] The greatness and the complexity of the event known as the Great Depression is undeniable. No "single-cause" explanation can lead to a satisfactory understanding of the events of the period 1927-1933. Indeed, the notion of cause is severely restricted in the complicated interdependence of parts of the system.

To understand the depression we must observe the behavior of a system of economic relations, rather than the behavior of a few elements. For example, an explanation of the depression depends not only on the decline in long term lending and the consequent decline in trade but also upon the failure of short term lending to increase and of governments to cooperate more fully.

Given the complexity of the problem, changes in economic understanding, changes in economic values, changes in the availability of data, and perhaps most important, the multitude of relevant questions which may be asked, it is surprising that we have so few different interpretations of the Great Depression.

There are a number of reasons for the variety of "explanations" of the depression. One problem in any explanation is determining where to begin. If one begins with the year 1927 it is proper to emphasize the role of long term lending. However, if one begins his analysis in 1930, emphasis of current account problems is more convincing, while one who begins with the year 1931 could not fail to be struck by the severe problems facing the

---

[1]Allan Nevins, The Emergence of Lincoln, Vol. II, p. 462.

reserve currency countries.

A second problem is a sort of historical myopia, the tendency to overgeneralize about the "interwar period". Thus the flight of short term capital of the period 1934 to 1939 and the current speculation of the period 1919 to 1926 have been extrapolated, without evidence, into the period between 1927 and 1930.

Diverse explanations also arise in response to different questions. For example, an author discussing the failure of world recovery may implicitly extend his argument to include the cause of the depression. Of course, the factors which led to the depression are not necessarily identical to the factors preventing recovery. Other writers discuss measures which might have prevented the depression; however, by similar reasoning, those measures which might have prevented the depression may deal with entirely different elements of the system from those which apparently plunged us into the depression.

This chapter has two purposes: we are interested in relating the various explanations of the depression to the behavior of long term capital flows, and in integrating these explanations into a general explanation of the depression. The first three sections concern the views of various writers, according to the part of the balance of payments to which their arguments seem directed: current account, capital account, and gold and reserve currencies. The fourth section will deal with explanations based on changes or defects in the structure of world economy.

a/ Current Account

The behavior of the current account has been held responsible for the world depression in a number of ways. Some have argued that the depression spread from the United States to other countries through the decline in

United States import demand. Heinz Arndt[1] observes the decline in imports by a number of industrial countries and bases this as much, apparently, on unfortunate coincidence as on inter-relation. Arndt and others have pointed critically to the failure of the United States to allow its current account to become more passive.[2] Heinz Arndt, W. Arthur Lewis, and Bertil Ohlin have given causal pre-eminence to the rapid decline in primary prices, attributed to the "over production" of primaries, and a move toward autarky by primary producers which reduced the demand for manufactured imports.[3] Carl Major Wright has suggested that the failure of transport rates to decline meant that the full burden of the decline in primary prices was borne by the primary producing countries and was translated immediately into a decline in the imports of manufactured goods.[4]

a-1/ The Role of the Decline in United States Import Demand in Causing the World Depression[5]

There can be no question about the importance of the contribution of the United States depression to the world depression. The United States and Germany suffered the most severe downturns among the industrial countries. The United States accounted for about 45% of the world's industrial output.[6]

---

[1]See section a-1 and a-2.

[2]See section a-6.

[3]See sections a-3 and a-4.

[4]See section a-5.

[5]See Arndt, The Economic Lessons of the Nineteen-Thirties, p. 31. Arndt argues that the world economy contained a number of internally unstable nations; the national declines were triggered by the U. S. slump.

[6]League of Nations, World Production and Prices, p. 23.

Nonetheless, economic conditions worsened in Germany and Britain during 1929, prior to the downturn in United States economic activity. Britain and Germany accounted for about 21% of world industrial output,[1] and the decline in their domestic investment occurred at the same time as the drop in new long term foreign lending by the United States. This drop in lending was reinforced by the deflationary policies introduced by these countries in order to maintain their external positions.[2]

In contrast to the increase in American imports during 1928 and 1929, long term capital exports declined during each of those years (chart 1). Furthermore, the decline in United States capital exports was clear by the second or third quarter of 1928,[3] and was primarily a product of the United States boom. The world depression began before the decline in American income and imports although imports of goods and services by the United States did decline by more than capital exports between 1930 and 1933.

a-2/ The Simultaneous Worsening of Conditions in the Industrial Countries

Heinz Arndt does not directly address the question of whether there were relationships among the industrial nations which were directly responsible for the depression.[4] Instead, he places primary importance on the common problems which faced the industrial countries: e.g., the legacy of war, over-production of primary products, the move toward autarchy, and the impact of structural changes caused by war debts and changes in the patterns of trade.

---

[1]League of Nations, World Production and Prices, p. 23.

[2]See ch. 3, pp.39-45, for a more detailed discussion of the relative importance of U.S. imports and capital exports to the U.K., Germany, and certain other countries.

[3]See ch. 3, pp. 32-35.

[4]Heinz Arndt, The Economic Lessons of the Nineteen-Thirties, pp. 9, 11, 31.

While all these are problems in the interwar period, the responses of Britain and Germany to the decline of United States lending in 1929 initiated the deflationary spiral. The reader may choose to regard the problems cited by Arndt as the more remote causes of the depression or, alternatively, to regard long term capital flows as the instruments through which these problems made their impact on the economies of the nations involved. We will discuss the plausibility of some of these assertions later. Nonetheless, it is clear that these nations did not react simultaneously to the more remote problems, but rather to the more immediate problem of the decline in lending. Furthermore, this decline in lending was initiated by the one country which was least affected by the problems described by Arndt.

a-3/ The Problem of Primary Overproduction

Some writers[1] have considered overproduction of primary products, with the subsequent sharp declines in primary prices and aggregate demand by primary producers, among the most important causes of the world depression. It is undeniable that the rapid increases in stocks, which began in 1930 and continued for a number of years, made the prospects of the recovery of the prices of primary products quite remote. This however, should not be confused with the proposition that increases in production initially reduced the prices of most primary products. In general, as we will discuss, the latter did not happen.

---

[1]H. Arndt, The Economic Lessons of the Nineteen-Thirties, pp. 56, 196: W. A. Brown Jr., The International Gold Standard Reinterpreted, p. 823; B. Ohlin, The Course and Phases of the World Economic Depression, pp. 99, 211; Royal Institute of International Affairs, The Problem of International Investment, p. 14.

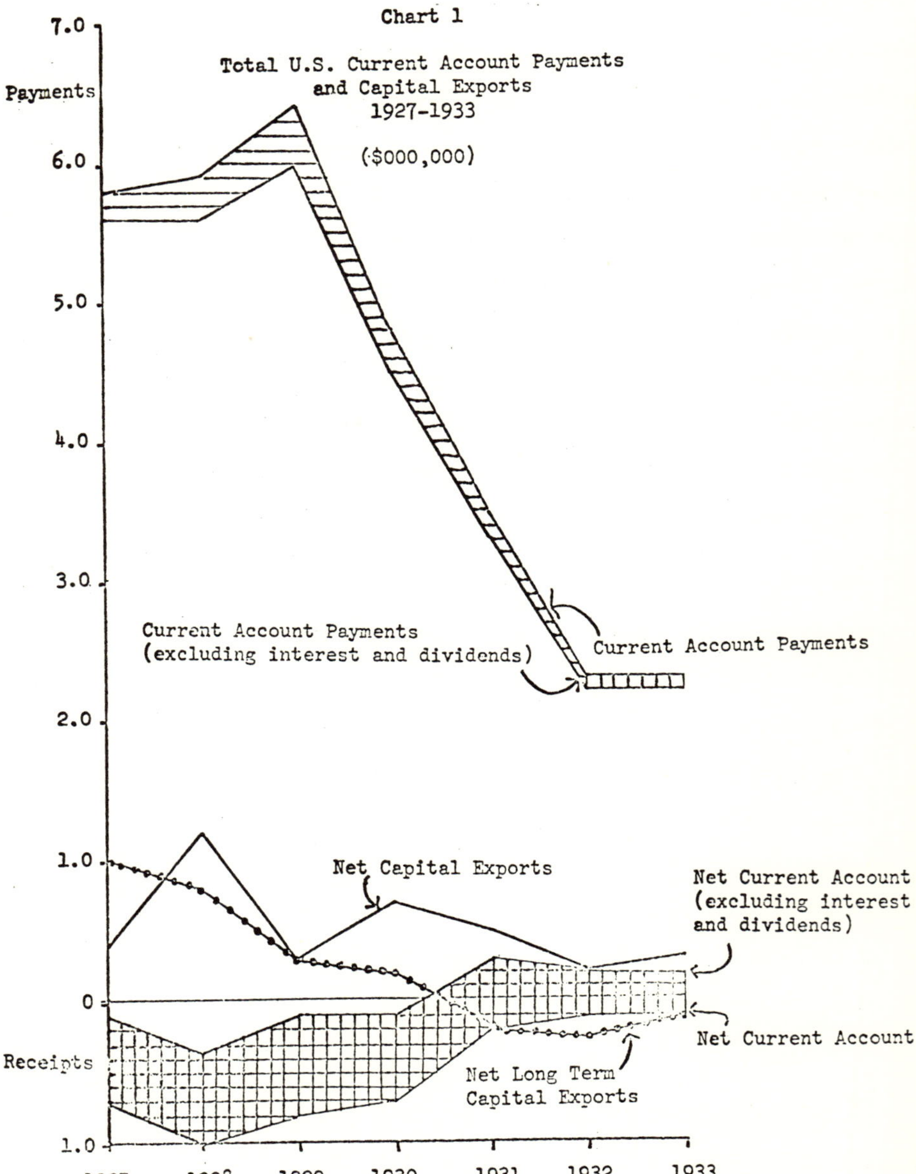

Source: Hal B. Lary, The U. S. in the World Economy, table I. However, I have moved amortization of war debt payments (see appendix 1, p. 48) from the current account and placed them in the capital account.

During the period from 1925 to 1929 the production of agricultural primary products rose less rapidly than industrial production while the production of non-agricultural primary products rose more rapidly; the weighted combined average of primary products rose less rapidly than industrial production (see chart 2 and table 1). There is apparently no index of world primary export prices during this period. However, the United States domestic price indices indicate that the prices of primary products rose in 1928 and 1929 from the levels of 1926 and 1927. In marked contrast, the consumer price index and the wholesale price index (excluding food and farm products) were lower in 1928 and 1929 than they were in 1926 and 1927 (chart 3).

On the whole, then, the primary sector was producing more and getting a better price in 1928 and 1929 than it was in 1926 and 1927. Inasmuch as the primary sector precipitated no world economic crisis in 1926 or 1927, it is difficult to see how such an argument can be made for 1929.

On the other hand the overproduction argument is somewhat relevant to the years 1930 to 1933. Again, however, it is clear that the problem lay in the decline in demand. Output of primary products tended to decline after 1929; however, it did not decline as rapidly as industrial output. The outcome of the situation is apparent in the precipitous decline of primary prices after 1929 (see chart 3). The sharp decline in primary prices and in the export earnings of primary producers was probably initially attributable to the decreased willingness to hold inventories, based on the high interest rates of 1929 and, probably more important, on pessimistic expectations about the likely course of industrial production. The other possible explanation, that a simultaneous increase in the production of most

Table 1

Percentage Change in Indices
of Primary and Industrial Production

1925 to 1929 and 1930 to 1933

	1929-1925 / 1925	1933-1930 / 1930
All Primary Products	+11.57%	- 3.88%
--Agricultural Primaries	+ 6.19%	0%
--Non-agricultural Primaries	+26.67%	-17.82%
World industrial output excluding the U.S.S.R.	+19.57%	-18.75%
World industrial output including the U.S.S.R.	+23.08%	-12.00%

Source: Calculated from data in League of Nations, World Production and Prices, p. 7.

Chart 2

Indices of Primary and
Industrial Production

1927-1933 (1925-1929 = 100)

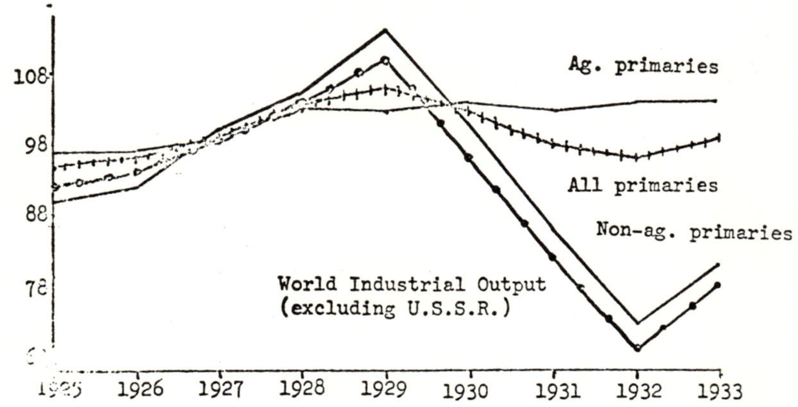

Source: League of Nations, World Production and Prices, p. 7.

Chart 3
Indices of Wholesale and Consumer Prices and Various Primary Commodity Prices 1927-1933 (for base, see notes)

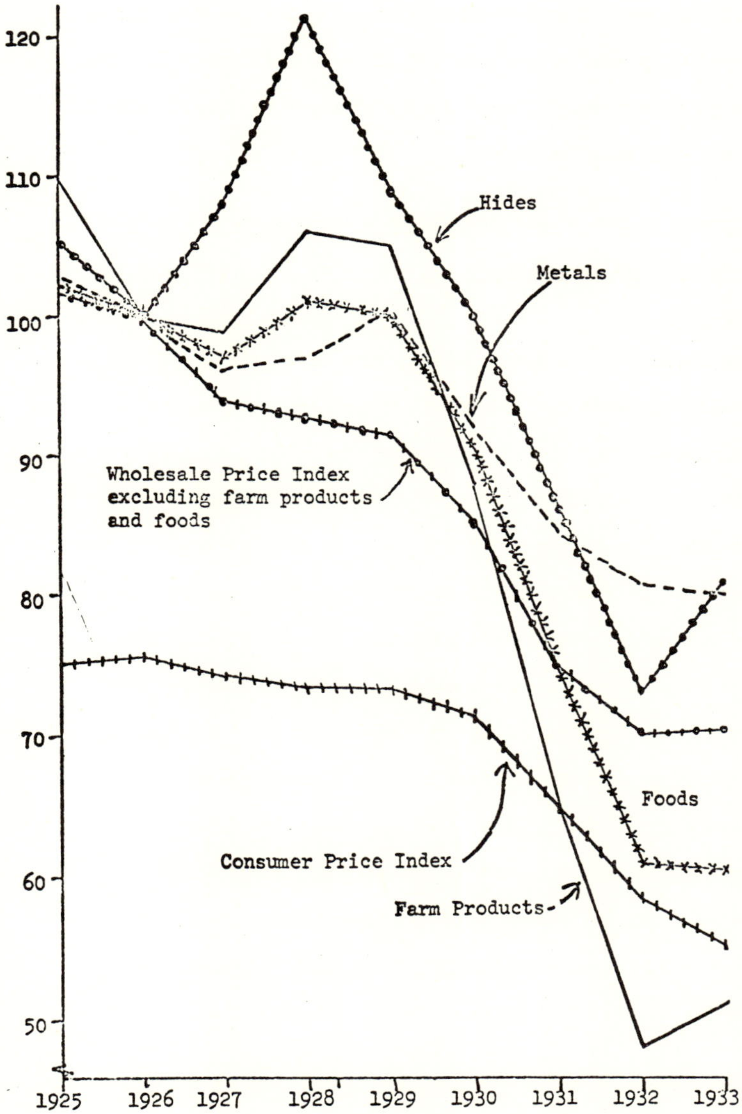

Sources: Bureau of Labor Statistics, Consumer Price Index, 1947-1949= 100; from Historical Statistics of the United States, 1961 ed., pp. 125-126. All other indices from Bureau of Labor Statistics, 1926=100; from Historical Statistics of the United States, 1961 ed., p. 116.

commodities in 1930 drove down primary prices, does not fit the facts in most cases. This argument does not contradict those who believed that a world commodity glut increasingly depressed the world economy. It simply denies that the glut originated independently of the behavior of national and international long term investment.

a-4/ The Disruption of the Traditional Pattern of Exports of Manufactured Goods to Relatively Underdeveloped Areas by an Increased Tendency Toward Autarchy.

A number of observers, including Arndt, have noted that World War I stimulated an existing trend toward protection and the development of domestic import competing industries, a trend which tended to lead away from international specialization and to disrupt world trade.[1]

This proposition has limited validity. It has been observed by many writers that the best customers of the industrial nations are each other. By this sort of reasoning, one would expect that as countries industrialize their demand for manufactured imports would increase. A study by the League of Nations in 1945 tends to confirm this.[2] Until 1930 demand for manufactured imports tended to rise most rapidly where domestic manufacturing was increasing most rapidly. To the extent that autarchy was responsible for the process of industrialization, autarchy stimulated aggregate demand for manufactured goods. Moreover, international trade increased more rapidly during the period 1925-1929 than it had during the period 1923-1925.[3]

---

[1]H. Arndt, op. cit., p. 11; Report of the International Economic Conference 5/4/27-5/23/27 cited, in part, in European Economic and Political Survey, May 31, 1927, vol. II, no. 18, p. 594.

[2]League of Nations, (Economic and Financial Section) Industrialization and Foreign Trade Series II.A.

[3]B. Ohlin, op. cit., Ch. 1.

However, Arndt's point is valid to the extent that the increased demand for manufactured imports was not felt uniformly by all industrial countries. It appears that substantial pressure was brought to bear on British textile industries, which suffered relatively more because of the relatively common tendency for countries to set up their own textile mills. British exports of cotton goods fell by about 50% between 1927 and 1933; during the same period Japanese textile exports increased by 100%.[1]

Nonetheless, while this is a consequence of autarchy, the failure of the British to readjust their economy to the new facts of international life largely reflects problems with capital flows. Among these are the structural characteristics of the British capital market which often made it easier for foreign firms to obtain long term capital than for domestic firms. Further complicating the problem were British interest rates, which, generally high until 1931, tended to discourage investment but were maintained at these levels for balance of payments purposes. Kindleberger has intimated that there were more serious problems in the British economy during this period, including a general failure of entrepreneurship[2]; nonetheless, high interest rates and capital scarcity, in principle, will discourage even the most dauntless entrepreneur.

It may be added that to the extent that increased tariffs distorted allocation, efficient allocation would have required greater movements of

---

[1]Royal Institute of International Affairs, The Problem of International Investment, p. 63.

[2]Kindleberger, C. P., Economic Growth in France and Britain, 1851-1950, ch. VI.

factors.[1] Since movements of labor were severely restricted by 1927 in comparison with the prewar years, long term capital flows would have assumed greater importance in insuring allocative efficiency.

a-5/ The Failure of Transport Rates to Decline

Carl Major Wright has argued that, in general, during depressions transport rates had fallen in such a way that the decline in primary prices at the point of consumption was greater than the decline in prices at the point of origin. This tendency enabled primary producing countries to maintain their ability to purchase imports from the industrial countries and thus helped to reduce the secondary effects (decline in exports) of depression on the industrial countries.[2]

Because of the decline in British coal exports, for the first time the balance of trade in terms of weight turned sharply in favor of the primary producers and freight rates rose between mid-1930 and mid-1931. Thus, the above stabilizing tendency was absent during the downturn of commodity prices after the summer of 1930.

---

[1]C. Iverson, Aspects of the Theory of International Capital Movements, p. 138. It should be noted that the presence of tariffs or change in the level of tariffs is not conclusive evidence of misallocation. The efficiency of allocation would depend as well on the other external costs and returns facing the developing nations.

[2]Carl Major Wright, "Convertibility and Triangular Trade as Safeguards Against Economic Depression", Economic Journal, September 1955.

Wright musters convincing evidence for his argument. However, this argument does not contradict the proposition that the decline in commodity prices was initiated by a decreased willingness to hold stocks due to expectations of decreasing industrial demand, which, in turn, were due to declining national and international long term investment. Moreover, the decline in commodity prices was so sharp[1] that even had the cost of shipping behaved in a stabilizing manner, export revenues of the primary producers would probably still have declined; while this does not contradict Wright's argument, it must be included in any estimate of the quantitative impact on the world economy of the failure of freight rates to decline.

a-6/ The Surplus on the United States Current Account

It was commonly argued that the United States exerted serious deflationary pressure on the world by running a surplus on current account while maintaining a net creditor position. For example:

> "For half a century before 1914 the U. S. A. had, with the assistance of foreign capital, built up her industry behind a tariff wall which had become a political institution while she had paid her creditors with agricultural and raw material surpluses. The war of 1914-1918 had compressed into a span of five years a process which without it might have taken a decade or two. In 1919 the U. S. A. was owed some \$2-\$4 milliard (billion) on private account, in addition to \$10 milliard of political debt. But no attempt was made to adjust the American balance of trade to the new position by turning her export surpluses into import surpluses".
>
> H. W. Arndt, *The Economic Lessons of the Nineteen-Thirties*, p. 71.[2]

---

[1]See chart 3.

[2]Arndt refers to this problem as "the most important cause of the economic instability of the world before 1929", Arndt, *op. cit.*, p. 12.

That this view was not uncommon during the interwar period[1] is indicated by the following statement of the Harvard Economic Service[2] in defensive agreement:

> "If the gold we received had produced its usual effect, it would have raised commodity prices somewhat and thus altered the terms of exchange in a manner favorable to our foreign debtors. As things have been, these debtors have sent us gold without securing thereby any alteration in the terms of exchange, and have then, at the next time of stress, sent more gold with a similar negligible result. This explains the statements of foreign critics that the United States is in the position of a creditor who refuses to take payment and makes his debtors borrow the money with which to pay current interest charges. These critics have overlooked the fact that since 1919 we have increased by $500,000,000 the amount of pay which we take in the form of services, and that we may continue to increase the amount which our debtors will pay us in this form. But it is nevertheless true, as our continued foreign loans and our continued gold imports show, that a maladjustment exists which sooner or later must be corrected."

The belief that a creditor country ought to run a deficit on current account seems derived ultimately from an argument by J. E. Cairnes.[3] Cairnes offers the simple example of the mother country commencing a loan of £1 million to a colony each year at 5% interest. At first, the inflow of capital will exceed the remission of interest payments leading, through the specie flow mechanism, to an import surplus by the borrowing-debtor country. After a time, twenty years in the example, the inflow of capital

---

[1]See also the Report of the 1927 World Economic Conference summarized in European Economic and Political Survey, May 31, 1927, p. 594; W. A. Brown, Jr., The International Gold Standard Reinterpreted, Vol. I, p. 546; C. Iversen, op. cit., p. 190.

[2]Harvard Economic Service, vol. VI, no. 29, July 23, 1927, p. 193.

[3]J. E. Cairnes, Some Leading Principles of Political Economy, (1874 ed.), pp. 359-363.

will equal the remission of interest payments; at this point the specie flow mechanism will lead to a balance of merchandise imports and exports. After this point, remissions of interest will exceed the inflow of capital and the current account of the debtor will grow progressively more active. Thus, the balance of payments of the debtor changes from passive to neutral to active while the balance of payments of the creditor passes from active to neutral to passive. This idea is cited by Carl Iversen[1] in 1935 and illustrated in a table in Charles Kindleberger's International Trade.[2] Thus, Cairnes's argument seems to have remained in sight during the past ninety years and presumably the rationale of the otherwise unsupported view of the persons earlier quoted, that creditors ought to have current deficits, lies with Cairnes.

This argument rests on theoretically misleading foundations, but even if theoretically valid, need not logically apply to the United States. In addition, although this contradicts neither Cairnes nor the critics, the United States had a large and continuing overall deficit with respect to Europe, the source of most of the criticism.

---

[1] Carl Iversen, Aspects of the Theory of International Capital Movements, p. 54.

[2] C. P. Kindleberger, International Trade: 1968 ed., pp. 483-486; 1958 ed., pp. 417-420; 1953 ed., pp. 367-369. See also, P. A. Samuelson, Economics, 1967 ed., pp. 636-637.

(1) The Theoretical Foundations of Cairnes's Notion of the Relationship Between the Current Account and the Net Foreign Asset Position of a Country Over Time.

There is a peculiar incongruity in Cairnes's discussion, which, when corrected, severely beclouds the obviousness of his conclusion. While Cairnes assumes that net foreign assets in the debtor country will increase indefinitely, he ignores the fact that these increasing foreign assets will accompany, and in part represent, an increase in the capital stock and output of the debtor country. Once this is taken into account, the process discussed by Cairnes and others has decreasing and ultimately negligible importance on the sign and size of the balance of payments.[1]

In Cairnes's example, total foreign investment, (K_t), by the mother country in the colony will amount to the annual investment, (I), times the number of years which have passed, (t). Thus, in the twentieth year another £1 million will be lent to the colony, bringing the total foreign debt of the colony to £20 million.

Total interest payments by the colony to the mother country, (R_t), will amount to the rate of interest, (r), times the total foreign debt, (K_t), of

---

[1]Curiously, as I read Cairnes, his intention seems to be to show that the balance on merchandise account cannot be predicted on the basis of the nation's status as a borrower or lender but also depends on its status as a debtor or a creditor and the relation between the two (see also Iversen, op. cit., p. 53). The erection of a new rigid framework involving stages seems to be a later oversimplification of Cairnes's views.

the colony. Thus, in the twentieth year, in Cairnes's example, total interest payments would equal 5% (the assumed rate of interest) of the total foreign debt of Ł20 million, or Ł 1 million.

The relationship between foreign investment and interest payments is shown in chart A and conforms to the verbal description of Cairnes's "stages" given earlier. The solid line shows the evolution of the debtor's balance on investment and interest payments, while the broken line shows the evolution of the creditor's balance on investment and interest payments.

Chart A

Balance of Investment and Interest Payments for the Debtor and Creditor Country

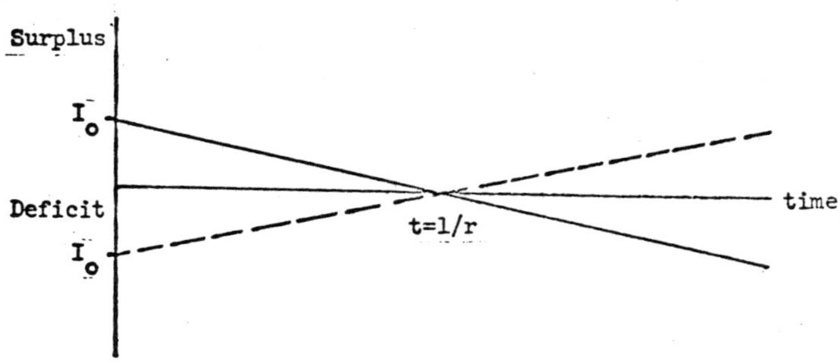

Source: See text for explanation.

It should be obvious that if exports (X) and imports (M) are initially equal, that chart A also describes the change over time in the two countries balances of payments. It should also be clear that interest payments will represent an ever-increasing share of total payments by the debtor over time, while foreign investment (I) will remain a constant share of the debtor's receipts, since in Cairnes's example investment is constant and imports and exports, by implication, do not change except to adjust to interest payments.

However, now we will allow for the growth of the capital stock and income of the debtor and creditor country. Let us suppose, given relative prices, that imports (M) and exports (X) are a function of the level of income (Y) in the two countries. At any moment in time, income (Y_t) will equal the initial level of income growing at a compound rate (g) for t years ($Y_t=Y_oe^{gt}$). Thus, the imports of the debtor country (M_t) will equal the income of the debtor country (Y_t) times the average propensity to import of the debtor (m) or $M_t=mY_t=M_oe^{g''t}$, where the rate of growth of the debtor's income is g''. Similarly, the debtor's exports (X) would always equal the average propensity to import of the creditor times the income of the creditor or, $X_t=X_oe^{g't}$, where the rate of growth of the creditor's income is g'.

If we suppose that the debtor's exports and imports are initially equal, and that the rate of growth of exports and imports are identical, then it is clear that the debtors exports will always equal his imports. Chart A would,again,describe the evolution of the debtor's and creditor's balances of payments.

However, unlike our earlier example, the importance of the stream of foreign investment will not remain unchanged but will decline as a percentage of the debtor's total receipts. This is quite obvious in Cairnes's example, since while investment remains unchanged, the debtor's exports increase at the rate of g' each year.

Precisely the same observation may be made about the relative importance of interest payments by the debtor. Interest payments will increase in direct proportion to the growth of the total foreign debt ($R_t = rK_t$); however, this means that interest payments will grow at a decreasing rate each year, while imports will grow at a constant rate each year.[1] In the long run, the total payments by the debtor will depend almost entirely on the size of his imports. This, parenthetically, is true regardless of the rate of interest, the rate of growth of either country, or the size of the annual investment.[2]

Given the increasing importance over time of imports and exports relative to the constant stream of investment or the increasing stream of interest payments, it should now be clear that if the debtor's imports initially exceed his exports then the deficit will ultimately increase at a steady rate each year. Conversely, if the debtor has an initial export surplus, that surplus will ultimately increase at a steady rate each year. Chart B illustrates some of the possible courses of evolution of the debtor's balance of payments.

---

[1]Given a constant level of investment equal to 1/year, the total debt of the debtor will increase arithmetically as 1, 2, 3, 4, 5, 6, ... However, the annual rate of increase will fall: (2-1)/1=100%, (3-2)/2=50%, (4-3)/3=33%, (5-4)/4=25% and so on. Ultimately it approaches zero. In contrast, the rate of growth of imports is constant and greater than zero.

[2]Total Payments $= M_t + R_t = M_o e^{g''t} + rIt$. The share of interest payments in total payments is equal to $(rIt)/(M_o e^{g''t} + rIt)$. The limit of the latter expression, as t approaches infinity, is zero.

Chart B

Balance of Payments of the Debtor Country, Assuming Initial Inequality of Exports and Imports

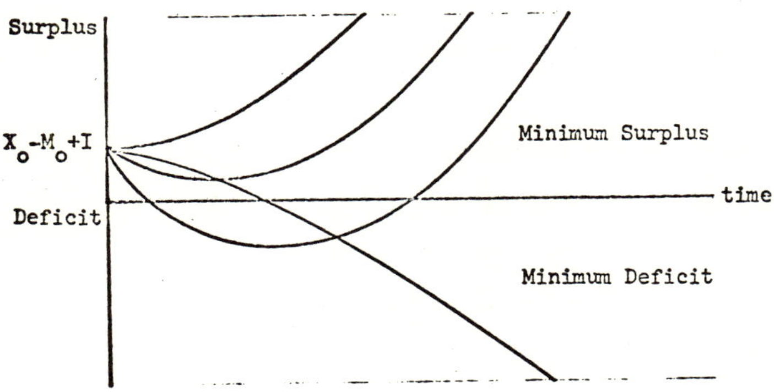

Source: See text for explanation.

Whether the debtor running an initial merchandise surplus ever passes through a deficit phase depends on the relative sizes of initial exports, imports and the annual investment together with the relative size of the rate of interest and the rate of growth. Whether the debtor initially running a merchandise deficit ever has an overall surplus depends on the relative sizes of the initial investment and the initial merchandise deficit.[1]

Consider now the implication that the rate of growth of the colony

---

[1] $B_t = X_o e^{g't} - M_o e^{g''t} + I - rIt$, $(g'=g''=g)$; $\frac{dBt}{dt} = ge^{gt}(X_o - M_o) - rI$;

$\frac{d^2B_t}{d^2t} = g^2e^{gt}(X_o - M_o)$.

exceeds the rate of growth of the mother country. If we take as given that in the long run capital tends to flow from the mother country to the colony, that implies that the rate of return on capital is greater in the colony than in the mother country [dY/dK colony > dY/dK mother country]. If we assume that the average propensities to save are equal in the two countries[1], [$S/Y=dK/Y$ colony = $S/Y-dK/Y$ mother country], then the rate of growth of the colony exceeds the rate of growth of the mother country [(dY/dK) (dK/Y) colony=dY/Y colony > (dY/dK) (dK/Y) mother country $dK/Y=dY/Y$ mother country].

This implies that the imports of the debtor colony will tend to grow faster than its exports, and that whatever the annual investment, the relative rates of growth, or the interest rate, the debtor will tend, in the long run, to have a deficit on merchandise account. Once, again, interest payments and investment become progressively less important in comparison to differences in relative rates of growth as time goes on.

We have so far neglected any discussion of the adjustment mechanism. Cairnes uses a simple specie flow mechanism with internal price adjustments bringing exports and imports into a relation such that, together with investment and interest payments, their sum is zero. The foregoing discussion could

---

[1]This is the strong Keynesian assumption that savings depends on income alone, coupled with the generally held empirical position that the long run consumption (and hence savings) function passes through the origin. However, assuming the dependency of savings on the rate of return on capital implies that the savings-output ratio in the colony would be greater than the savings-output ratio in the mother country. In either case we preserve the strong inequality which follows above.

be coupled with any adjustment mechanism: internal price, exchange rate, income, or changes in relative rates of growth. If we assume, as in our example, that investment is exogenous[1] then clearly in equilibrium the merchandise account must adjust to the balance on investment and interest payments. Thus, in equilibrium all cases would approach Cairnes's example. However, this is quite different from the position that it is the relationship between investment and interest payments which is the powerful factor calling into play balance of payments adjustment. In short, we may observe a debtor country with a persistent tendency toward deficits but the explanation of these merchandise deficits lies not in the factors which Cairnes discusses, but in the relative sizes of incomes in the two countries, their relative average propensities to import, and their relative rates of growth.

It should be made explicit that there are a great many other pertinent questions which we have ignored in this discussion. Among these are the effects of different rates of technical progress and population growth, different production functions in the two countries due to the presence of inalienable factors, different and changing relationships between the

---

[1]Changes in relative price levels, relative exchange rates, relative incomes, and relative rates of growth affect the relative rates of return on capital. Thus, the same factors which lead to changes in the merchandise balance would probably lead to changes in the level of foreign investment. Although a relatively great amount of attention has been paid in the literature to the process of transfer and the manner in which exports of capital affect the merchandise balance, almost no attention has been paid the manner in which changes in the merchandise balance and accompanying internal changes affect the long term capital flows. The theoretical reasons for believing that the latter connection exists are precisely as good as for the former. See, for example, John Knapp "The Theory of International Capital Movements and Its Verification", <u>Review of Economic Studies</u>, Vol. X, No. 2, pp. 115-121.

average propensity to import and the average propensity to save,[1] different price and income elasticities of demand for different internationally traded products, amortization of loans[2], and the effects on lending of changing differences between the marginal products of capital of the two countries. Therefore, in no sense should the foregoing exercise be regarded as a complete theoretical discussion of the factors determining the evolution of a balance of payments over time[3]. We have tried to restrict the discussion

---

[1]Knapp, op. cit., pp. 115-121.

[2]The reader may be able to see intuitively that introducing the assumption that loans are repaid does not substantially modify the conclusions we have reached. If we maintain our assumption of a constant stream of loans, each maturing in n years, the outstanding debt of the colony will equal $tI - \frac{It(t-1)}{2n}$ for $t < n+1$ and will equal $tI - \frac{It(t-1)}{2n} + \frac{I(t-n-1)(t-n)}{2n}$ for $t > n+1$. For the case of $t<n+1$, K_t reaches a maximum of $\frac{I(n+1)}{2}$ for t (integer) = n and n+1; for the case of $t>n+1$, K_t remains constant at $\frac{I(n+1)}{2}$. If the net foreign debt remains constant, then there is no net outflow of capital from the debtor unless new investment ceases. Then, of course, the outstanding debt of the debtor will be reduced through amortization payments.

In either case, the inflow of capital declines to zero or less; therefore it will be even less important in total receipts of the debtor than in the case explored where the inflow of capital remained constant. Similarly, interest payments by the debtor will remain constant or decline; these will be less important in expenditures than in the case studied where interest payments increased at a decreasing rate.

[3]The pioneering work in this field is E.D. Domar's "The Effect of Foreign Investment on the Balance of Payments" (American Economic Review, December 1950, pp. 805-826). Domar discusses the question of the sign and size of the balance on new investment, amortization, and interest payments, given various assumptions about the type of amortization, the rate of growth of the economy, and the rate of interest. Harry Johnson has considered the relationship between the rate of growth of imports and exports and the overall rate of growth, and the relation between different rates of national economic growth in "Equilibrium Growth in an International Economy" (Canadian Journal of Economics, November 1953, pp. 478-500). Dudley Seers has discussed, under various assumptions, the effect of different income elasticities of demand for exports of different regions in "A Model of Comparative Rates of Growth in the World Economy" (Economic Journal, March 1962, pp. 45-78).

to pointing out that the very assumptions necessary for Cairnes to explain the evolution of the equilibrium balance of payments position of a debtor over time imply that international lending and interest payments are progressively less important in explaining the type and extent of adjustment which a country undergoes.

If the long run tendencies are so theoretically unclear, all manner of additional complications emerge when we introduce intermediate and short run factors such as business fluctuations, wars, stock market booms, and so forth. It is not surprising that "the developmental stages worked out in this scheme do not fit history neatly".[1]

(2) Was the United States a "Mature" Creditor Country?

Even if this framework isolated the important factors determining the sign and size of the balance of payments, it is difficult to see why the United States should be placed in the category of mature creditor country with a passive balance of payments during the interwar period.

The United States was, admittedly, the largest net creditor in the world. That fact might theoretically imply that the marginal product of capital was lower in the recent past in the United States than in the rest of

---

[1]C. P. Kindleberger, International Trade, 1958 ed., p. 419; the question of historical verification does not appear in the 1968 edition of this book.

the world.[1] However, this fact alone tells us nothing about the current difference in the marginal products of capital in the United States and the rest of the world and the rate of movement of funds in response to that differential. If the marginal product of capital in the United States was still lower than in the rest of the world, then whatever the size of the net creditor position, the United States would still properly be a net foreign investor with an active trade balance. That is, the United States would properly be classified as a "young" creditor country with an active balance of payments.

To reiterate, even the popular classification schema does not dictate that the United States be a net deficit country on current account.

(3) Was the United States Balance of Payments Passive or Active?

More temperate critics of the United States current account position noted that her current account position became steadily less active during the twenties[2] (although the sum of the current balance and net amortization

---

[1]The effects of the war would seriously qualify any conclusions on this question.

[2]A fact, incidentally, which tends to confirm the greater importance of relative income growth over the net asset position. Rising U. S. foreign investment implies a rising current account surplus, particularly if the rate of growth of foreign investment is greater than the rate of growth of interest and amortization payments. The fact that the U. S. current account surplus fell indicates that, at least during the twenties, relative rates of income growth were more important than the U. S. net foreign asset position in determining the sign of the U. S. balance of payments.

payments was always positive). Perhaps the most curious fact in this entire affair, however, is that the overall balance of payments of the United States with respect to the major source of criticism, Europe, was passive. As we have noted, gold flowed persistently from the United States to Europe.[1]

This, in a sense, does not speak directly to the criticism of the United States, which was essentially that it should import, rather than lend, to refinance interest and amortization payments. This might well have been in Europe's interest in 1928 and 1929 given the volatility of United States foreign lending compared with United States imports. However, it does speak to the implication that United States trade policy somehow trapped European borrowers in an unsatisfactory predicament.

In short, these criticisms imply that continuous United States lending was a problem, at the same time that we argue that the problem was that United States lending was not continuous.

---

[1]Ch. 2, p. 7.

b/ Long Term Capital Account

Three types of explanations of the depression have been based on the behavior of the long term capital account. Bertil Ohlin has emphasized the drop in new lending; this and other positions were summarized in chapter 1 and examined in chapter 3. Some writers have placed foreign speculation at the root of the United States stock market crash of 1929 and that crash at the root of the depression.[1] Others have suggested that the war debts were an important source of financial instability.[2]

b-1/ Foreign participation in the stock market

There was, and to an extent still is, a school of depression analysis that bases the events of the thirties on speculation and the collapse of the New York stock markets. There is yet another part of this school which argues that foreign liquidation was responsible for the stock market crash, and presumably, for the domestic depression.

It is difficult to evaluate the impact of the stock market decline on the events which followed. Most proponents of the stock market thesis argue that the main impact was on expectations and investment plans of businessmen. The consensus among economists now is probably that the stock market and businessmen's plans each reflect the same underlying elements of the economy. The majority of economists probably believe that the stock market is not the cause of any basic change in the level of economic activity.[3]

However, the stock market was much more central to the economic life of the nation in 1929 than it is today. If there is an economic focus in

---

[1]See section b-1.

[2]See section b-2.

[3]See for example Paul A. Samuelson, Newsweek, 3/18/68, p. 89.

today's economy, it is probably Washington and not New York. The effect of the decline in values on entrepreneurial confidence may have been greater in 1929 than it would be today.

Furthermore, the total decline in 1929 of the value of stocks traded on the New York Stock Exchange was at least $30 billion[1]. Some studies suggest that consumption varies by .05 to .07 of the change in wealth[2], if the change in wealth is not transitory. By these measures, the stock market decline of 1929 alone would have reduced consumption by $1.5-$2.1 billion, and national income by more. Since the decline in personal consumption in 1930 was about $8.0 billion[3], the stock market decline would explain an appreciable part of that decline.

The impact of the 1929 crash on the outlook of businessmen and on the spending plans of consumers compounded the problems already facing the economy. The tight money policy initiated by the Federal Reserve system in early 1928, the decline in the rate of population growth, and the decline in the rate of growth of the key electrical and automotive industries all represented serious problems prior to the decline in the values of equities. In summary, other factors pointed toward an economic

---

[1]Broaders Mitchell, Depression Decade, p. 27.

[2]John J. Arena found the wealth coefficient equal to approximately .05 [$C = .5Y + .05W$]: (Arena, "The Wealth Effect and Consumption: A Statistical Inquiry", Yale Economic Essays, Fall 1963, pp. 274-276, 282). Albert Ando and Franco Modigliani found the wealth coefficient equal to .073 for the years 1900-1928, while the coefficient for changes in wealth amounted to .047 [$C = 0.755Y + 0.073A$, $R^2 = .995$; $\Delta C = .731\ Y + 0.047\Delta A$, $R^2 = 0.44$]: (Ando and Modigliani "The 'Life Cycle' Hypothesis of Saving: Aggregate Implications and Tests", American Economic Review, March 1963, reprinted in American Economic Association, Readings in Business Cycle Theory, Vol. X, p. 423.

[3]U. S. Department of Commerce, Historical Statistics of the United States, p. 178.

slowdown in the United States, and it is likely that these were more important than the effect of the stock market decline on business expectations and investment plans. The role of foreign liquidation in the stock market decline was probably very limited, although, curiously enough, it is very difficult to devise a workable test of this rather simple proposition. It is most simple to compare the foreign and domestic position in the stock market and observe that foreigners held a maximum of \$5.4 billion in United States equities[1] while the total value of stocks on the New York Stock Exchange was about \$87 billion in early October of 1929[2]. It is difficult to believe in the face of these relative asset positions that foreigners as a group could have had more responsibility for the direction of prices than domestic shareholders. The entire value of foreign assets in the United States was probably no greater than the total sales on the New York Stock Exchange during September 1929, a month of strongly rising prices[3]. I suspect that even the most diehard operationalist would entertain the suspicion that foreign liquidation would be insufficient to reverse a bull market sustained by domestic buying.

While it is clear that foreign liquidation (maximum \$917 million)[4] was smaller than domestic sales (\$9.6 billion-\$24.9 billion)[5], it is

---

[1]See appendix 3, notes 1 and 2.

[2]George Soule, <u>Prosperity Decade</u>, pp. 70-72.

[3]Sales on the New York Stock Exchange probably amounted to \$2.5 - \$8.3 billion during September 1929, with a reasonable guess closer to the high side than the low. See appendix 3, note 2 for sources and estimating techniques.

[4]See appendix 3, notes 1 and 2.

[5]See appendix 3, notes 1 and 2.

difficult to interpret this insofar as the intention of the transactor is concerned. We can "measure" the desire of foreigners to dispose of United States securities by observing that maximum foreign sales of such securities were $917 million. We have no analogous measure of American "intentions" since stocks sold by Americans were in large part purchased by Americans. We are left with the position that domestic sales were clearly more depressing than foreign sales, but that domestic purchases were more important than foreign purchases in supporting the market.

The same sort of problems beset us in interpreting the likelihood that foreign sales were a smaller fraction of foreign-owned equities than American sales were of domestically owned equities.[1] However, Bloomfield, presumably on the basis of independent evidence, states that foreigners tended not to liquidate during 1929 because they had made fewer purchases on margin.[2]

We could, of course, construct a more sophisticated hypothesis about foreign participation which might have foreigners selling at key points in sizeable quantities; that is, we might postulate that foreigners led the decline. Such a hypothesis would be extremely difficult to test; however, there are no plausible grounds for believing that such an explanation might be true.

---

[1]Foreign sales represented between 17% and 50% of foreign holdings of U. S. equities, with a reasonable guess much closer to 17% than to 50%. Domestic sales represented were between 11% and 29% of the total value of shares outstanding with a reasonable guess much closer to 29% than to 11%. The estimating and data problems are discussed in notes 1 and 2 to this chapter.

[2]Bloomfield, Capital Imports and the American Balance of Payments, 1934-1939, pp. 12, 99.

b-2/ War Debts

War debt amortization and interest payments were not great compared to international flows of long term capital. Private amortization payments to the United States exceeded the combined inflow of interest and amortization payments on war debts, while the decline in long term lending in 1929 exceeded both (see chart 4).

It is important to note, though, that the largest payments of war debt interest and amortization payments were made to the United States by Britain, while the brunt of reparations payments were naturally borne by Germany. In this respect, the burden of payment bore mainly on those countries which were the first to collapse and thus, from the interest of the world economy, it might have been advisable to have readjusted that burden earlier.

However, most explanations of the depression which emphasize the centrality of war debts revolve around the psychological impact of changes in war debt settlements. Although the annual payments of amortization and interest on war debts were small compared to the other elements and changes in the elements of the long term capital account, these payments were funded over a long period of time and their capitalized value was immense: France and the United Kingdom alone owed $8.6 billion to the United States[1]. In contrast, total U. S. private portfolio assets in 1929 amounted to less than $8.1 billion[2].

---

[1]Moulton and Pasvolsky, World War Debt Settlements, p. 374.

[2]Cleona Lewis, America's Stake in International Investments, pp. 652-655, not adjusted for transactions in outstanding securities.

Chart 4

Imports and Exports of
Capital and War Debt Payments, 1927-1933

($000,000)

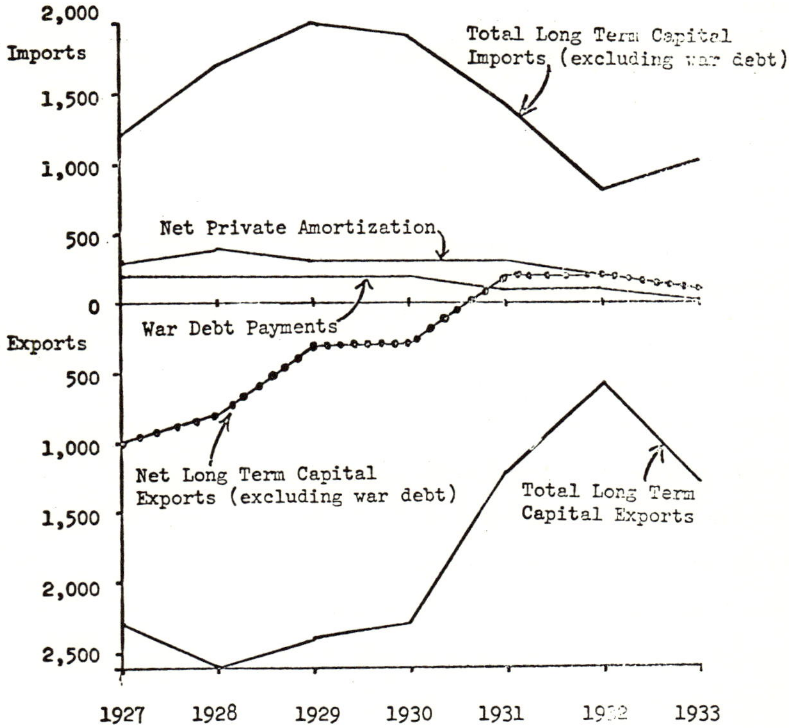

Source: See appendix 1, pp. 35-53 passim.

In some cases this psychological factor was measurably evident: during the Young plan negotiations there was a substantial outflow of short term funds from Germany followed by a large inflow during the first half of 1929 after the report of the experts[1].

However, in most cases it is not clear how the author is measuring the psychological impact of the war debt. In 1924 Strong wrote that he did not believe that any measures for the return to the gold standard would be successful so long as the "immense weight of international debt" hung unadjusted over the nations of Europe[2]. In 1931 Gustav Stolper observed that the problem of international debt was the source of many of the world's difficulties and, in particular, that "the Young plan lies badly placed on all the loan markets, an insurmountable obstacle to every additional expansion of commerce."[3] Angell has claimed that United States insistence on the resumption of war debt payments, at the end of the June 20, 1931 one-year moratorium, caused "tension and disturbance" in international finance.[4]

It is difficult to test these arguments, depending as they do on the impact on expectations of the size and changes in the debt, and in turn, on the effect of changes in these expectations on trade and investment. However, the case of those who have felt that war debts were an important factor in the depression would be considerably stronger had the Hoover moratorium produced some positive effect on the world economy.

---

[1]Brown, op. cit., Vol. II, p. 821.

[2]Strong letter to Block, May 16, 1924, cited in Chandler, Benjamin Strong, Central Banker, p. 269. During this period the argument has considerable merit inasmuch as the U. S. Department of State informally prohibited lending to most countries which had not settled their war debts with the United States.

[3]Gustav Stolper, Harvard Business Review, March 1931, p. 298.

[4]J. W. Angell, Financial Foreign Policy of the United States, pp. 120-122.

c/ Short Term Capital Account

Robert Triffin has pointed to currency speculation largely in its role as complicating the problems of the reserve currency countries (chiefly Britain and the United States during this period).[1] Heinz Arndt has argued that "the gold standard was wrecked by the large and increasing movements of short term capital..."[2] We will first consider the role of short term capital speculation in the international economic relations of the United States with the rest of the world. Next we will briefly discuss the size and consequences of movements of short term funds among third countries. Finally, we will discuss other explanations for the decline in short term assets and liabilities between 1930 and 1933.

---

[1]See R. Triffin, The Evolution of the International Monetary System, p. 25. Triffin refers to "the acceleration of U. S. capital outflows and reserve loans, prompted by speculative expectations of possible changes in gold prices and exchange rates, as well as by the differential evolution of earning prospects and interest rates in Europe and in the United States..." in a list of phenomena in the postwar period which he feels parallels the events of the late twenties and early thirties. I may be reading too much into Triffin's statement, but he does seem to imply that speculation against the key currency countries was one of the important events of the period. However, where he discusses the events of the interwar period (pp. 21-23) he does not mention speculation.

[2]Arndt, op. cit., p. 14. Arndt also points out that the depression alone would have made maintenance of the gold standard increasingly difficult. He concludes the quote cited in the text with the statement "...which (short-term capital) constituted an altogether new and disturbing phenomena of the post-war period". This is an extremely curious statement in light of capital flight from Germany during the 1920-1923 inflation, speculation against the French and Belgian francs during the 1923 occupation of the Ruhr, the movement into sterling on the rumors of impending stabilization in 1925, and the return of capital to France after the 1927 stabilization.

c-1/ Speculative Movements of Short Term Funds To and From the United States

There is little evidence that speculation, in the form of the shifting of short term balances among financial centers in such a way as to gain from a change in exchange rates, played an important part in United States economic relations with the rest of the world.

If there were such speculation one would reasonably expect it to show up prior to the German capital embargo in July 1931, the British devaluation in September 1931, and the United States devaluation in March 1933. Charts 5 and 6 show United States short term assets and liabilities with respect to Britain and Germany, together with the covered and uncovered interest arbitrage incentives.[1] In the case of Britain it is clear from chart 5 that during 1931 there was an incentive to move funds from New York to London. Consistent with this incentive, British balances in New York were drawn down during this period. United States balances in

---

[1]Covered arbitrage is the purchase of spot foreign funds to place in interest bearing instruments while selling an equivalent amount of forward exchange to guard against the risk of devaluation. The condition for covered arbitrage from B to A is that $\frac{Ef}{Es}(1 + i_A) > 1 + i_B$ where Ef is the forward exchange rate, Es is the forward exchange rate, Es is the spot exchange rate (quoted in units of B currency/unit A currency), i_A is the interest rate in center A and i_B is the interest rate in center B. (We are assuming the transaction is costless).

Uncovered arbitrage is the purchase of spot foreign funds to place in interest bearing instruments without selling an equivalent amount of forward exchange. The condition for uncovered arbitrage from B to A is $\frac{E(Es)}{Es}(1 + i_A) > 1 + i_B$ where E (Es) is the expected value of the spot rate at some time in the future. So, for example, if sterling were at the gold export point, U. S. lenders might not cover their sterling purchases since they would anticipate no further decline in the price of sterling and might profit from an increase in the rate. We assume that uncovered arbitrage takes place only when the currency is expected to remain freely convertible and within the gold points.

London decreased by $93.4 million between March 31 and August 5, in rough correspondence to the decline in the arbitrage incentives. Between August 5 and September 16, United States balances in London increased by $119.3 million, in rough correspondence to the increase in the arbitrage incentive. In light of the September 19th devaluation of the pound, intelligent speculative behavior would have dictated precisely the opposite course of action.

Similarly, prior to the May devaluation of the German mark there was an incentive to shift funds to Germany under both covered and uncovered arbitrage. Consistent with this, German balances in the United States declined by $109 million between December 31, 1930 and July 29, 1931 (see chart 6). We have data for United States balances beginning in March 1931 and these indicate that she slightly reduced her short term position in Germany from $542.0 million on March 31, to $534.8 million on July 29.[1] Again, intelligent speculative behavior would have dictated opposite behavior by Germans and more extreme action by Americans.

American assets in foreign countries continued to decline gradually after March 1930 (see chart &). There is no evidence of large movements of funds prior to February 1, 1933, although the gradual $120 million increase in United States assets between the end of August 1932 and the beginning of

---

[1]The reader should observe, though, that in the interim U. S. assets in Germany had declined and risen by about $50 million (see chart 6). This may have represented some U. S. flight from the mark.

February 1933 might represent the movement of speculative funds (see chart 7). Foreign assets in the United States exhibit no clear trend during the six months preceding the gold embargo.

The behavior of short term assets and liabilities was radically different for a brief period before and after the gold embargo. American assets overseas, largely in Britain and France, increased by $90 million in the first week in March, while foreign assets in the United States declined by $118 million during the last week in February and the first week in March.[1]

There are some quite subtle questions of interpretation of this data, but it is by no means clear that the proposition that the outflow of capital forced the decision to devalue is a better description of the causal chain than the proposition that capital flowed out once it became clear that a devaluation was likely. If the latter is the correct description of events, one can hardly argue that speculative short term capital flows were responsible for wrecking the gold standard in the United States. The problem is further complicated by the "March" banking crisis, which actually began in late 1932 and reached its peak in late February and early March of 1933. Whatever the expectations about the exchange rate, the bank situation would probably have caused some short term flows in the same directions as those observed.

---

[1]Calculated from weekly short-term foreign liability and asset data in Banking and Monetary Statistics, 1943 ed., pp. 574-576, 585-587.

Chart 5

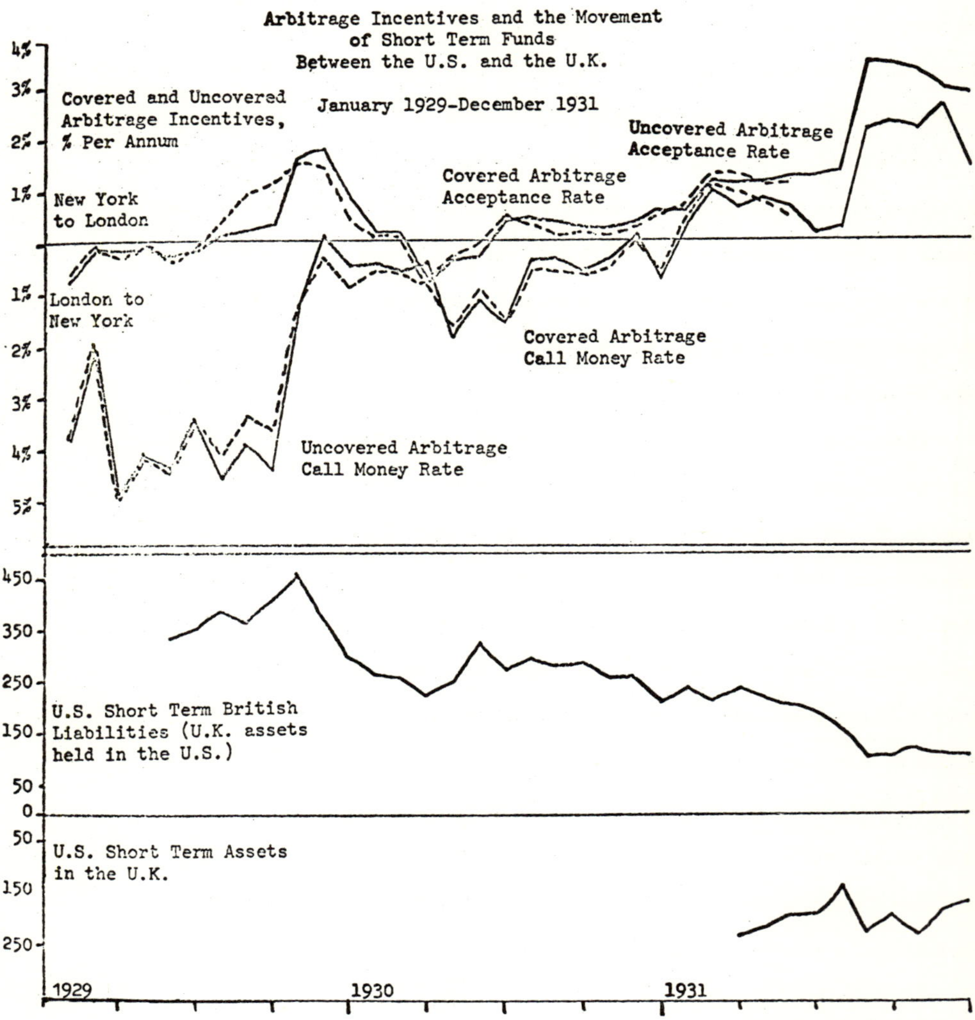

Source: Arbitrage incentive calculated according to formulas shown on p. 35, with the actual spot rate 90 days in the future used as proxy for the expected value of the spot rate $[E(E_s)]$. Spot and forward rate data was taken from Einzig, Theory of the Forward Exchange, Appendices, passim. Data for mutual short term liabilities and assets of the U.S. and the U.K. were taken from Banking and Monetary Statistics, 1943 ed., pp. 574-576, 585-587.

Chart 6

Arbitrage Incentives and the Movement
of Short Term Funds
Between the U.S. and Germany

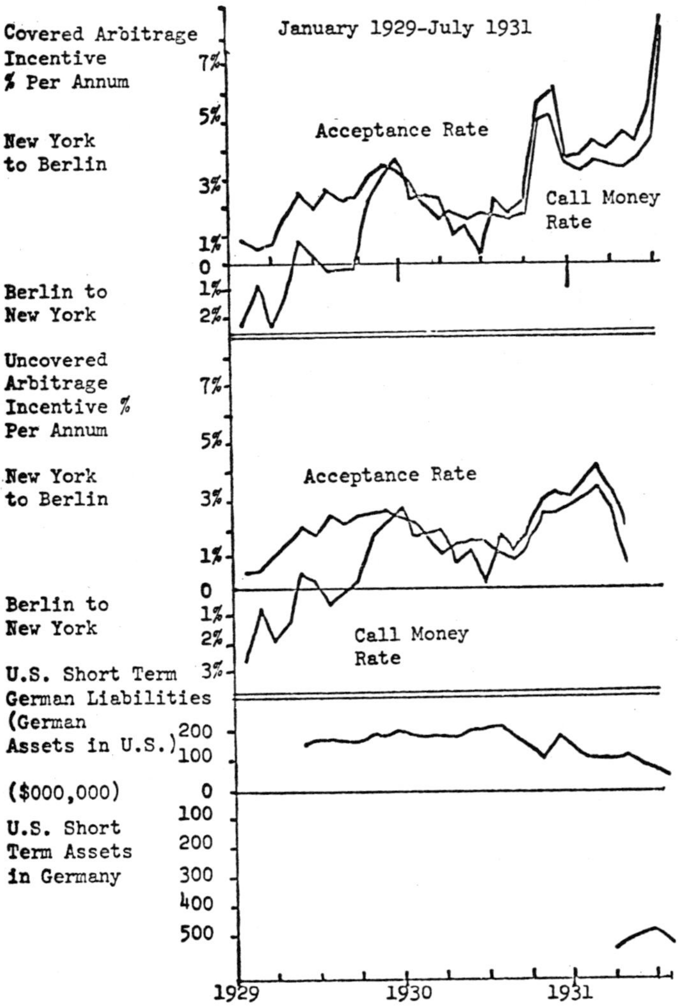

Source: Arbitrage incentive calculated according to formulas shown on p. 35, with the actual spot rate 90 days in the future used as proxy for the expected value of the spot rate $[E(E_s)]$. Spot and forward rate data was taken from Einzig, Theory of the Forward Exchange, Appendices, passim. Data on mutual short term liabilities and assets of the U.S. and Germany were taken from Banking and Monetary Statistics, 1943 ed., pp. 574-576, 585-587.

Chart 7

U.S. Short Term Assets and Liabilities,
End of Month Data

December 1929 - June 1933
($000,000)

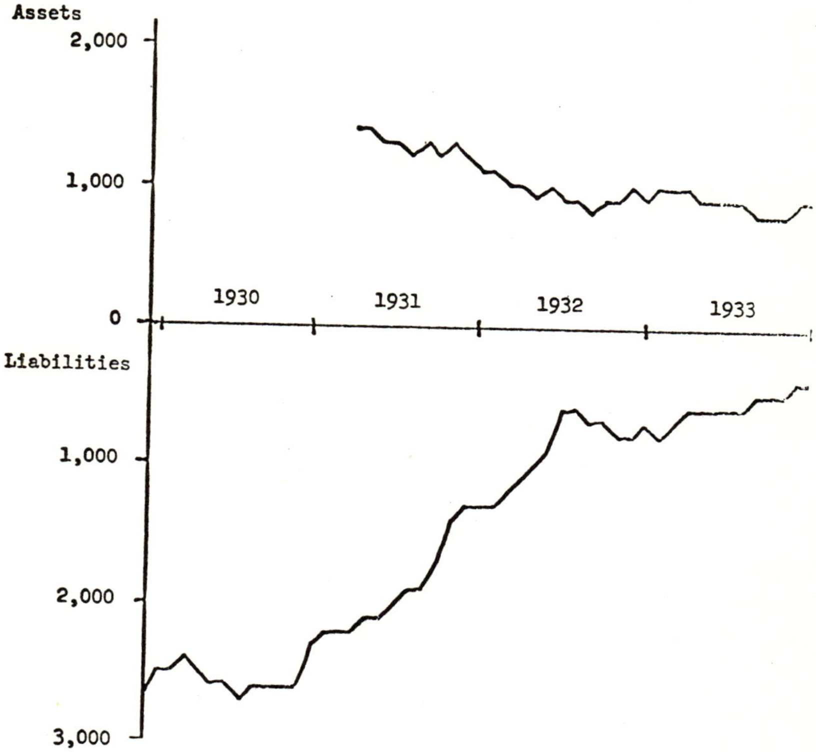

Source: Banking and Monetary Statistics, 1943 ed., pp. 574-576. There are no monthly data for U.S. foreign assets prior to March 1931.

Finally, it is important to keep in mind that when we spoke of changes in long term capital flows from the United States we spoke of declines of the order of $1.3 to $5.0 billion dollars sustained over a year.[1] Here we are speaking of flows which amounted to, at the most, $200 million and which took place in a period of two or three weeks.[2] Not only can't we be sure how much of this movement represented speculation against the dollar or even flight from the dollar[3], but we have considerably stronger evidence concerning the detrimental effects of the decline in United States long term capital exports on the international and domestic financial positions of various countries than we have on the detrimental effects of the outflow of short term funds on the international or domestic financial position of the United States in 1933.

In summary, there is no evidence of substantial speculation or capital flight involving the movement of short term funds to or from the United States for the purpose of gaining from a change in relative exchange rates. However, this conclusion must be interpreted with care.

It is possible that speculative short term capital movements occurred outside normal channels and escaped the rather crude enumeration procedures of the government. However, the existence of sharp changes in the enumerated flows discussed, around the time of the American gold embargo, implies that

---

[1]See chapter 3, pp. 32-33.

[2]Or, if we include the increase of $120 million in U. S. foreign assets between August 1932 and February 1933, a flow of $320 million over a period of seven months.

[3]In contrast to flight from the instruments of a collapsing banking system.

the data do include some movements of speculative and flight capital.

Furthermore, we have used data for short term balances held in the United States and abroad, and have not treated the question of speculation in the forward exchange market. There are no data for this period on positions or changes in positions in the forward exchange market. Inasmuch as the arbitrage incentives from New York to London and Berlin were positive and rising prior to the peaks of their exchange crises, we can say that any forward market speculation which was present was insufficient to reverse the arbitrage incentive. Nonetheless, this does not prove the absence of speculation in favor of dollars and against pounds and marks.

Finally, and perhaps most important, these data say nothing about movements of speculative or flight capital among third parties. The apparent absence or relative smallness of such flows between New York and Berlin or between New York and London does not tell us anything about the nature or size of flows between other countries and Berlin and London or between Berlin and London.

A Digression on Short Term Capital Movements Among Other Centers

Although a thorough treatment of short term capital movements among other financial centers is beyond the scope of this study, we might discuss briefly the probable magnitude of such flows during 1931, their impact relative to the impact of changes in long term flows, and their impact on Britain and Germany during the year.

We have estimated, with a wide allowance for probable error, that net withdrawals of short term funds from Germany prior to July 1931 amounted to \$150-\$450 million[1] and that net withdrawals of funds from Britain prior

[1]See appendix 3, note 3.

to September 1931 amounted to about $650 million.[1]

Withdrawals of short term funds from Germany seem to have been undertaken primarily by France, the United States, the United Kingdom, and the Netherlands. Withdrawals of funds from the United Kingdom seem to have been undertaken primarily by France, the Netherlands, Belgium, Switzerland and Italy.

There are two grounds on which one might reasonably argue that these outflows of short term funds were less important than the decline in net long term lending by the United States and other leading creditors. In the first place, the outflow of short term funds in the case of Germany was probably less than the decline in long term lending. Secondly, the outflow of short term funds was smaller and probably had a less deflationary effect than the decline in long term lending which led to the rise in interest rates, the decline in German and British domestic new issues, and the decline in primary product prices and the import demand of primary producing countries.

The decline in the net inflow of long term funds to Germany in 1929 was probably more than $216.9 million.[2] This represented the decline in new long term lending by the United S-ates alone and takes no account of the decline in new lending by other centers or of possible German participation in the rising stock markets of the United States, Canada, and France. The decline in German domestic new issues in 1929 amounted to

---

[1]See appendix 3, note 4.

[2]See ch. 3, chart 2.

$376.1 million.[1] The decline in German exports between 1929 and 1931 was $925.2 million.[2]

Total new long term portfolio lending to Great Britain was probably not great; however, the British were probably large participants in the American stock market boom.[3] In addition, British domestic new issues declined by $290.1 million[4] during 1929 while British merchandise export revenues declined by $2.0 billion between 1929 and 1931.[5]

Thus, not only had the decline in long term lending had its effect by 1931, but a large part of the reason for the increase in short term borrowing by these centers lay in the effects of the decline in long term investment. We might observe finally that the decline in net United States long term lending occurred at a time when the domestic situations of these countries was clearly better than they were in 1931; therefore the decline in long term lending might most reasonably be held responsible for the ensuing deflation.

In the evaluation of such runs, there is probably a tendency to overestimate their importance simply because when they occur they tend to occur only when a country is weak; because of that weakness, the run is sufficient to cause a policy alteration of great significance. This is entirely different from the position that the run was the cause of the

---

[1]Calculated from the League of Nations Statistical Yearbook 1933-1934, p. 226.

[2]Commerce Yearbook, 1935, pp. 372-373.

[3]See chapter 3, section b.

[4]Calculated from the League of Nations Statistical Yearbook 1933-1934, p. 226.

[5]Commerce Yearbook, 1935, pp. 374-375.

weakness. Although a complete study of the British and German economies would be required before a solidly supported conclusion could be reached, the impression is inescapable that the international positions of both Britain and Germany were steadily worsening and that some dramatic change in policy would ultimately have been required whether or not there had been a run on their currencies.

c-3/ Other Factors Contributing to the Liquidation of Short Term Assets

U. S. short term assets and liabilities declined between 1931 and 1933. Overall, United States foreign assets declined less than foreign liabilities from 1931 to 1933.[1] This was consistent with outward arbitrage incentives during most of this period.

Foreigners erratically reduced their balances in New York. It is difficult to determine how much of the reduction in United States foreign liabilities was due to lack of confidence in the dollar. Of course, the liquidation movement may be so explained. However, a number of other explanations are consistent with the observed data.

France and the gold bloc nations had publicized for a number of years their intention to return to a pure gold standard and to cease holding gold exchange.[2] This strategy may well have been accelerated by doubts

---

[1]According to the flow estimates in Lary, op. cit., table IV, the U. S. increased its short term assets during this period; according to the stock estimates in Banking and Monetary Statistics, pp. 585-587, U. S. assets declined, but by less than liabilities.

[2]The act of June 25, 1928 forbade further acquisition of foreign exchange by the Bank of France. It was silent concerning the disposition of existing stocks of foreign exchange (Brown, op. cit., pp. 458, 464). These stocks were reduced each year from the end of 1928 to the end of 1933, except during 1930 when they increased by a negligible amount (League of Nations, Statistical Yearbook 1933-1934, pp.210-212. See also, Nurkse, International Currency Experience, p. 39).

about the soundness of the dollar; however, it was not based on doubts about the dollar. In addition, though, with short term money rates in New York at extremely low levels relative to other centers[1], the incentive to hold exchange instead of gold was greatly diminished. Finally, foreign official liquidation of exchange reserves reflected, probably more frequently, attempts to stave off their own payments problems rather than fears about the United States position. About 30% of foreign short term balances in New York were held as exchange reserves by foreign central banks[2].

Private balances would also tend to be reduced by factors having nothing directly to do with sentiment about the soundness of the dollar. The diminution in world trade reduced the need for the maintenance of trade financing balances. Short term balances held in the United States declined to about 15% of their 1929 level by 1933, while the value of world trade declined to 33% of its 1929 value during the same period.

The proceeds of long term loans floated in New York were often deposited in short term instruments until the borrower needed the funds[3]; other short term funds were working capital for investment in the New York Stock Exchange. With the reduction in United States lending and the decline in

---

[1] Banking and Monetary Statistics, 1943 ed., pp. 440-441, 656-660.

[2] Lary, op. cit., pp. 113-115.

[3] See Chandler, Benjamin Strong, p. 88; Bloomfield, Capital Imports and the American Balance of Payments, 1934-1939, p. 125.

trading on the New York Stock Exchange, this demand for short term funds was curtailed.

In summary, while there is evidence of some speculation and capital flight at work in the United States short term capital market, the actual behavior of the market may be explained as well by other economic forces; much the same might be said of Great Britain. Perhaps more significant in the case of the United States is the apparent smallness of speculation when there should have been a clear incentive for speculation and capital flight, prior to the German capital embargo and the British devaluation. Finally, and most important, the size and the timing of most of the short term capital flows leaves us with the impression that these changes could not be considered the initiating factors in the world depression: they served rather to deliver the economic coup de grace.

If fault is to be found with the short term capital market it lies more with the apparent limit on the amount of funds the short term capital market was able to muster in response to arbitrage incentives in favor of countries, such as Germany and Britain, that desperately needed funds. The constraint on the amount of funds available may have reflected fear of capital loss due to exchange control or collapse of the borrowing bank, the need for short term funds due to the intermittent banking crises in the United States, or simply the constraint of portfolio balance considerations by the lending banks. In any case, while arbitrage incentives pointed, in general, toward countries in distress and while the direction of flow of funds was also correct, it is clear that the amount of funds actually moved was quite inadequate.

d/ Gold and Reserves

Gold and the gold-exchange standard have been held by some writers to be responsible in various ways for the dislocation of the period. Ragnar Nurkse and Robert Triffin have pointed to the shift out of foreign exchange and into gold as an important factor contributing to the problems of the reserve currency countries and to the instability of the period.[1] Robert Triffin has spoken more generally, as well, of the instability of the gold exchange standard.[2] A number of writers have spoken about the problem of the "maldistribution" of gold.[3]

d-1/ The Shift Out of Foreign Exchange Into Gold

The trend out of foreign exchange and into gold, documented by Nurkse,[4] was unmistakeable (see chart 8). It is also clear from the series on exchange reserves that the greatest pressure on the reserve currency countries was exerted in 1931 and 1932, although about $500 million in exchange reserves were also liquidated in 1929 and 1930.

As important as the decline in the holding of currency reserves is the failure of the demand for exchange reserves to increase in 1929, thus depriving reserve currency countries, particularly Britain, of an important source of deficit financing.[5] The major run on the key currency countries

---

[1]See section d-1.

[2]See section d-3.

[3]See section d-2.

[4]Nurkse, International Currency Experience, pp. 39-41.

[5]A variation on a point made by Nurkse. Nurkse (op. cit., p. 64) observes that the U. K. bore part of the effects of price fluctuations in agricultural countries through changes in sterling reserves held by these countries. The implication is that in the absence of the sharp declines in primary prices, sterling area agricultural producers would have increased their foreign exchange reserves, helping the financing of British deficit.

Chart 8

Gold Exchange Reserves,
By Region and Total, 1926-1933
(end of year data; $000,000,000)

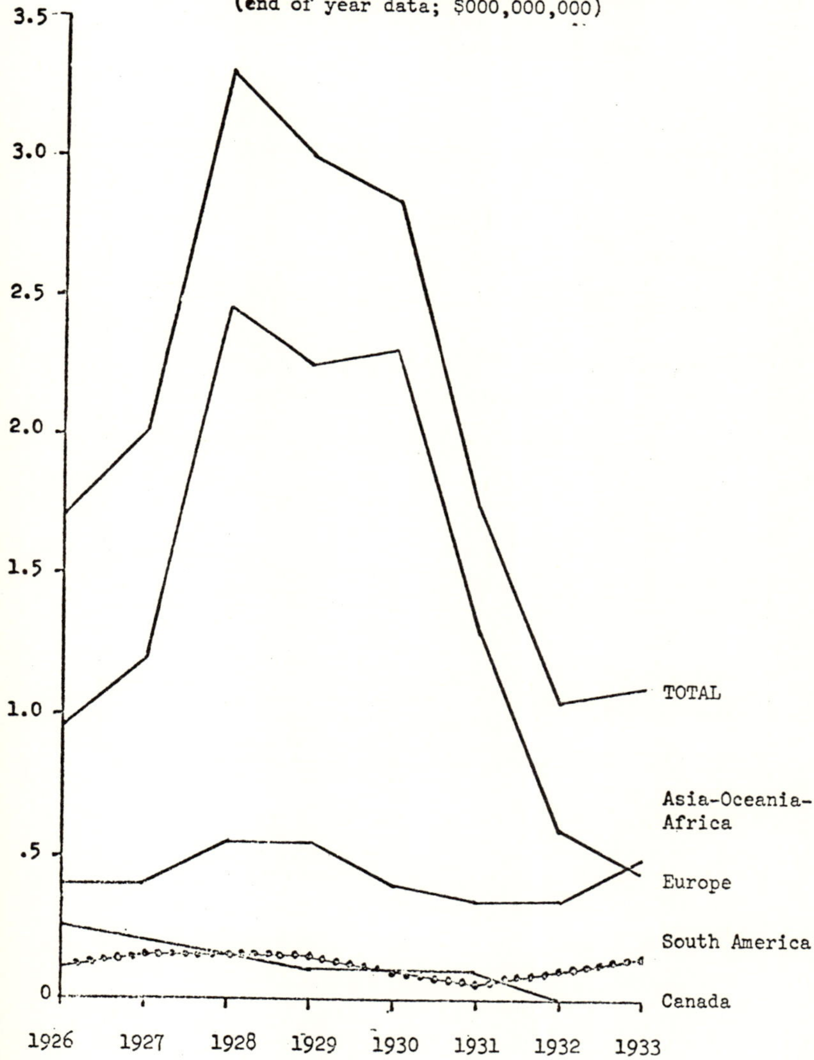

Source: Calculated from data contained in the League of Nations Statistical Yearbook 1933-1934, pp. 210-212.

Chart 9

Percentage Share of Gold and Gold Exchange in Assets of Foreign Central Banks, 1926-1933

(end of year data)

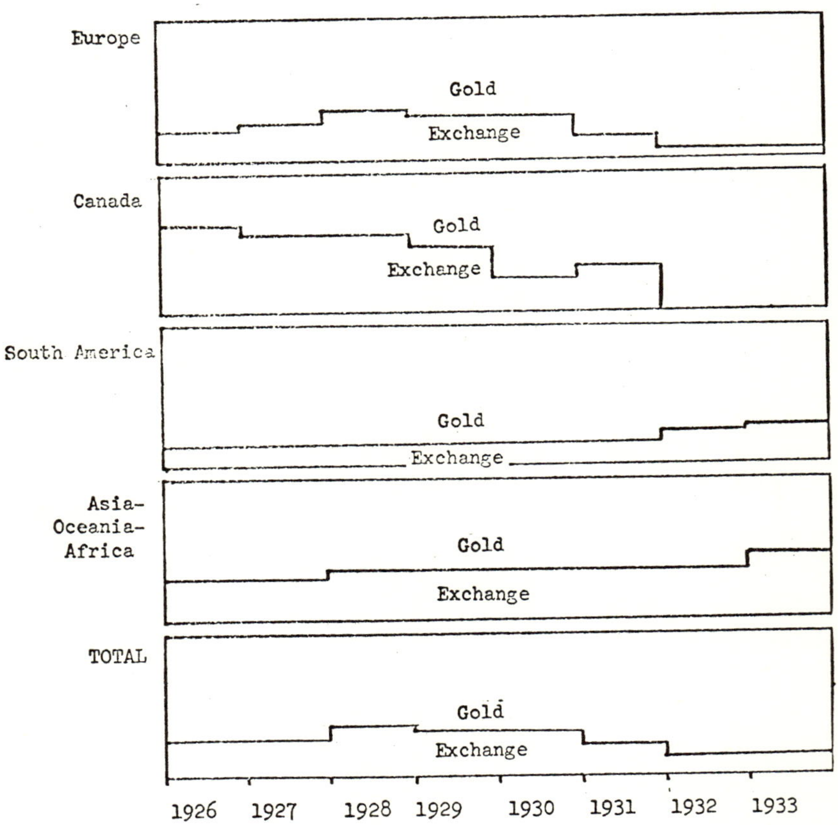

Source: Calculated from exchange reserve data from the League of Nations <u>Statistical Yearbook 1933-1934</u>, pp. 210-212 and gold data from <u>Banking and Monetary Statistics</u>, 1943 ed., pp. 544-555.

occurred after the gravity of their economic positions became obvious. It does not appear that a run on the key currency countries was a major factor in initiating their problems.

It is unlikely that the entire decline in foreign exchange reserve assets was due to a lack of confidence in the reserve centers. Short term interest rates were generally extremely low in reserve centers between 1931 and 1933.[1] The drop in reserves during this period also reflects the decline in the surpluses of British colonies and primary exporters in the sterling area, and reflects in general the international payments problems faced by gold-exchange standard countries.

Finally, we have the announced intention of France to convert her foreign exchange balances to gold. This reflected, at least at its outset, the intention of parliament to have the Bank of France switch out of foreign exchange, the general belief that "first-rate" financial powers hold gold rather than gold-exchange, and a profound unwillingness on the part of France to support, in any way, British objectives in Central Europe. At some point the reasons for the conversion may have changed to the understandable central bank fear that the reserve currency would devalue. Nonetheless, the conversion would probably have continued irrespective of the conditions of the British or American economies.

---

[1]Except of course during the British exchange crisis in August and September 1931 and prior to the American gold embargo in March 1933. See Banking and Monetary Statistics, 1943 ed., pp. 440-441, 656-660.

Attention has also been focused on the total amount of reserves.[1] While the total amount of reserves declined by about 5% during the period 1930 to 1933, trade declined by about 56%.[2] Since the decline in trade preceded the decline in reserves it is unlikely that the attrition of reserves was the cause of the downturn in trade. The distribution of reserves is quite another question, and to that we turn next.

d-2/ The Maldistribution of Gold

Proponents of this argument generally made their cases along the following lines: the distribution of gold (shown in chart 10) was determined by the "abnormal" considerations of war and the immediate post-war years. This "abnormal" distribution of gold, because of the link between gold and the domestic money supply, made expansion by some countries quite difficult. Thus, some redistribution was necessary and desirable to expand world economic output.[3]

However, in almost every country it was possible to expand the money supply

---

[1]Nurkse, op. cit., p. 41.

[2]Total reserves by region are shown in chart 9; world export statistics taken from Commerce Yearbook, 1935, pp. 372-373.

[3]Royal Institute of International Affairs, The International Gold Problem, pp. 147, 207, 211. In one sense, this argument is trivial. Obviously if everyone had an unlimited supply of gold (and if in such circumstances gold could retain its position as an international medium of exchange), then everyone would be free from the internal or external constraints imposed by their gold supply and could expand at will.

through the use of gold exchange. Even if national statutory requirements limited the amount of gold exchange which could be held, all gold exchange was freely convertible to gold, at least until September 1931.

The lack of both gold and gold exchange indicated, then, either the lack of a balance of payments surplus or an insufficient accumulation of past surpluses. Conceive, for example, of a country in external balance but with domestic unemployment. Assume that the only policy instrument which it can use is expansion of the money supply. However, given its supply of gold and gold exchange it has expanded the money supply to the maximum permissable[1]. What are its options?

Proponents of the "maldistribution of gold" position advocated some plan for the redistribution of gold. This is a puzzling choice of policy options. Domestically, any country had the option of changing the legal ratio of reserves to the money supply. Internationally, any country had the option of borrowing the gold exchange necessary to move to the optimum money supply. Either of the latter alternatives, while not politically or economically uncontroversial, would probably have a greater chance of success than negotiations to change the distribution of gold -- about which discussions dragged on fruitlessly for years.

The fact that few "maldistribution" proponents argued that there was

---

[1]The reader may imagine a number of variants of this problem. For example, a country with a small balance of payments surplus might be able to generate a sufficient base for the money supply over a period of years but policy makers would like a sufficient base for the money supply in the present year.

Chart 10

Percentage Regional
Distribution of Gold and
Total Reserves, 1926-1933

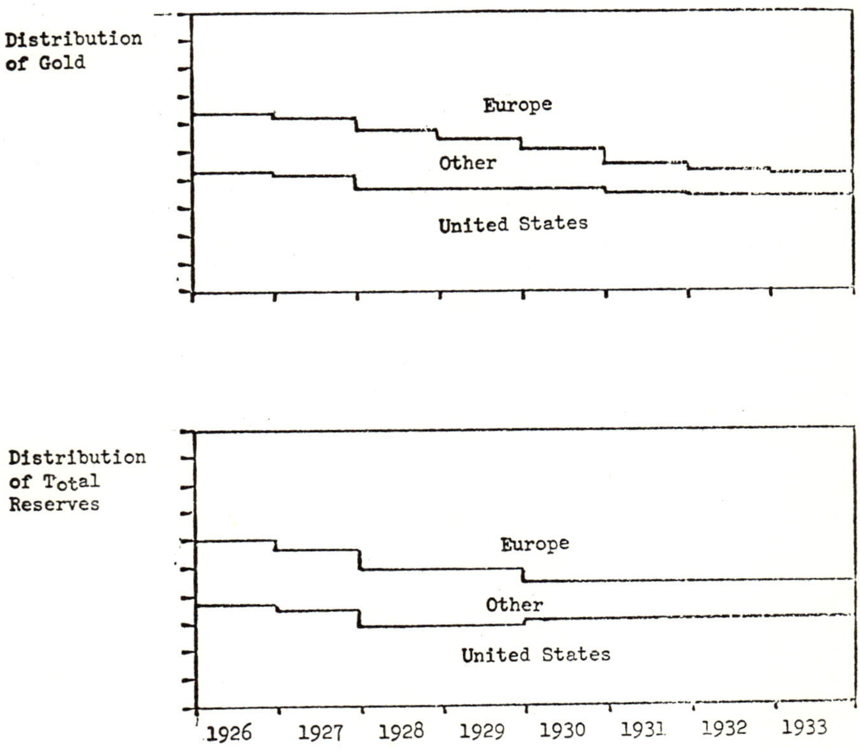

Source: Calculated from Banking and Monetary Statistics, 1943 ed., pp. 544-555 (Gold) and League of Nations Statistical Yearbook 1933-1934, pp. 210-212 (Gold exchange).

an overall scarcity of gold and gold-exchange[1] indicates even more strongly that the failure, in contemporary terms, to which they addressed themselves was the failure of the surplus countries to adjust in such a way as to ease the problems of the deficit countries. If such is the case, speaking about the "maldistribution" of gold is a rather confused and confusing way to treat the problem. If this sort of argument has any importance and impact on the events of the period, it is probably only with respect to countries on the gold-exchange standard who announced their intention of switching ultimately to the pure gold standard. The impact of this policy has been discussed.

d-3/ The Inherent Instability of the Gold-Exchange Standard

The leading proponent of this point of view is Robert Triffin[2]. Briefly, he argues that the maintenance of world trade requires an increase in "international money" in some relationship to the increase in world trade. Gold cannot fulfill this demand perfectly since gold simply does not emerge in perfect response to the needs of trade.[3] Because of

---

[1]Hawtrey argued that there was no gold shortage ("...if there is not a redundancy..there is a sufficiency") and yet subscribed to the maldistribution thesis (Royal Institute of International Affairs, The International Gold Problem, pp. 99, 207).

[2]R. Triffin, Gold and the Dollar Crisis, p. 70.

[3]Gold emerges in response to mineral discoveries and technological advances in recovery. Given the state of the arts, more gold is forthcoming the greater the price; however, increasing the price implies devaluation of currencies tied to gold. Furthermore, it is possible in principle to have a situation where insufficient gold would emerge regardless of the price; i.e. there may be a physical limit on the amount of gold we have.

this, certain currencies which are generally believed to be freely convertible to gold come to be used in addition to gold in international dealings. However, these currencies are only generally believed freely convertible so long as confidence is maintained in the ability of these countries to control imbalances in their balance of payments. Any chronic imbalance in the balance of payments, or a situation in which the stock of outstanding gold-exchange begins to exceed the gold stock of the reserve currency country, tends to reduce confidence in the issuing country. From this point one of two outcomes may be expected: (a) the reserve currency country cannot adjust its balance of payments deficit, total liabilities continue to exceed the gold stock, and a run on the country in the form of the mass conversion of reserves for gold leads to depreciation; (b) the reserve currency country adjusts its balance of payments, the growth of international currency declines, and the problem of the inadequacy of international currency again appears. In either case, the outcome for the world economy is undesirable.

It it unlikely that either of the horns of Triffin's dilemma spurred the events of the depression. We have already considered the propositions that an overall decline in reserves or runs on the key currency countries initiated the events of this period; we found that the overall decline in reserves was probably nowhere a relevant constraint. The main run on the key currency countries occurred after the downward move in economic activity was apparent to even the most casual observers.

While the events of the early years of the world depression do not conform with Triffin's idealized model, these events nonetheless more than confirm the drift of his argument. The instability of the gold exchange standard which Triffin cites is only one of the problems facing a sporadically unstable world economy. In general, uncontrolled flows of private international investment are no more capable of maintaining the world economy at full employment than these same flows are capable of maintaining the domestic economy at full employment. Specifically, the events of the period 1928 to 1931 were aggravated by attempts by central bankers and governments to avoid the outcomes predicted by Triffin. Thus, the world never reached Triffin's dilemma in the early years of the Depression, not because that dilemma was avoidable, but rather because the main forces determining the depression had played out their roles before that dilemma was faced.

e/ Structural Change and Reform

A number of writers have centered their attention on the structure of the international economy during this period as the prime source of instability. These explanations deal with two types of phenomena: apparent changes in structure which seemed to have caused instability and the question of whether other changes in structure might have prevented the Depression.

Monetary and financial arguments of this sort have been made by Milton Friedman, Anna Schwartz, and Ragnar Nurkse. Friedman and Schwartz have attributed the severity of the world depression to the rigid links among nations provided by the gold exchange standard; had rates been allowed to fluctuate freely, the world depression would have been less severe.[1] Ragnar Nurkse has cited those who attributed much of the instability of the period to the failure of national economies to adjust their

---

[1]See section e-1.

levels of economic activity in a way dictated by the movements of gold, that is, to a general failure to "abide by the rules of the game" of the gold exchange standard.[1] W. A. Brown has claimed that the gold standard could no longer function well because of an inefficient division of function between New York and London.[2] In a related vein, many have pointed to the supposed undervaluation of the franc and/or overvaluation of the pound.[3] Other investigators have designated as complicating factors the move toward autarchy, the technological obsolescence of certain commodities, declining population growth, and a decline in the international mobility of people.[4] Finally, political factors were present in many international economic problems.[5]

e-1/ <u>The Role of Fixed Exchange Rates in the World Depression and the Advantages and Disadvantages of the Introduction of Flexible Rates</u>

While hypothetical history is considered by some to be unworkable and by most to be quite difficult[6], we can discuss some of the likely outcomes of the introduction or the existence of flexible exchange rates on the types of problems encountered during the period 1927 to 1933. Milton Friedman and Anna Schwartz are, to my knowledge, the only proponents of the view that flexible exchange rates would have ameliorated the problems of the thirties[7].

---

[1]See section e-2.

[2]See section e-3.

[3]See section e-4.

[4]See section e-5.

[5]See section e-6.

[6]Hypothetical history of the sort "If U. S. foreign lending had been maintained..." is sanctified by the body of economic theory. However, we have no economic theory which would explain a change in the structure of international payments from fixed to flexible rates. Therefore nothing now stands between us and the scorn of traditional historians.

[7]Friedman and Schwartz, <u>Monetary History of the United States</u>, p. 353.

Whether a system of flexible rates could have eased the problems of the period from 1927 to 1933 is problematic. The initial problem facing the world economy was the decline in long term investment. The substantial drop in United States lending in 1925 and 1929 presumably would have caused an increase in the dollar exchange rate. This increase might have reduced the inflow of long term funds to the New York stock markets, but if the increase in stock prices was greater than the appreciation of the dollar, additional funds would have flowed.

An increase in the dollar rate might have increased the value of United States imports and eased the problems of the industrial countries. However, European export expansion would probably not have taken place quickly. To the extent that the United States was large enough to force a decline in the price in terms of dollars of primary commodities, dollar revenues of primary exporters would probably have declined because of the price-inelastic demand for their product. Moreover, one can question the political feasibility and the economic wisdom of allowing huge changes in trade; full compensation for the $1.3-5.0 billion decline in long term capital exports would have required a 50%-100% increase in United States imports.

---

[1]See J. M. Keynes, A Treatise on Money, p. 196.

We discussed earlier the impact of changes in the exchange rate on the profitability of international investment. In general, we decided, appreciation of the dollar should have increased or left unchanged the incentive to invest in foreign countries. However, if United States investors had waited to see how far foreign exchange would depreciate, a further increase in the dollar exchange rate would have been likely. As before, declining exchange rates imply rising interest rates; however high interest rates and tight money in foreign countries probably contributed to the decline in domestic investment in those countries and hence to the depression.

There would probably have been a tendency to hedge American holdings denominated in foreign currencies, which would have further reduced the value of foreign exchange. If the hedging took place in the forward market then, given the relative interest rates of the United States and the center under discussion, the incentive to move funds in covered interest arbitrage to that center would be less[1]. Given uncertainty about the movements of rates, uncovered arbitrage would probably disappear. If we choose to give investors perfect expectations, then it would be rational to shift funds into dollars, further exasperating the situation.

It is therefore not immediately obvious that a system of flexible rates would have reduced the impact of the events of 1928 and 1929 on the world economy. The events of 1930 concerned the continued fall of long term investment coupled with a severe decline in commodity prices attributable to the

---

[1]Inasmuch as Central Banks are now supposed to operate without foreign exchange reserves, they would be unable to purchase their outstanding currencies in the spot market and would be able to influence the forward rate with support operations for only a brief period of time.

decreased willingness to hold stocks due to worsened expectations about conditions in consuming nations. Since flexible exchange rates did nothing substantial to change investment, there is no reason to believe that the same price reaction would not have set in.

Flexible exchange rates would add the new element of a decline in the value of the foreign exchange of the primary producing countries. Despite massive devaluation by primary producers the prices in consuming countries of world traded commodities would tend to be unchanged to reduced. If the prices were unchanged, then flexible rates would do nothing to change the situation, except to increase the prices of imports in primary producing countries and increase the pressure on developed countries. If primary prices were further reduced, the price inelasticity of demand of such commodities would ensure that foreign exchange earnings of primary supporters would be reduced, further reducing their import demand. The major problem of 1930 was the rapid fall of primary prices relative to industrial prices; flexible exchange rates would have tended to increase or leave unchanged that difference.

In summary, had a system of flexible exchange rates prevailed during this period, the effect on the system during 1929 would be indeterminate; the situation in 1930 would probably have been worse. It is clearly not obvious that flexible rates would have saved the day. We have not considered some of the more standard objections to flexible exchange rates: the possibility of destabilizing speculation, the increased cost of trading in a world where all trade must be hedged, the increased cost of lending in a world where all loans must be covered, and the possibility that a relatively high rate of inflation in one economy will be met ineffectively by perennial depreciation of that nation's currency. We are concerned here with the question of the superimposition of flexible exchange rates on nations as they are, taking as given the degree of domestic price flexibility, varying types of demand for different commodities, and the political rivalries of the day. If the argument for flexible exchange rates concerns far-reaching changes in other relationships, then evaluation of such a program is outside the bounds of this study

e-2/ The Failure to Abide by the "Rules of the Game"

Ragnar Nurkse[1] argued that many nations failed to follow the "rules of the game" of the gold-exchange standard. Thus, some countries losing gold did not take action to further reduce their money supplies, while other countries, receiving gold, did not take action to further expand their money supplies[2].

The view that failure to follow the rules of the game was responsible

---

[1] R. Nurkse, International Currency Experience, pp. 68-88.

[2] A number of questions have been raised concerning the proper interpretation of Nurkse's data. Arthur Bloomfield (A. Bloomfield, Monetary Policy Under the International Gold Standard: 1880-1914, pp. 47-51) observes that according to Nurkse's measure violations of the rules of the game occurred with about the same frequency during the period 1880-1914 as they did during the period 1922-1938 which Nurkse studied.

Robert Triffin has observed (R. Triffin, The Evolution of the International Monetary System, pp. 5-6) that despite an inverse corellation between changes in international and domestic assets of central banks, there may be a positive correlation between international assets and sight liabilities which would produce a multiplied impact on the private banking system through customary and legal reserve requirements.

for the instability of the international economy[1] was stated strongly in the Report of the Committee on Finance and Industry (the Macmillan Committee) in 1931[2] and with mild qualification in the Report of the Gold Delegation of the League of Nations[3].

There is little reason to believe, in the absence of consistency

---

[1]Curiously, Nurkse, to whom this view has been frequently appended, appears to have been quite skeptical about it. After describing a rather idealized view of the "rules of the game" and the international adjustment mechanism, he states quite explicitly: "There was a wide belief in the early 'twenties' that the monetary upheavals of that time were due to the absence of the equilibrating mechanism enforced by the gold-standard rules of the game. Whether this picture affords a satisfactory account of what happened even in the best days of the gold standard before 1914 is a question that may be touched on later" (Nurkse, op. cit., pp. 66-67). Later he indicates that an income adjusting system probably better describes the world than a price adjusting system (ibid, pp. 103-105), and points to the contradiction which frequently occurs between the goals of domestic stability, full employment and external balance (ibid, p. 105). He then advocates that a country suddenly facing a passive balance of payments settle the discrepancy through the shipment of reserves and otherwise do nothing, for to deflate in the face of increased exports from another country in a recession would be detrimental to world stability: "...the use of international currency reserves coupled with comprehensive 'offsetting' through changes in domestic expenditure---seems preferable in all respects; but it obviously presupposes the existence of adequate buffer stocks of international means of settlement" (ibid, p. 112). Advocacy of increasing domestic expenditures to offset the effect of an increase in imports and an outflow of reserves hardly seems to be the position of a man enchanted by the "rules of the game".

[2]Report of the Committee on Finance and Industry, Paragraphs 153 and 185; cited by Nurkse, op. cit., p. 87.

[3]Report of the Gold Delegation of the Leqgue of Nations; cited by Nurkse, op. cit., p. 87.

between internal and external balance, that a more assiduous adherence to the rules of the game would have resulted in a substantially improved international situation.[1] The United States, consistent with the outflow of gold in early 1928, did pursue a tight money policy which apparently had detrimental effects on the system and on the country. Britain, facing a balance of payments deficit and a gold outflow during the years 1928 and 1929, pursued a tight money policy which aggravated its internal problems and reduced the amount of long term lending.

Those countries in surplus, which were later to become the Gold Bloc, generally pursued easier money policies than the United States and Britain during the period 1927 to 1929. However, with most of their domestic economies fully employed under conditions of stable prices, the domestic incentive of any of these countries to change their domestic policy in a significant way was minimal.

In short, any principle such as the "rules of the game" is less than fully workable if the surplus countries are in internal balance but are supposed to expand while deficit countries already suffering from internal recession, are supposed to contract. Moreover, while such a policy might preserve exchange stability in the short run, it would do so at the expense of domestic output and price stability. If so, it may set into operation forces which ultimately are disturbing to the structure of exchange rates

---

[1]H. W. Arndt has taken a similar position: "What really matters, however, is that these countries had good reasons for their refusal to observe these rules, and, furthermore, that it is very doubtful whether even the most rigid adherence to them could by itself have maintained and restored international equilibrium." (Arndt, op. cit., p. 287).

and to income and price stability. Thus, the British policy of maintaining the pound contributed in the longer run to the British contraction, then to the decline in primary prices and, ultimately, to the devaluation of the pound.

e-3/ A Gold Standard Without a Center

W. A. Brown argues that one of the most critical factors undermining the stability of the interwar world economy was the incomplete transfer of the role of the gold standard center from Britain to the United States.[1] Prior to the war, London was the principal source of trade financing balances and long term loans, the major market for goods and securities, and the world's leading exporter of manufactured goods. In the interwar period the United States was becoming or had become preeminent in each of these fields.

Prior to the war Britain could exercise a great degree of control over the international economy. However, because the transfer of function was incomplete, neither Britain nor the United States could exercise such control after the war. Upon the more fragile structure of international payments were superimposed unusually severe economic disturbances (war debts, reparations, overproduction, among others), and the result was collapse.

Any provocative argument usually creates more questions than answers, and critical gaps remain despite Brown's extensive documentation. In particular, despite mounting research in the field, we still do not know precisely how the gold standard functioned in the latter half of the nineteenth century. The tentative consensus of serious research in this field is that relative price adjustment was not an important

---

[1]W. A. Brown, The International Gold Standard Reinterpreted; particularly see volume I, ch. 17, pp. 493-534 and volume II, ch. 21, pp. 773-806.

factor.[1] However, it is difficult to bring this information to bear on Brown's thesis: for undetermined is the extent to which all of these countries responded to common stimuli[2] albeit in different degrees, and thus undetermined is the extent to which the apparent control exercised by the Bank of England was illusory and represented only the British response to these common factors.

A second problem about which we know little is the extent to which any actual loss of coordination might be due to a general decline in the willingness to be "coordinated" rather than to a decline in the power to coordinate. Nurkse has spoken explicitly[3] of the increase in the importance placed on domestic stability and full employment relative to the importance placed on exchange stability. His observation is confirmed by other writers who simply observe that the rules of the game are defective because they do not guarantee these domestic goals.[4] Such a change in goals might convincingly be argued to be based on the increase in the number of national governments and the rise of participatory democracy after World War I.

On these grounds one might have serious reservations about a thesis which attributes increased instability to the loss of a centralized international monetary system. It is doubtful that these reservations could

---

[1] See, for example, A. I. Bloomfield, _Short Term Capital Movements Under the Pre-1914 Gold Standard and Monetary Policy Under the International Gold Standard, 1880-1914_; Robert Triffin, _The Evolution of the International Monetary System_; Jacob Viner, _Canada's Balance of International Indebtedness, 1900-1913_; Harry D. White, _The French International Accounts, 1880-1913_; John H. Williams, _Argentine International Trade Under Inconvertible Paper, 1880-1900_.

[2] Such as technological change or the gold discoveries.

[3] Nurkse, _op. cit._, p. 22; Keynes, _Essays in Persuasion_, 1932 ed., pp. 199-200.

[4] See, for example, Arndt, _op. cit._, p. 287.

be resolved on the basis of current knowledge.

Brown also suggests the existence of certain problems facing the world economy because of the rise in importance of New York as a financial center. These problems were the shift of trade financing to New York, the growth of the New York securities market, the growth of the United States as a trading center, and the growth of New York as an exporter of long term capital.

The question of competitive challenge and actual damage to the British export position has important bearing on the problems of the interwar period. This has less to do with the operation of the gold standard than with the world's critical need of a rising flow of international investment during the interwar years. To the extent that Britain's balance on current account directly or indirectly limited British lending, the problem was serious[1].

The effect of the shift of trade financing balances to New York is more problematic. Brown argues that this shift increased the need for international reserves and that increases in trade consequently required

---

[1]See chapter 4, section e-4/1.

relatively larger trade financing balances. Whether or not the demand for reserves would have so increased,[1] this increased demand would have to be weighed against the increased supply of international reserves attributable to the extension of the gold exchange standard.[2]

Brown in unclear about the reason for the significance of the rise in the relative importance of the New York securities markets. Possession of such a market by a country implies that other creditor countries will remit funds to this center for investment elsewhere. On the other hand, since both potential center countries, Britain and the United States, were long term net lenders in the long run, the security market should have reflected this and there should have been a net outflow of funds in transactions in outstanding securities, except in times such as the boom on the New York stock exchanges. It is difficult, though, to see the relationship between the boom and the split gold standard. This argument does reflect on the size and movement of short term balances between the center countries, since some short term balances were maintained for the purpose of

---

[1]If we believe that international reserves are a constant fraction of international transactions ($M_i = k'Y_i$) then a division of trade financing, or a change in that division, would not change the total demand for international reserves unless the center which was receiving funds maintained a larger fraction (k') of reserves to trade then the center losing funds. On the other hand, if we believe that transactions balances are not a constant proportion of international transactions, than an increase in the number of centers would require an increase in the amount of reserves (e.g. $M_i = \sqrt{k'Y_i}$ (Baumol-Tobin) or $M_i = a + k'Y_i$.) Only knowledge of the precise relationship can tell us whether <u>increases</u> in trade would require larger <u>increases</u> in reserves under a split standard. This would be true if $M_i = \sqrt{k'Y_i}$, but it would not be true if $M_i = a + k'Y_i$.

[2]This is true despite the fact that the trade financing countries operate only on gold reserves, for gold exchange could be used by the peripheral countries.

investment in long term securities. Similarly, a split gold standard would not affect the size or direction of new long term lending, but it would affect the size and location of the short term proceeds of such loans.

It seems that most of Brown's argument can be reduced to the question of the size and location of short term balances. In the interwar period short term assets and liabilities could be shifted between two major centers, while prior to the war according to Brown, these balances would of necessity, be located primarily in London. Thus, neither center could control the flow of short term balancing funds. In particular, London was sporadically deprived of short term funds by events in Paris and New York. It was once said that a 10% Bank Rate could draw gold from the ground; yet in 1929, 6-1/2% couldn't draw gold from New York.

The factors described by Brown may help explain the failure of short term funds to flow in times of stress between 1929 and 1931. However, the stress itself is best explained by the sudden decline in net long term lending.

e-4/ Improper Valuation of Exchange Rates

(1). The Overvaluation of the British Pound

It was agreed, by even those who set the rate, that the pound was overvalued. From a vantage point of forty years it also seems that the pound was overvalued, that there was no particularly good reason for it to have been overvalued, and that the effects of the overvaluation on Britain and on the world economy were quite damaging.

Semantic dangers and conceptual voids lurk everywhere in the definition of the term "overvalued currency". A currency is overvalued if, given the exchange rate, autonomous transactions on current and long term capital accounts produce chronic net inflows of accomodating items on the short term capital or gold accounts[1]; or if, in the absence of such accomodating flows, the autonomous flows produce domestic deflation of prices, output, or employment.

Despite the implication, the possessor of an "overvalued" currency needn't devalue. On the contrary, devaluation might well be his least desirable option. He may instead reduce autonomous investment, increase

[1]The treatment of long term capital flows and current account items as "autonomous" and gold and short term capital as "accomodating" is an empirical generality with glaring exceptions. For example, French conversions of foreign exchange to gold, flight capital, speculation, and the U. S. drive to build an acceptance market, among others, have been discussed earlier.

exports, decrease imports, or accept deflation until his currency ceases to be overvalued. Which option is best depends on the costs and returns to the individual country and the world; moreover, it is not always true that a policy consistent with the welfare of the former will be consistent with the welfare of the latter.

In order to maintain the pound at the rate set in May 1925, Britain pursued a vigorous tight money policy aimed at deflating internal prices[1], and briefly attempted to restrain new foreign lending as well[2]. Inasmuch as this policy also produced substantial domestic unemployment, it is clear, at least as we have defined matters, that the pound was overvalued. The value of the pound was set in 1925 with the understanding that a policy of deflation would have to be followed. The architects and the critics of that policy differed primarily on questions of probably consequence.

---

[1]The Report of the Committee on the Currency and Bank of England Note Issues (February 5, 1925) stated that a return to gold at parity was possible if credit control was used to reduce domestic prices and if foreign investment were restrained. Inasmuch as this had not been accomplished by May 13, when the Gold Standard Act was passed, the pound was at that time overvalued [Report of the Committee on the Currency and Bank of England Note Issues (Cunliffe Committee), Sec. 10-13; cited by Brown, op. cit., Vol. I, p. 375].

[2]An embargo was placed on new foreign lending in November 1925 and remained in effect until November 1926 (Brown, op. cit., Vol. I, p. 378).

The consequences of that policy were that Britain endured a high degree of unemployment throughout the period between the 1925 stabilization and 1929, and maintained a tight money policy which presumably reduced the rate of increase of new long term foreign lending. In contrast, it is not obvious that a British devaluation would have had a deflating effect on the world economy through the British current account. A state of affairs in which a devaluation increases the current account surplus and permits monetary loosening might result in absolutely larger imports,[1] exports,[1] current account surplus and long term lending, thus bringing Britain into balance while being net stimulating to the world.

J. M. Keynes and Reginald McKenna[2] argued against the policies of Baldwin and Churchill with force and prescience, Keynes at one point presenting a prediction not only of the consequences of the policy but of the historiography of the consequences:

> "And since the public always understands particular causes better than general causes, the depression will be attributed to the industrial disputes which will accompany it, to the Dawes Scheme, to China, to the inevitable consequences of the Great War, to tariffs, to high taxation, to anything in the world except the general monetary policy which has set the whole thing going."
>
> Keynes, "The Economic Consequences of Mr. Churchill" (1925)[3]

---

[1]Assuming that the income effects outweigh the price effects.

[2]President of the Midland Bank.

[3]Reprinted in Keynes, Essays in Persuasion, 1932 ed., pp. 263-264.

Continued attacks based on the blatant lack of success of the tight money policy erupted in June 1927 with a Labor motion to investigate the Bank of England. Winston Churchill, Chancellor of the Exchequer, replied:

> Our policy, like that of every other set of Ministers who have been responsible, has been the re-establishment of the gold standard, and the maintenance, as far as we can, of the stability of the currency and the stability of our international exchange...
>
> It is true that there is an alternative policy...That is the view put forward by Mr. McKenna and also put forward to some extent, but in a different form, by Mr. Maynard Keynes...
>
> In one form or another, and in the most seductive terms, they suggest that just a spice of inflation would be advantageous--so long as it is called by some other name...
>
> For good or ill we have taken our course, right or wrong, and in these currency matters it is essential to pursue a course with some consistency and persistency for a certain number of years"..
>
> Churchill to Parliament June 27, 1927[1]

On the following day Reginald McKenna stated that "Mr. Churchill's statement is in itself sufficient proof of the need for an inquiry".[2] Inquiry into this and related matters was finally begun in 1931 by the Committee on Finance and Industry (the Macmillan Committee). Questioning by Macmillan and Keynes of officials of the Bank of England indicated that these officials felt the overvaluation of the pound was due primarily to two events: the decline in the value of the franc after the stabilization of the pound[3] and the artificial stimulus given to the British coal

---

[1]European Economic and Political Survey, vol. 2, no. 21, July 15, 1927, p. 706.

[2]European Economic and Political Survey, vol. 2, no. 21, July 15, 1927, p. 708.

[3]Report of the Committee on Finance and Industry (Macmillan Committee), 1931, questions 3353-3363; cited in Brown, op. cit., vol. 1, pp. 611-612.

industry by the occupation of the Ruhr during 1923 and 1924.[1]

The position that the events which led to the overvaluation of the pound were unforseen and unforseeable is not convincing. The price of francs in terms of dollars had declined by about 12 1/2%[2] during the nine months preceding the January 1925 decision to seek loans from the United States in order to smooth the return to gold; the price of francs in terms of pounds declined by 20.2% during the same period. Between the end of January and the April 28 announcement that the Gold and Silver (export control) Act would not be renewed in December,[3] signalling the return to the gold standard, the price of francs in terms of dollars declined by 3.8%; the price of francs in terms of pounds declined by 4.1%. The Gold Standard Act was passed on May 13, 1925; between the end of April and the end of May, the dollar-franc rate declined by .47% while the sterling-franc rate declined by 1.7%.

---

[1]Report of the Committee on Finance and Industry (Macmillan Committee), 1931, questions 7621-7625, 7633-7635; cited in Brown, op. cit., vol. 1, pp. 614-615.

[2]All exchange rates and exchange rate changes are calculated from Banking and Monetary Statistics, 1943 ed., pp. 670, 681. The sterling-franc rate was calculated by multiplying the dollar-franc rate by the reciprocal of the dollar-sterling rate [($/fr.) (£/$)=£/fr.] Morganstern claims that during the period 1914-1931 actual rates and cross-rates of exchange show no permanent differences, indicating a highly efficient currency arbitrage market. He used a similar procedure to derive exchange rates (Morgenstern, International Financial Transactions and Business Cycles, pp. 224, 276).

[3]Authorities emphasized the necessity to act on the question of the return to gold before the expiration of the Gold and Silver (export control) Act in December 1925 (Brown, op. cit., vol. 1, p. 612).

With few improvements in the French economic situation in prospect,[1] it was considerably more likely that the franc would continue to decline, which it did, than that it would stabilize or rise, which it did not. In any case, the position of those such as Keynes who wanted to wait as long as possible before returning to gold seems to have been quite reasonable if you were of the mind that the sterling-franc rate was critical. Such a position would have been well-rewarded since the franc reached 3.9¢, the level at which it was ultimately stabilized, in November 1925, a month prior to the expiration of the Gold and Silver Act. It appears that British authorities were not terribly concerned about the sterling-franc rate, underestimated the conseqquences of a further depreciated sterling-franc rate[2], or underestimated the difficulty of internal adjustment to changes in that rate.

Similar observations may be made about the quantity and value of British coal exports. Exports of coal and coal products declined by 31.2% in 1924 and 24.2% in 1925 (see chart 11). Surely if this was considered an important element in the British external position, the rapid decline of these exports during 1924 and 1925 must have given some hint that the levels of 1923 would not be maintained. Moreover, both the quantity and value of coal exports seem to have settled approximately at 1925 values after stabilization[3]; thus, further decline in these exports could not

---

[1]The evacuation of the Ruhr occurred in November 1925.

[2]Although, as we discussed earlier, there is no overwhelming evidence that the franc was undervalued, and hence that the sterling-franc rate was more critical than the general level of the sterling rate.

[3]The decline in exports during 1926 was due to the British general strike.

have been an important cause of British difficulties in the late twenties.

Chart 11

Quantity and Value of British Exports
of Coal and Coal Products, 1923-1930

($000,000)

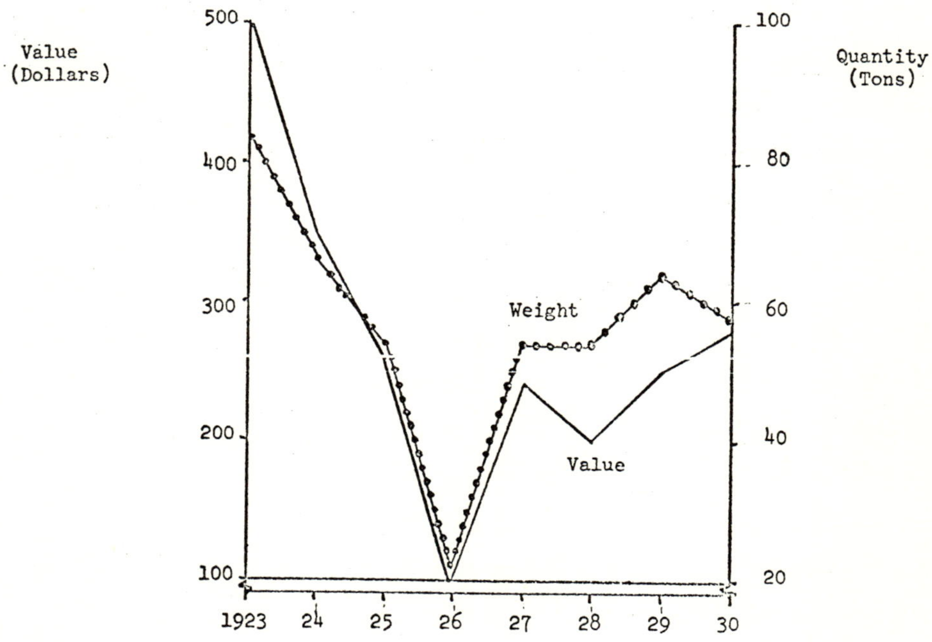

Source: U.K. Coal exports for the years 1923-1930 were taken from the U.S. Department of Commerce, Commerce Yearbook for the following years [1923 data, 1923 Yearbook, p. 565; 1924 data, 1924 Yearbook, p. 614; 1925 data, 1926 Yearbook, Vol. II, p. 541; 1926-1927 data, 1928 Yearbook, Vol. II, p. 643; 1928-1930 data, 1932 Yearbook, Vol. II, p. 289].

When Lord Macmillan asked Montague Norman, Governor of the Bank of England, "And if these circumstances which have supervened had been foreseen it may be that you would not have reverted to the gold standard at the time you did?", Norman replied, "I will not say that".[1] To W. A. Brown this implied "that even had the subsequent history of the French and Belgian francs been foreseen, the date of the British return to gold and the choice of the old par would not have been altered. The foundations of that choice were far too deeply laid in the character of British banks and British bankers, and in the traditional policies of the British government".[2]

The foundation of that choice may have rested on nothing less ephemeral than considerations of "prestige", "national honor", or those curious shards of morality that come to be patched on to assorted precepts of economic theory.[3] However, it might be kept in mind that the British government held its assets in sterling but its liabilities (war debts, stabilization loans) in dollars and, therefore, that a devaluation of sterling relative to the dollar would have tended to reduce its net asset position in terms of gold, or equivalently, have increased the burden of the war debt in terms of gold. In addition, a devaluation of sterling would have tended to reduce

---

[1]Report of the Committee on Currency and Finance, 1931, questions 3353-3363; cited in Brown, op. cit., Vol. 1, pp. 611-612.

[2]Brown, op. cit., Vol. 1, p. 612.

[3]See, for example, Keynes, Essays in Persuasion, pp. 242 and 223-243 passim.

the gold value of the vast amounts of sterling-denominated long term foreign loans, and the gold value of the net asset position of the private British lending community.

Whatever the ultimate reasons for the choice of the rate and time of return to the gold standard, the method of adjustment selected, involving tight money, domestic unemployment, and reduced international lending, was already a drag on the world economy when the rapid decline in net long term lending by the United States commenced in mid-1928.

(2). The Undervaluation of the French Franc

Like "maldistribution of gold", "undervaluation of the franc" and "overvaluation of sterling" became catch phrases of the period and it is rather difficult to determine precisely what was generally deemed to be the problem. Most people seem to be referring to the level at which, and the manner in which, the franc was stabilized during 1926 and 1927. For a number of reasons, bear speculation among them, the franc declined sharply from 4.7¢ in July 1925 to 2.5¢ in July 1926.[1] However, economic measures by the newly elected Poincare government in mid-1926 reversed this situation and the franc, in terms of dollars, appreciated from 2.5¢ to 3.9¢ during the remainder of the year.[2] The appreciation of the franc was believed by French authorities to have caused a minor recession during 1926. This, together with the sentiment that the appreciation of the franc was largely due to bull speculation, led France to stabilize the franc at 3.9¢.[3]

However, at this rate funds continued to flow into France, perhaps in anticipation of a further increase in the franc rate. Fearing that this inflow of funds would lead to inflation, French authorities engaged in one of the early classic forward exchange operations: they sold francs in

---

[1] Banking and Monetary Statistics, 1943 ed., p. 670.

[2] ibid.

[3] The position that short term capital inflows to France represented repatriated capital is stated by a number of authors: Brown, op. cit., p. 444; Nurkse, op. cit., p. 38. Benjamin Strong, head of the New York Federal Reserve Bank, apparently believed large sums of French capital in the U. S. and the U. K. would return to France upon stabilization of the franc (Chandler, Benjamin Strong, p. 363).

Emile Moreau, head of the Bank of France, apparently believed that the franc was appreciating because of speculative buying (Chandler, op. cit., p. 372). Paul Einzig claims that this was generally believed in France, that the initial depreciation of the franc between 1919 and 1926 was caused by bear speculation, and that British and German banks did in fact take bear positions in francs (Einzig, Behind the Scenes of International Finance, pp. 28-29; this book is profoundly unsympathetic to the French).

the forward market, keeping the franc from appreciating, and absorbed the proceeds of the francs thus sold with the purchase of foreign short bills, thus preventing domestic liquidity from increasing sharply.[1] In the process of making these sales of forward francs, French authorities acquired huge amounts of foreign exchange. Additional foreign exchange flowed in due to the French current account, which was in surplus from 1927 through 1930. This surplus was offset in part by known long term capital operations (see chart 12).

The hypothesis that the franc was undervalued has two different implications. If the implication of the argument is that France exerted deflationary pressure on the world economy through her known overall surplus, the answer is qualifiedly affirmative. However, it should be observed that France's current account surplus had declined by about $170 million in 1929, about 35% of its 1928 value. It should also be observed that French long term lending was apparently reduced by the reluctance of borrowers to borrow at the high rates of 1928 and 1929. Had French long term lending remained at 1927 or even 1930 levels during 1928 and 1929, France's overall surplus would have declined more rapidly than it in fact did. Therefore, the "drain" exerted by France through her current and capital accounts is not an independent phenomena, but related to the decline in net United States lending and the resulting tight money rates which we discussed earlier.[2]

---

[1]Nurkse, op. cit., p. 36.

[2]Inasmuch as net known long term lending by France amounted to $162 million in 1927 and declined by $132 million during 1928 (League of Nations, Balance of Payments Yearbook, 1929, pp. 88-89) while U. S. net lending between July 1928 and September 1929 declined by $1.3-$5.1 billion (ch. 3, p. 32), it seems likely that the behavior of U. S. net long term lending, rather than that of the French, better explains the tight money conditions of 1928 and 1929.

Chart 12

French Current and Known[1]
Long Term Capital Accounts 1927-1933

($000,000; gold = $20.67/oz.)

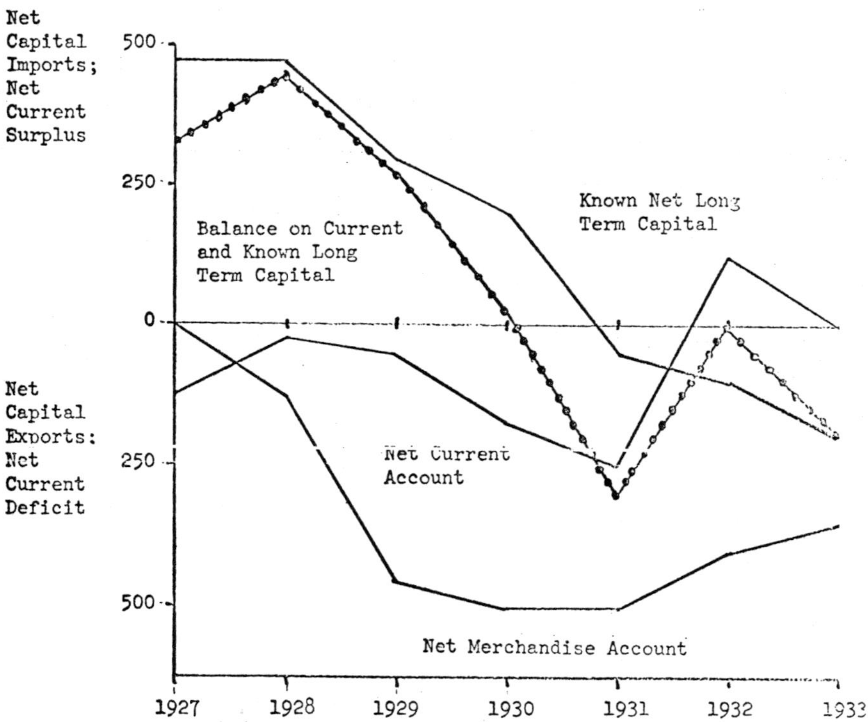

Source: 1927-1929 data taken from League of Nations, Balance of Payments Yearbook 1929, pp. 88-89; 1930-1933 data from the League of Nations Balance of Payments Yearbook 1933, pp. 82-83. Converted to gold dollars at 1 franc = 3.9¢.

---

[1] Data are available only for new issues and some special loans; there are incomplete data for transactions in outstanding securities. Some amortization was included with interest payments. See balance of payments citations above for further information.

However, if the implication is that the vast financial power exercised by France, particularly at times of inconvenience for Britain and the United States, was attributable to current account surpluses,[1] then it must be tightly circumscribed: for cumulative current account surpluses are insufficient to explain the size of French holdings of gold and foreign exchange. If we plot the cumulative net current account proceeds against the increase in gold and foreign exchange holdings of the French central bank and government, the latter are generally greater than the former (see chart 13). While the relationship is not constant, cumulative surpluses never accounted for more than 70% of the increase in reserve assets while in the critical years of 1928 and 1930-1932 they accounted for less than 57% of the increase in reserve assets (see chart 12).[2]

Short term capital movements and unreported long term capital movements were generally as or more important than current account surpluses in contributing to French holdings of international reserve assets. There is considerable question about how much of these short term flows to attribute to the "undervaluation" of the franc. French international

---

[1]After speaking about the undervalued franc, Arndt states that "an almost regularly active balance of trade and a high surplus on invisible exports enabled France to accumulate a very large gold reserve after 1928..." (Arndt, op. cit., p. 24).

[2]Speaking of the apparent lack of success of devaluations in the thirties, Nurkse observed that "no country succeeded in gaining an advantage comparable to that which France enjoyed during the years 1927-1930" (Nurkse, op. cit., p. 107). Yet in 1930 only 54.1% of French international reserve assets could be accounted for by cumulative balance of payments surpluses from 1927 (see chart 13).

Chart 13

Cumulative French Surpluses on
Current and Known Long Term Capital Account
and Change in Total French International Reserve Assets,
1927-1933

($000,000)

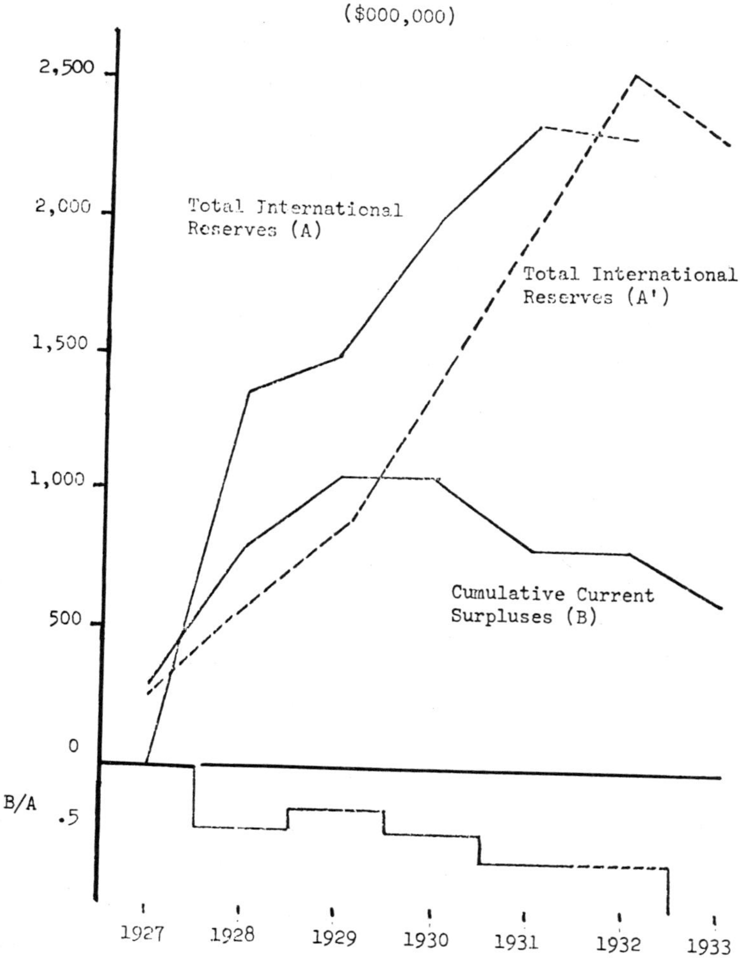

Source: See chart 11 for source of current plus known capital balance. A and A' are two estimates of French international reserve assets. See the following page, note 1 for a discussion of these estimates.

reserves rose sharply during 1928 as a result of the official operations which were aimed at offsetting the effects of the large inflow of short term funds.

There are two unproved hypotheses about the origin of this foreign exchange: one is that the inflow of foreign exchange was due to foreign speculation; the other is that these funds represented the return of French assets which had fled earlier to avoid loss due to the depreciation of the franc during the years 1919-1926. Inasmuch as there was no subsequent substantial withdrawal of funds from France, such as one might expect once speculators became aware that France was actually stabilizing the franc at 3.9¢,[2] it seems likely that these funds were largely repatriated capital.

If these funds represented repatriated capital, then their return was less a function of the level of the exchange rate than of the conviction of

---

[1]Estimates of French central bank and government holdings of gold and foreign exchange were taken from the Bank for International Settlements, The Gold Exchange Standard, cited in Brown, op. cit., vol. II, pp. 740-741. These were used in preference to the estimates of the League of Nations (League of Nations Statistical Yearbook 1933-1934, pp. 210-212) in this case because of the claim that official Bank of France estimates of gold and foreign exchange holdings were underestimated in the late twenties. (Brown, ibid, p. 736). The Bank for International Settlements estimates end in September 1932. I have included the League of Nations estimates so that the reader may see the difference. The reader should note that use of the League of Nations estimates would tend to increase the importance of the current surplus during the years 1927-1931 and decrease it during the years 1932-1933, relative to the estimates used in the text.

[2]The franc was held close to 3.9¢ throughout 1927 and legally stabilized at that level in mid-1928. There is no reason either to believe that these funds represented capital flight from any other major currency.

the repatriators that the franc had ceased depreciating[1]. Hence, the "undervaluation" of the franc may have been irrelevant in determining the cause of the 1927-1928 inflow of short term funds.

The next large inflow of funds appears to occur from 1930 through 1932. This inflow presumably reflects the economic disorder in Britain, the United States, and on the Continent. One might observe, initially, that in 1931, of the four major financial centers, New York, London, Berlin, and Paris, only the latter had not suffered from either (or both) a payments crisis or the collapse of important segments of its banking system[2].

It is unlikely that the undervaluation of the franc had much to do with these circumstances. It is rather obvious that the level of the exchange rate of the United States, overall or relative to France, was not an important factor in the dollar's problems. The level of the exchange rate in Germany appears to have been much less important than the decline in foreign long term lending and the effect of that decline on domestic business

---

[1]We could argue that the belief of repatriators that another wave of depreciation would not occur was positively correlated with the lowness of the franc rate. However, then we would have to explain why the money remained in France as the current account worsened between 1927 and 1930. Furthermore, the other examples of capital flight which we discussed seem to have occurred during periods when the economic conditions of the countries involved were clearly on the verge of disaster. If it is so that people in the habit of setting capital in flight do not act until they are in the midst of a crisis, then it seems quite likely that they would be perfectly satisfied with exchange rate stability and the absence of visible internal economic and political disorder.

[2]This is generally taken for granted, but of course if you are exporting capital for the purpose of maintaining or increasing its real value, then you are not only interested in the soundness of the currency of the recipient nation but, as well, in the soundness of the recipient institutions and their instruments.

conditions and Germany's international payments position[1]. In the case of Britain, it would appear that the general overvaluation of the pound was a considerably more serious problem that the general undervaluation of the franc[2].

France avoided, for a couple of years, the problems facing these other countries because of her relatively smaller dependence on trade and foreign investment and her consequent ability to avoid monetary self-strangulation in 1928 and 1929 rather than because of the lowness of her exchange rate. Funds moving to France between 1930 and 1932 were probably based more on apparent French soundness than on the low franc rate, which does not appear to have been the main determinant of that soundness.

The glittering displays of French financial might, occurring primarily in 1927 and 1928 and again in 1931 and 1932 rested invariably on the ability of France to lend, based on her large reserves, and on the willingness of France to convert gold exchange for gold--frequently at times embarassing for Britain and the United States. The amount of such reserves which France

---

[1]There is naturally disagreement about this. Bloomfield states that the Gold Bloc was undervalued relative to the pound and that badly chosen exchange rates led to disequilibrium (Bloomfield, Capital Imports and the American Balance of Payments, pp. 14, 18). Nurkse, on the other hand, said that "the French balance of payments no doubt contributed, though probably to a minor degree, to the forces making for depression in the rest of the world at the turning-point of the business cycles in 1929-1930" (Nurkse, op. cit., p. 38). Keynes, writing in 1926, after the stabilization of the pound, said that the franc should be set between 3.3¢-4.0¢; in editing his essays in 1932 he noted merely that "this was a happy guess" (Keynes, Essays in Persuasion, 1932 ed., p. 111).

[2]See chapter 4, pp. 126-134.

could manipulate was attributable at least as much to flows of short term funds as it was to current account surpluses based on an "undervalued" franc; French desire and willingness to engage in such operations is best explained by neither the surplus on the current or the short term capital account.[1]

e-5/ Other Structural Explanations[2]

(1). Technological Obsolescence of Some Commodities

The most important case during this period of the technological obsolescence of a primary export is the substitution of petroleum for coal.[3] The decline in the coal market primarily affected Britain.

It is clear that whatever the initial impact of these problems, they were aggravated by restrictive monetary policies aimed at external balance. Given the decline in long lending and the need to switch from the production of these commodities, precisely opposite policies would probably have been more beneficial.

(2). The Decline in Population Growth

The decline in the rate of population growth has been held responsible by some authors for the decline in demand and the subsequent depression.[4] Inasmuch as population growth and technological progress (construed loosely) are the ultimate determinants of long term investment, it is likely that a more rapid rate of population growth in societies where the remaining apparatus of growth was present would have had a buoyant effect on the world economy. Given the increase in interest rates and the reduction in the quantity of funds available for long term loans, the size of the decline in investment probably depended in part on the decline in the rate of population growth.

---

[1]The economic basis of the French conversion of gold exchange for gold is discussed in this chapter, section c-3. The political basis for the French conversion is discussed in this chapter, section e-6.

[2]We have discussed the question of the move toward autarchy in chapter 4, pp. 10-12.

[3]Royal Institute of International Affairs, The Problem of International Investment, p. 34.

[4]ibid, p. 14.

(3). The Decline in Migration[1]

The substantial decline in migration during the period 1919 to 1929 was mainly due to increased restrictions on immigration by developed countries. Inasmuch as part of the problem of the period was the failure to export capital, it is probably true that some of the consequences of this failure might have been offset by migration: if the capital can't be moved to the people, then move the people to the capital.

Increased immigration to the United States prior to 1929 might have offset the negative effects of the declining rate of population growth and postponed or reduced the domestic depression. To the extent that immigrants would have been drawn from rural areas in Southeastern Europe, there might have also been a net gain to the world. However, had the immigrants come mainly from England or Germany, any imporvement in the United States might have been offset by a decline in economic activity in the country of emigration.

e-6/ Intergovernmental Lending and Cooperation

Private lending and borrowing led to a situation incompatible with world economic growth at full employment, largely because many of the decisions made by private lenders and borrowers ignored factors which were crucial to these objectives.[2] Despite the diversity of the explanations discussed earlier in this chapter, most shared the trait that the private market solution to the economic problem was inconsistent with world economic growth at full employment.

The divergence between private interest and social interest is the

---

[1] The decline in migration as an economic problem of the interwar period was described by Arndt, op. cit., p. 278.

[2] See chapter 3, passim.

classic ground for government intervention in a market economy. However, government intervention in the problems we have described was sporadic and, ultimately, ineffective.

During the years 1927 and 1928, lending for stabilization purposes to the countries of Central Europe was an important intergovernmental activity. There was a great deal of friction between the Bank of England and the Bank of France concerning their relative positions in administering these loans with the United States.[1]

As important was the attempt to synchronize and reduce the discount rates of Britain, France, Germany, and the United States. Such an agreement was concluded during July 1927 in New York.[2] Reduction of the British bank rate had a salutary effect on the British economy: toward the end of 1927 British domestic production reached the highest level since 1920[3] while the sterling-dollar rate reached the United States gold export point at a time when sterling was usually seasonally weak.[4] This agreement apparently ended with the increase in the United States discount rate in February 1928.

---

[1]Chandler, Benjamin Strong, ch. 11, passim.

[2]ibid, p. 376.

[3]Harvard Economic Service, Weekly Letter, Vol. 6, no. 43, October 29, 1927, p. 281.

[4]ibid, no. 44, p. 286.

French withdrawals of funds from Austria, due to French opposition to recently revealed plans for a customs union including Germany and Austria, contributed to the collapse of the Austrian Credit Anstalt in May 1931[1]. An emergency loan of $14,070,000 was financed by a consortium of eleven Western nations operating through the Bank for International Settlements[2].

On June 17, 1931 France declared publicly that a previously promised loan to Austria of $25,000,000 was contingent on Austrian renunciation of any plans for economic union with Germany[3]. In part as a protest against this condition and its attendant humiliating publicity, the Austrian government resigned; Britain filled the breach with a loan of £5,000,000 (about $24,324,315)[4].

The short term capital policies of both France and Germany were affected, and sometimes determined, by the desire to gain an advantage on the reparation question. Hjalmar Schacht, head of the Reichsbank, was disturbed that continued inflows of short term funds would give the German balance of payments an appearance of excessive strength and lead to demands for increased reparations payments.[5] France, on the

---

[1]Arndt, op. cit., p. 29.

[2]Federal Reserve Bank of New York, Annual Report for 1931, p. 23.

[3]Einzig, Behind the Scenes of International Finance, pp. 75-79.

[4]Ibid, p. 79; see also the Royal Institute of International Affairs, The Problem of International Investment, p. 218. The average sterling-dollar rate for June 1931 was $4.864863 (Banking and Monetary Statistics, 1943 ed., p. 681); at this rate, £5,000,000 is equivalent to $24,324,315.

[5]European Economic and Political Survey, vol. 2, no. 16, April 30, 1927, p. 504; vol. 2, no. 23, August 15, 1927, p. 758.

other hand, was reluctant to lend money on short term to Germany[1], and at first was unwilling to aid in the flotation of the Dawes Loan[2] , the purpose of which was to facilitate the payment of reparations. This apparent contradiction may be resolved by noting that when Emile Moreau, Governor General of the Bank of France, informed Poincare that Montague Norman's assistance might be obtained in the flotation of the Dawes Loan, Poincare replied that flotation of the full Dawes loan would hasten the time when French troops would have to leave the Rhineland, and that this was not in the best interest of French security[3].

There are reports that during 1929 France withdrew funds from Germany in order to force Schacht to accept the schedule of reparations payments in the original Young Plan[4]. and withdrew gold from Britain when that country indicated unwillingness to have its share of reparations further reduced[5].

---

[1]Einzig, Behind the Scenes of International Finance, p. 60. The Bank of France charged an additional 1/2% to discount bills drawn on German banks and apparently informed private banks that lending to Germany was not favored.

[2]Clarke, Central Bank Cooperation: 1924-1931, p. 67.

[3]Moreau, Souvenirs d'un Gouverneur de la Banque de France, p. 320: "Je poursuis mon exposé en disant au président que nous pourrions essayer d'obtenir de M. Norman son appui en Europe, notamment pour l'émission des obligations Dawes. M. Poincaré me repond qu'il ne desire pas, pour le moment, qu'on émette plus qu'une partie de ces obligations, car si l'émission était totale, il nous faudrait evacuer la Rhénanie. Or, M. Poincaré ne veut pas évacuer la Rhénanie tant que notre frontière ne sera pas en état de défense et militairement organisée."

[4] Brown, op. cit., vol. 2, p. 936.

[5] Einzig, op. cit., p. 49.

France withdrew $209.6 million in gold from Great Britain between January and July 1931, $110.1 million during July alone[1]. According to Einzig, France sought to demonstrate to Germany that any assistance for her external problems could only be gained by cooperation with France[2]. The Darmstadter and National Bank, one of the most important banks in Germany, had suspended payments on July 13[3]. This coming in the wake of the failure of the Credit Anstalt, led to increased liquidation of short term balances in Germany. During May and July of 1931 about 30% of foreign short term assets in Germany were withdrawn.[4]

On June 26, 1931 the Bank of France, the Bank of England, and the Federal Reserve had granted Germany a $100,000,000 loan which was to be repaid on July 16, 1931[5]. When the loan was exhausted Germany turned to France; again the terms involved public renunciation of economic union with Austria[6]. Germany refused the loan, closed the banks on July 14th and later instituted a capital embargo and exchange control.

---

[1] Federal Reserve Bulletin, February 1932, p. 113.

[2] Einzig, Behind the Scenes of International Finance, p. 100.

[3] Stolper, et al., The German Economy: 1870 to the Present, p. 114. The bank failure was due largely to the bankruptcy of a large Bremen textile firm, the Norddeutsche Wollkammerei, in which the bank had extensive investments.

[4] Federal Reserve Bank of New York, Annual Report for 1931, p. 23.

[5] ibid.

[6] Einzig, op. cit., p. 86.

French withdrawals of gold from Britain declined sharply in August 1931.[1] Britain received a $250,000,000 loan on August 1, which was divided evenly between the Bank of France and the Federal Reserve. A further loan to Britain of $400,000,000 was made on August 28, divided evenly between private lenders in France and the United States.[2] These efforts failed, and on September 21, 1931 Britain announced the cessation of gold payments and allowed sterling to depreciate.

President Hoover proposed a moratorium on intergovernmental debt on June 20, 1931, reiterating the position that there was no connection between the payment of reparations and the payment of war debts, although both were included under the proposed moratorium. The moratorium was planned as an attempt to restore international confidence; essentially though it served to sacrifice the public debt in order to increase the chance of saving the private debt.

The moratorium was not generally agreed upon until July 6, 1931. Its effectiveness was decreased by delays in acceptance by France and the United States Congress. France wanted assurances that reparations payments would be resumed, while Congress had similar concern over war debt payments. Einzig claims that France drew heavily on United States gold at the end of 1931 in order to get American support for the continuation of reparation payments.[3]

---

[1] Federal Reserve Bulletin, February 1932, p. 113.

[2] Federal Reserve Bank of New York, op. cit., p. 12.

[3] Einzig, op. cit., p.135.

Some Reflections

Neither the United States nor the United Kingdom was in a position to undertake unilaterally, or even in concert, substantial loans to assist deficit countries with the degree of financial security possible had they been able to gain the cooperation of the Gold Bloc and preeminently, of France. Together, these three nations controlled 62% of the world's international reserves in 1931 (see table 2).

Table 2

International Reserves of the U. S., U. K., and France, December, 1931

($000,000)

		France	U. S.	U. K.	Total
1.	Exchange	$ 838.5	-----	-----	$ 838.5
2.	Gold	$2699.4	$4051.5	$ 587.6	$ 7338.5
3.	World Gold	($11370.0)	($11370.0)	($11370.0)	$11370.0
4.	2. ÷ 3.	23.7%	35.6%	5.2%	64.5%
5.	1. + 2.	$3537.9	$4051.5	$ 587.6	$ 8177.0
6.	World Reserves	($13109.0)	($13109.0)	($13109.0)	$13109.0
7.	5. ÷ 6.	27.0%	30.9%	4.5%	62.4%

Source:
Data on gold reserves are taken from Banking and Monetary Statistics, 1943 ed., p. 544; data on exchange reserves are taken from the League of Nations Statistical Yearbook, 1933-1934, pp. 210-212; total reserves are calculated from these sources.

Understanding the failure of intergovernmental cooperation during this period involves understanding the actions of France. As we have seen, French international financial policy was based, in part, on a variety of political factors. A full treatment of the political background to the economic events of this period is beyond the scope of this paper. However, it is useful to place French policy in perspective.

The major economic-political questions concerning the United States and Europe were war debts, reparations, the link between war debts and reparations and the domination of Central Europe. We have seen that French gold and lending policies bear on each of these questions. In contrast, the United Kingdom and the United States have frequently been described as acting from internationalist motives in these matters[1].

On consideration, all this is somewhat strange. The economic weapon is a traditional foreign policy instrument of wealthy nations. Trade embargoes, loans to foreign governments, economic penetration as a method of control -- all these can be as effective as troops in achieving a political end. Neither the United States nor Britain were strangers to these techniques. Britain had used trade discrimination as a weapon against the United States in the late 18th and early 19th centuries. The United States had used economic measures at least since the beginning of the twentieth century, when control of capital flows to the Caribbean and Central American nations was used to fortify a general policy of political and military intervention. The question, then, is not whether France alone used such instruments of policy, but whether France alone used them during this period.

---

[1] See, for example, Einzig, Behind the Scenes of International Finance, p. 5 and passim; The Royal Institute of International Affairs, The Problem of International Investment, p. 21; Leuchtenberg, The Perils of Prosperity (paperback 1962 ed.) p. 256.

War debts, reparations, and the question of their repayment were subjects controversial in the extreme during the interwar period. The United States was the major creditor on account of war debts at the time of the armistice (see table 3).

Table 3

Intergovernmental Debt of Major Allied and Associated Powers at the Time of the Armistice

($000,000)

Owed to:	U. S.	U. K.	France	Total (B)
Owed by:				
U. S.	-----	-----	------	-----
U. K.	$3696.0	-----	------	$3696.0
France	$1970.0	$1682.8	------	$3652.8
Other	$1411.1	$5425.1	$2237.6	$9073.8
Total (A)	$7077.1	$7107.9	$2237.6	$16516.9
Net Credit on War Debt (A-B)	$7077.1	$3411.9	-$1415.2	
Loans to Russia	$ 187.7	$2471.8	$ 955.2	
Net Credit on War Debt Excluding Russia	$6899.4	$ 940.1	-$2370.4	

Source: Calculated from Moulton and Pasvolsky, World War Debt Settlement, p. 426.

Excluding Imperial Russian obligations, which were not honored by the Soviet government, the United States and Britain were net creditors to the extent of about $7.0 billion and $1.0 billion respectively, while France was a net debtor to the extent of about $2.4 billion.

During the early twenties, there was widespread support among European Allies for a general cancellation of war debts.[1] As part of the general official American opposition to such a prospect, the State Department informally prohibited loans to governments of countries which had not negotiated a final settlement of their war debts[2] As the British economic historian, A. J. Youngson recently put it:

> "Everybody was in debt to everybody else: and above all everybody had run up an immense account with the great Sir Galahad of the West, whose bill did not seem to be any smaller because his heart was pure."[3]

The inter-governmental debt figures discussed take no account of final war debt settlements, reparations, or rehabilitation and stabilization loans. We can get a rough idea of the relative positions of various governments during the years 1927-1930 by observing relative total

---

[1] European Economic and Political Survey, vol. II, no. 2, p. 33; ibid, no. 17, p. 567.

[2] Angell, op. cit., pp. 99-101.

[3] Youngson, The British Economy, 1920-1957, p. 52.

payments and receipts[1] as of December 1931[2] (see table 4). The United States was still the largest net creditor overall, having a net position more than six times greater than France, and more than twenty times greater than the net position of Britain. However, if reparations are excluded, both France and Britain become net debtors, with the net debt of France nearly three times greater than the net debt of Britain, while the net creditor position of the United States remains virtually unchanged.

---

[1]Estimating total war debts would be extremely difficult. War debt settlements were concluded by the United States with various countries during the period between the end of the war and the end of 1927. The fraction of the total debt paid to the United States was determined, in part, on the basis of the ability to pay. These debts were then funded in different ways, and often at different interest rates, for each country. No change in the terms of payments could take place without renegotiation or default.

Each country faced a stream of interest and amortization payments fixed in time. Thus, with each change in the interest rate, the capitalized value of the war debt would change. Furthermore, long term interest rates were at different levels and changed by different degrees in different countries. Therefore, the capitalized value of the war debt payments would not be identical in the debtor and the creditor country.

The present value of the war debt in terms of gold would be subject to the above problem and to changes in the gold value of the creditor's currency in those cases where the debt was denominated in the creditor's currency.

The real value of the war debt and changes in the real value would be difficult to calculate because of different price levels and changes in levels in debtor and creditor countries.

[2]I have no data for 1927 or 1928. In 1929 the Young plan resulted in a reduction in German reparations but an increase in the French share. Therefore, total German obligations were greater in 1928 than shown in table 3, but total payments due France may have been greater or smaller. However, the relative sizes of various obligations was probably not significantly changed.

Therefore, the discontinuation of reparations would not directly affect the American government's net international asset position but would transform the French government's net credit into a debit three times as large. Nonetheless, the United States, to the end, refused to accept the French contention that the payments of war debts were contingent on the payment of reparations.

Reparations due France from Germany were more than twice those due both the United Kingdom and the United States. In contrast, Germany was a much more important customer of goods and credit of the United States and Britain than was France. In 1928, for example, Britain's merchandise exports to Germany were 60% greater than her exports to France, while during the same year the United States exported almost twice as much to Germany as to France. Germany was Britain's most important customer on the continent and her fourth largest export market in the world; Germany was also the most important continental customer of the United States, and America's third most important customer in the world. In absolute terms, French exports to Germany in 1928 were about $186.7 million; combined United States and British exports to Germany in 1928 were about $710.4 million.[1]

---

[1]U.K. exports were $235.8 million; U.S. exports were $474.6 million. Total merchandise exports were taken from the League of Nations Balance of Payments Yearbook 1927-1929, pp. 88, 175, 187. Germany's percentage share of these countries exports was taken from the League of Nations, International Trade Statistics 1931 and 1932, pp. 331, 335, and 345. The conversion rate used for the franc was 3.9¢; for the pound, $4.85.

Table 4

Total Scheduled Intergovernmental Debt Payments
July 31, 1931

($000,000)

Owed to:	U.S.	U.K.	France	Germany	Other	Total(B)
Owed by:						
U.S.	---	---	---	---	---	---
U.K.	9754.2	---	---	---	---	9754.2
France	6647.7	3820.2	---	---	29.2	10497.1
Germany	237.6	4871.9	13414.5	---	7085.6[1]	25609.6
Other	4183.2	1993.7	441.3	.2	262.2	6880.6
Total (A)	20822.7	10685.8	13855.8	.2	7377.0	52741.5
Scheduled Net Receipts (A-B)	20822.7	931.6	3358.7	-25609.4	496.4	
Net Scheduled Receipts Excluding German reparations	20585.1	- 3940.3	-10055.8	---	- 6589.2	

Source: Calculated from Moulton and Pasvolsky, War Debts and World Prosperity, Table I.

Notes: 1. Belgium $1,450.2 million; Italy $3,943.2 million.

Britain and the United States had a much larger net investment position in Germany than France. Of a total of $768 million in foreign long term lending to Germany during the years 1927 to 1929, $576 million came from Britain and the United States while less than $10 million came from France[1]. On September 30, 1933, the United States and Britain were the

---

[1]Calculated from the League of Nations Balance of Payments Yearbook 1927-1929, p. 108.

source of $1.5 billion of Germany's total $3.5 billion in foreign long and short term loans, while France was the source of $.2 billion[1]. If we assume that these shares were the same at the time of the proposed Hoover Moratorium, then the United States was Germany's net creditor to the extent of $1.7 billion, Britain was Germany's net creditor to the extent of .7 billion, and France was Germany's creditor to the extent of $.3 billion. To the extent that the moratorium on reparations facilitated German servicing of private debt and maintained German imports, the United States had the most to gain and the least to lose while France had the least to gain and the most to lose, with England in an intermediate position on both counts.

Let us consider a plan whereby German reparations would cease, German private debt would be paid, but nothing else would change. The present value of the net intergovernmental creditor position, in July 1931, of the United States was about $6.9 billion, $3.4 billion for France, and $.9 billion for Britain[2]. If the elimination of reparations leads to the payment of private German debt, the creditor positions of these countries are changed as follows: the U.S., $8.6 billion; the U.K., $-.6 billion; France, $-3.0 billion.

---

[1]Calculated from the League of Nations Balance of Payments Yearbook 1933, p. 92.

[2]Moulton and Pasvolsky estimate the present value of the war debts due the United States at $6.9 billion, assuming a rate of discount of 4.25% (Moulton and Pasvolsky, War Debts and World Prosperity, p. 101). This is an approximation and is subject to the estimating problems we discussed earlier. Assuming that the payment structure of debts of other powers was similar to the structure of payments to the United States, we can calculate the present value of the debts and assets of Britain and France by assuming that the present value of their debt is in the same proportion to their total payments (see table 4) as the present value of the debt of the United States is to the payments due the United States.

Obviously the burden of such a plan falls most heavily on France. Nonetheless, German reparations were reduced by 90% according to the Lausanne Agreement of 1932.[1] Consideration of the question of downward adjustment of war debts was postponed until the World Economic Conference of 1933; the position of the United States remained,however, that there was no connection between war debts and reparations.

It makes little sense to talk about these questions in terms of economic interests alone. However, to the extent that economic interests can be isolated, the relatively soft positions on reparations of the United States and Britain did not reflect the "disinterest" of these countries but rather the fact that their economic interests lay elsewhere.

Moreover, quite like France, both the United States and Britain were capable of using economic tools to secure these ends. Thus, from 1925 to 1929 the United States enforced an embargo on private lending to the French Government until a war debt settlement was concluded,[2] while in 1927 French flotation of some refunding loans in New York was made contingent on successful French flotation of its share of the Dawes Loan.[3] Even the apparent parallel of British and American interests with German interests was not without deviation. The settlement at Paris following the war provided for the confiscation of most of the

---

[1]Moulton and Pasvolsky, War Debts and World Prosperity, p. 362.

[2]Angell, op. cit., p. 102.

[3]Clarke, op. cit., p. 67.

German merchant marine,[1] ostensibly to reimburse the British and the Americans for wartime shipping losses, but dovetailing nicely with the interest of the two leading maritime powers in increasing their advantage over their leading competitor.[1]

Differences between France and Britain on the question of Central Europe were most clearly reflected in the Locarno Pact of 1925, which guaranteed the western border of Germany (and hence Belgium and France) but conspicuously did not guarantee the eastern border of Germany. Bilateral agreements between France and several Central European countries seem to indicate a desire by France to contain Germany. The stabilization loans should be viewed in this context.

Political considerations were a factor, to one degree or another, in each stabilization loan. One of a number of examples is the 1927 stabilization of the Italian lira. The Bank of France was not consulted about Italian stabilization loans until all arrangements had been made by Montague Norman and Benjamin Strong.[2] Yet in December 1926, Mussolini had made a series of bellicose speeches concerning Italians living in North African areas under French mandate and massed Italian troops on the French border. During the same month Italy concluded a treaty of Arbitration and Conciliation with Germany and it appeared at that point that two rival treaty

---

[1]Stolper, op. cit., p. 75. Confiscated were the entire German navy, all German merchant ships of more than 1600 tons gross tons, half of all merchant ships of 1000-1600 gross tons, and one-fourth of the German fishing fleet.

[2]Chandler, op. cit., pp. 382-389.

organizations were growing up in Europe. One was headed by France and included Czechoslovakia, Yugoslavia, Rumania and Belgium; the other, headed by Italy, included Spain, Rumania, Albania, and Germany.[1] Thus, the actions by Britain and the United States, whatever their political motivation, were equivalent to thwarting French aims in Central Europe and abetting those of Italy and Germany.

France viewed with similar disfavor the expansion of German banking activity into Central Europe. Between 1925 and 1927 the German "D-Banks" gained extensive financial control in Austria and Latvia, and moved into Holland, Luxenbourg, Hungary, Bulgaria, and Spain.[2] The expansion of German Banks into central Europe was displeasing to the French both because it indicated further German economic penetration and made the German balance of payments look less strong and thus less capable of bearing reparations payments. French political conditions placed on loans to Germany and Austria during 1931 are part of a continuing French effort to confine German influence, while the British replacements of those loans were part of a persistent frustration of those French efforts. Thus France would periodically shift financial pressure to Britain.

---

[1] European Economic and Political Survey, vol. II, no. 7, December 15, 1926, pp. 166, 170; ibid, vol. II, no. 10, January 31, 1927, p. 234.

[2] ibid, vol. II, no. 23, August 15, 1927, p. 755.

It is difficult to understand precisely what British motives in these matters were. At minimum, Britain seems to be attempting to prevent the establishment of a French foothold in Central Europe and thus avoid the political and economic tension on the continent which was likely to result from a French effort to prevent German expansion. At maximum, it might be interpreted as a British attempt to gain influence in Central Europe. Emile Moreau, Governor General of the Bank of France, believed the latter.[1]

It is clear that France was not alone in using economic instruments to secure what she believed to be her economic and political interest. However, it is difficult to judge whether international economic cooperation failed during this period because of divergent national economic and political interests or because governments failed to understand the consequences of lack of cooperation. The existence of intergovernmental loans, albeit insufficient, indicates that governments were aware that the problems of this period could not be handled by the private market. We might ask this, though, in discomforting conclusion: if differences in national interest can bring nations to war, why can they not lead to unconstructive economic action, even when nations are aware of the consequences?

---

[1]"J'expose au président du Conseil que l'Angleterre ayant été le premier pays européan à retrouver une monnaie stable et sûre, après la guerre, a profité de cet avantage pour jeter sur l'Europe les bases dûne veritable domination financière. ...Les remèdes (proposed by the British for countries with monetary difficulties) appliqués comportent toujours l'installation auprès de la Banque d'Emission d'un controleur d'une partie de l'encaisse de la Banque d'Emission à la Banque d'Angleterre, ce qui sert à la fois à soutenir la livre et à fortifier l'influence anglaise." (Moreau, op. cit., entry for February 6, 1928, p. 488).

Summary

We have attempted to examine the validity of these various explanations of the depression and to compare their importance with that of the decline of net American capital exports between 1928 and 1929. We have found some of these arguments empirically or logically lacking. The trend toward autarchy did not reduce manufactured exports, the United States was not a drain on the world economy because it failed to run a current account deficit, the French franc was not markedly undervalued, and the "maldistribution of gold" was largely the reflection of the change in size and direction of long term lending.

Other problems represent the "given" of the situation, the context in which international capital movements took place: the overvaluation of the British pound, the technological obsolescence of certain commodities, the decline in population growth and the decline in migration. In general, these factors would have tended to reduce the rate of return on capital and make the world more sensitive to any increase in interest rates. In particular, the overvaluation of the pound would have tended to increase the alacrity with which British officials tightened money to correct for balance of payments problems created directly and indirectly by the American tight money policy and reduction in lending.

A number of other problems contributed to the depression but because of their lateness, or because of their comparative smallness, they cannot be considered the cause of the depression. Primary overproduction did not appear until industrial demand declined. Short term capital speculation does not seem to have been a problem in the relations of the United States with the rest of the world and it seems to have occurred among other nations only when their economies had reached a point of serious depression. The bulk of the shift out of foreign exchange into gold did not occur until the economy of Britain and the United States were clearly in serious condition. The failure of transport rates to decline eliminated a characteristic of the system which might have dampened the effect of the price decline on the import demand of developing countries but was clearly not the cause of the initial fall; and it would have been of questionable importance in dampening a large part of the decline in primary commodity prices.

Finally, we have a number of propositions which are difficult to compare with the decline in long term lending. We cannot measure the quantitative impact of the decline in the stock market on long term investment, or the quantitative impact the war debts and changes in the war debts on international lending and payments. It is also difficult to measure the impact of some suggested changes in the international economy. We cannot be sure that a centralized international economy would have led the center country to provide short term funds to compensate for the decline in long term lending. There is little reason to believe that flexible exchange rates or conformance to the rules of the game would have prevented or compensated for the decline in American lending and the world tight money situation.

However, of those things which we can measure, it does seem that the decline in American long term lending and the concomitant tightening of the world monetary situation, by their size and timing,provide better explanations of the roots of the world depression.

Chapter 5

Summary and Conclusion

In early 1928 the rate of population growth and migration were declining, there was dislocation due to economic development and technological progress; and Great Britain, the second largest lender and creditor and the third largest industrial nation in the world, faced an overvalued exchange rate. In this context, the decline in the net outflow of capital from the United States accompanied by deliberate Federal Reserve action to raise the interest rates and reduce the quantity of money was the major factor which set in motion the series of events which culminated in the Great Depression.

The effect of tight money and the decline in long term lending were evident by 1928 and 1929 as many countries reduced domestic investment, foreign investment, and imports. The superimposition of the stock market crash on an already serious recession led to a worldwide decline in primary commodity prices which reduced the domestic value of raw material output in the industrial countries and the value of their exports to the developing countries.

It was clear by the end of 1930 that a depression of unusual severity was underway; meanwhile, long term capital flows and the long term portfolio exerted additional deflationary pressure on the world economy. Debtor countries, attempting to remedy their balance of payments problems through import reduction, faced further declines in new portfolio and direct investment, rigidly fixed payments of interest and amortization to the creditors, and a flow of funds back to the creditors in order to repatriate their outstanding debt. Their attempt to adjust by reducing imports reflected deflationary pressure back on the industrial countries while their defaults, which followed their failure to adjust their merchandise accounts, contributed to the constriction of new lending and the paralyzing atmosphere of crisis.

The industrial nations, for their part, faced continued contraction as their domestic investment and exports declined. Finally, when the seriousness of their economic situation became obvious, they faced in addition, the withdrawal of the short term funds which had been financing their deficits.

We have given American monetary policy, lending, and the response of the world to these policies a central role in the depression and have tried to construct this account in a way to which economists have become accustomed. Yet, in an important sense, the question of what caused the depression is unanswerable. The decline in American long term lending is no more the "cause" of the depression than is the failure of American short term lending to increase by an amount sufficient to offset the decline in long term lending. This is a problem quite distinct from the apparent circularity of problems involving simultaneous determination. If $C=a + bY$, $I=c + dY$, and $Y=C + I$, then consumption, depends in part on income and income depends in part on consumption. We address instead here this question: if Y increases, does C increase because Y increased or because a failed to decline? The fact that economists may assume that a is constant, or that economists know empirically that a is constant has nothing to do with determining that the change in Y and not the failure of a to change is the "cause" of the rise in C.

We can, like many historians and physicists, discard the search for the "cause" and replace it with a set of questions, the answers to which are analytically richer. We may ask, for example, which element of the system changed most significantly prior to the decline in world aggregate output; that element was the American net long term lending. We may ask next which of the elements changed in such a way as to move the world away from a position of full world resources employment; again, that element was the decline in net American long term lending.

Third, we may ask why the other elements of the system responded, or failed to respond, to the decline in lending in such a way as to fail to push the world back to a point where resources were fully employed? The answer to this question is scattered throughout the previous pages, but we may briefly summarize some of the most relevant points.

Consider first the formative years of the depression, from 1927 to 1930. Long term foreign lending and borrowing among other countries failed to offset the decline in American lending because foreign monetary authorities responded to that decline with tight money policies in order to maintain their balances of payments; private foreign lenders shifted funds to the American securities markets; and foreign borrowers found interest rates too high or faced quantity restrictions. The short term capital market failed to respond because investment opportunities for short term capital in the United States were excellent; countries with balance of payments problems generally do not seem to have been able to attract short term funds to finance deficits because of risk, and authorities seemed interested in spreading adjustment over all accounts rather than solely financing with short term funds and they therefore attempted a combination of internal adjustment and financing. The current account did not adjust because price and income adjustment could not take place quickly enough to offset the large and rapid changes in the patterns of international lending; primary product exporters could reduce imports but could not have increased exports; and because either of these adjustment methods tended to be deflationary. Finally, reserve expenditure did not offset the effects of the decline in lending because many countries had insufficient reserves to accomplish that and because most authorities began taking deflationary steps to adjust other elements of their international accounts to reduce the outflow of gold.

We may ask the same questions about the second phase of the depression, which lasted from 1930 to 1933. Long term lending failed to revive because direct investment was adversely affected by the same deflating factors which reduced domestic investment, potential portfolio lenders faced a world of defaulting debtors, outstanding securities produced no large net outflow of funds because prospects of appreciation or higher yield were universally bad, and debtors had an interest in repatriating their outstanding securities. The short term capital market failed to exert inflationary pressure because creditors repatriated funds from countries which appeared to be on the verge of drastic economic measures, internal conditions in creditor countries created a heavy demand for liquidity on the part of banks subject to runs, and because central banks which desired to hold gold converted gold exchange which they feared would become unredeemable. The current account failed to improve the situation because the decline in world income swamped the effects of any differential price reduction, countries levied tariffs to reduce foreign competition, and countries facing price-inelastic demand for their exports had no positive price effect to offset the negative income effect. Reserve expenditure failed to help the system because most countries with serious deficits had already expended their reserves while those countries with excess reserves were unable, for the most part, to inflate their own economies.

The final question, then, is how could this set of events have been avoided. To the extent that the weakness of the system was in part due to the lack of a centralized gold standard, institution of a centralized gold standard would only have provided a weak guarantee that short term deficit financing would have occurred. The replacement of fixed rates with flexible rates would not, at least as far as we could tell, have substantially changed the outcome of the situation. A more general conformity to the "rules of the game" might have been deflationary.

What was needed was some sort of change in the system which either would have prevented or compensated for the large decline in foreign investment. Somehow the system had to deal with the fact that private foreign investment was riddled with externalities: the British investor sending funds to the New York stock exchange did not consider as part of his cost the effect of the resulting tight money policy on the British economy; the private borrower in the debtor country did not consider the effect on his country of his refusal to borrow at high rates; the private lender in the industrial country did not consider the effect on his country's exports if he refused to lend to a debtor country with a balance of payments problem. In a market economy it is proper that individuals ignore such considerations since individuals cannot rationally include such factors in their investment decisions. Because of this, it is now considered proper that the government attempt to guide investment by instituting monetary and tax policies and to compensate for fluctuations in investment with government expenditures and tax policy.

However, private international lending created externalities even at the national level: Britain's policies to offset the reduction in American net capital exports further decreased the flow of long term funds to other countries and ultimately reduced British exports; import restriction by the underdeveloped countries contributed to the reduction in aggregate demand in the industrial countries leading to a further reduction in the value of the exports of the underdeveloped countries.

Externalities at the national level can be dealt with only by international action. The action taken by the international body should have been such that it offset the effect of the decline in international investment and kept world resources fully employed. It might have done that by changing the pattern of trade to conform to the new pattern and size of long term lending. However, it was likely that international capital would have again changed swiftly in size and direction while trade quantities and patterns would have changed slowly in size and direction. Moreover, since the costs of readjustment of trade patterns tend to be large,it would not have been an efficient solution. The international body might have increased the value of international reserves. This would have given all countries more time to finance the new patterns of payments based on the change in the size and pattern of long term international lending. However, this would have been inefficient to the extent that some nations' reserves might not have increased sufficiently while other nations' reserves might have increased excessively. This problem might have been solved by increasing nations' reserves by the precise amount needed to finance their new payments deficits. However, this would have been equivalent to international lending to compensate for fluctuations in private long term lending or to lending by surplus countries to deficit countries. Not surprisingly, this would have been an international solution closely analogous to the one which modern capitalist economies have constructed to offset fluctuations in their domestic private investment.

This solution was tried sporadically throughout the period 1927 to

1933 with little success. Governments attempted to synchronize policies and to lend to each other to offset the effects of the private capital market. As we have discussed, these policies may have failed partly because nations may have been ignorant of the consequences of lack of cooperation. However, a clearly critical element in their failure was the continual intrusion of questions of national political and economic interest. Differences in these interests were sufficient to block cooperation at critical times, and explain to a large extent the failure of the nations of the world to solve their mutual problems.

APPENDIX 1

Notes to Chapter 2, "United States Net Exports of Long Term Capital: Background and Description"

Note 1: Estimated Changes in Monetary Gold Assets by Region and by Cause of Change.

a/ Regional composition of changes in government monetary gold assets.

Monetary Gold Stock by Region

($000,000,000)

1.	12/26	12/33	Change (12/33-12/26)
Europe	3.4	6.9	+ 3.5
U. S.	4.0	4.0	0
Rest of World	1.8	1.1	- .7
Total	9.2	12.0	+ 2.8

Source: Banking and Monetary Statistics, pp. 544-545, 550-551.

2. The change in gold stock is attributable to gold production and international settlements. The composition of this change by region is shown in the following table.

Composition of Changes in Monetary Gold Stock by Region
December 1926 - December 1933
($000,000,000)

	Production	International Settlements	Change
Europe	0	+ 3.5	+ 3.5
U. S.	.4	- .4	0
Rest of World	+ 2.4	- 3.1	- .7

Source: Total monetary gold stock by region and production derived from Banking and Monetary Statistics, pp. 544-545, 550-551. It was assumed that no gold was produced in Europe (Europe, throughout this paper, excludes the Soviet Union).

3. Composition of the change in gold stock attributed to international settlements.

Change in Gold Stock Due to International Settlements
December 1926 - December 1933
($000,000,000)

Imports by: from:	Europe	U. S.	Rest of World	Total Imports
Europe	_____	+ 1.8*	+ 1.7	$ 3.5
U. S.	- 1.8*	_____	+ 1.4*	- .4
Rest of World	- 1.7	- 1.4*	_____	- 3.1

Imports (+)
of Gold

Source: Total imports derived as shown in table 2.

U. S. data, marked with (*), are derived below in note 3. The remainder of the table can be determined algebraically.

b/ Gold and gold exchange reserves of the Gold Bloc and "other" Europe are shown in the following table.

Total International Reserves of the Gold Bloc
and Other European Countries
December 1927 - December 1933
($000,000)

	12/27	12/28	12/29	12/30	12/31	12/32	12/33
Gold Bloc	1557.5	1923.4	2365.6	2879.7	4162.4	4817.7	4534.3
Other Europe	2283.8	2500.8	2408.0	2455.7	2062.0	2040.9	2368.5

Source: Gold reserve data were taken directly from Banking and Monetary Statistics, pp. 544-545, 550-551.

Exchange reserve data, in units of national currency, were taken from the League of Nations Statistical Yearbook 1933/34, pp. 210-212, and were converted to gold dollars according to the annual average dollar exchange rate for each year; exchange rates were taken from the League of Nations Statistical Yearbook, pp. 201-204.

Note 2: Measuring the Constancy of U. S. Monetary Gold Assets.

The U. S. gold stock was always within 10% of $4 billion: i.e., 3.6 billion < gold stock < 4.4 billion. As the following table indicates, the stock at the end of each year was greater than $3.6 billion and less than $4.4 billion; hence, the variation was less than 10%.

U. S. Gold Stock
December 1927 to December 1933
($000,000)

12/27	12/28	12/29	12/30	12/31	12/32	12/33
3,977	3,746	3,900	4,225	4,052	4,044	4,012

Source: Taken directly from Banking and Monetary Statistics, p. 544.

Note 3: United States Imports and Exports of Gold.

Table 1 shows gold earmark statistics by region; I am indebted to Mr. Ralph Bryant of the International Finance Division of the Federal Reserve Board for his help in obtaining these data.

Table 1

U. S. Earmarks of Gold for Foreign Account

($000,000)

	12/26	12/27	6/28	1/30	12/30	1/32	12/32	12/33
Europe	N. A.	N. A.	104	128	138	400	51	55
N. Am.	N. A.	N. A.	3	___	___	___	___	___
S. Am.	N. A.	N. A.	___	5	___	14	7	2
A-O-A	N. A.	N. A.	___	___	___	19	16	2
Total	39	199	107	133	138	433	74	59

Source: Federal Reserve Board
Note: Year end data were given where available; apparently much of the data for this period has been lost.

It is necessary to obtain estimates of the regional distribution of gold earmarks for December 1926 through December 1933. We are given the regional distribution of earmarks for December 1930, 1932 and 1933.

a. Estimating the regional distribution of earmarks for December 1931.

The observed distribution closest to December 1931 is that of January 1932 (table 1). Total earmarks in December 1931 were $459 million; hence, we must estimate the regional composition of the decline of $26 million in earmarks during the month of January.

Earmarks to each region declined during 1932. By assuming that earmarks to each region declined uniformly during the year, we obtain an estimate of the composition of the decline during January. This same distribution was applied to the $26 million decline of the month of January; in this way the entire decline in earmarks was attributed to Europe (table 2).

b. Estimating the regional distribution of earmarks for December 1929.

The observed distribution closest to December 1929 is that of January 1930 (table 1). Total earmarks in December 1929 were $135 million; these declined by $2 million to $133 million in January 1930. Inasmuch as both total and European earmarks increased between January and December 1930 while South American earmarks decreased, the $2 million decline was attributed to South America (table 2).

c. Estimating the regional distribution of earmarks for December 1928.

The observed distribution closest to December 1928 is that of June 1928 (table 1). Total earmarks declined from $107 million in June 1928 to $79 million in December 1928. The only region from which most of this decline could have come (earmarks cannot be negative) is Europe, since earmarks for South America and Asia-Oceania-Africa are zero and earmarks for North America are only $3 million. We assume that the entire decline took place in European earmarks (table 2).

d. Estimating the regional distribution of earmarks for December of 1926 and 1927.

The observed distribution closest to December 1926 and 1927 is that of June 1928 (table 1). Unfortunately, we have no earlier distribution with which we can interpolate. However, with the exception of the observed distribution of December 1932, Europe's percentage share of earmarks is always above 90%. We will attribute to Europe its average 96% share (excluding the 69% observed in December 1932); the remainder will be attributed to North America since it is the only other region observed to have had earmarks at the closest date for which we have data.

Table 2

Final Estimate of Regional Distribution of Gold Earmarks

	12/26	12/27	12/28	12/29	12/30	12/31	12/32	12/33
Europe	37	191	76	128	138	426	51	55
N. Am.	2	8	3	___	___	___	___	___
S. Am.	___	___	___	7	___	14	7	2
A-O-A	___	___	___	___	___	19	16	2
Total	39	199	79	135	138	459	74	59

Source: Total earmarks were taken from the Federal Reserve Board Annual Report (1927-1929 data were taken from the Annual Report for 1929, p. 82; 1930-1933 data were taken from the Annual Report for 1933, p. 139). The regional distributions of gold earmarks for December of 1930, 1932 and 1933 were obtained from the Federal Reserve Board; estimates for other years were made according to the procedure described in the text.

From the final estimate of the regional distribution of gold earmarks, we can calculate the annual change in earmarks by region. These are shown in table 3. Gold shipment statistics are shown in table 4 while earmarks and shipments are combined in table 5.

Table 3

Changes in Gold Earmarks, by Region[1]

($000,000)

(-)indicates decline in earmarks	1927	1928	1929	1930	1931	1932	1933
Europe	154	-115	51	10	288	-375	4
N. Am.	6	- 5	- 3	___	___	___	___
S. Am.	___	___	7	- 7	14	- 7	- 5
A-O-A	___	___	___	___	19	- 3	- 14
Total	160	-120	55	3	321	-385	- 15
(Total[1]	160	-120	55	2	321	-458	- 1)

Source: Derived from table 2.

[1]Change in total earmarks obtained from H. Lary, "The United States in the World Economy", (U. S. Department of Commerce, Office of Business Economics, Economic Series , No. 23), Table I.
I cannot explain the discrepancy between Lary's 1932 and 1933 estimates and those taken from the Federal Reserve Board Annual Report. Lary, op. cit., p. 207, note to chart 25, cites the Annual Report as his source for gold earmark statistics. In the following pages the Federal Reserve Board's estimates will be used.

Table 4

Gold Shipments, by Region[1]

($000,000)

	1927	1928	1929	1930	1931	1932	1933
Europe	- 27	367	- 4	76	390	701	259
N. Am.	- 34	- 80	- 73	- 7	- 81	- 65	- 20
S. Am.	87	100	- 87	-165	-203	- 53	- 11
A-O-A	- 32	10	- 7	-184	-250	-134	- 55
Other	___	- 5	- 4	___	- 1	- 3	1
Total[2]	- 6	392	-175	-280	-145	446	174
Total[3]	- 6	392	-175	-280	-145	447	174

[1](-) indicates import of gold.

[2]Total and regional gold shipments are taken from the Federal Reserve Board *Annual Report* for 1929 and 1933 (1927-1929 data from the *Annual Report* 1929, p. 82; 1930-1933 data are from the *Annual Report* 1933, p. 139).

[3]H. Lary, *op. cit.*, table I.

Table 5

Combined Gold Earmarks and Shipments, by Region[1]

($000,000)

	1927	1928	1929	1930	1931	1932	1933	Total 1927-1933
Europe	127	252	47	86	678	326	263	1,779
N. Am.	- 28	- 85	- 76	- 7	- 81	- 65	- 20	- 362
S. Am.	87	100	- 80	-172	-189	- 60	- 16	- 330
A-O-A	- 32	10	- 7	-184	-231	-137	- 69	- 650
Other	___	- 5	- 4	___	- 1	- 3	1	- 12
Total	154	272	-120	-277	176	61	159	+ 425

[1](-) indicates net inflow of gold.

Source: Derived from table 3 and table 4 above.

Note 4: New Long Term Capital Issues for Foreign Account by European Lending Nations.

The following table shows new issues for foreign account by the major international lending nations other than the United States.

New Issues for Foreign Account
by Major International Lending
Nations Other than the United States

($000,000)

New issues for foreign accounts

	27	28	29	30	31	32	33
U. K.	674	696	461	529	209	102	125
Netherlands	145[a]	107[a]	45[c]	103[c]	16[c]	10[c]	__[b]
Sweden	38[a]	18[a]	21[c]	60[c]	20[c]	30[c]	__[b]
France	N/A	N/A	43[c]	55[c]	146[c]	65[c]	16[b]
Total	857	821	570	747	391	207	141

Sources:

a/ League of Nations Balance of Payments Yearbook, 1927-29, p. 26.
b/ League of Nations Balance of Payments Yearbook, 1933, p. 17.
c/ League of Nations Balance of Payments Yearbook, 1931-32, p. 14.
U. K. 1927-1932 data League of Nations Balance of Payments Yearbook, 1931-32, p. 16.

1933 data League of Nations Balance of Payments Yearbook, 1933, p. 169.

Note 5: The Size of U. S. Net Long Term Capital Exports Relative to U. S. Domestic New Issues.

Domestic new issues of the United States in 1927 were $6.7 billion;[1] the outflow of long term capital from the United States in 1927 was $1.0[2] billion. Therefore, United States' long term capital exports were equivalent to 16-2/3% of domestic new issues.

---

[1]League of Nations Statistical Yearbook 1930/1931, p. 250.

[2]H. Lary, op. cit., table I.

Note 6: New Domestic Issues for Selected European Countries. Estimates of European domestic new issues for 1927, in national currencies, were obtained for these countries: Germany, Austria, Belgium, Denmark, Finland, France, Italy, Latvia, Norway, Netherlands, Poland, Rumania, United Kingdom, Sweden, Switzerland, and Czechoslavakia.[1] These figures were converted to dollars at the average exchange rate for 1927 and amounted to $3 billion. Hence, U. S. long term lending in 1927 was equivalent to about 33-1/3% of domestic issues for these countries, which account for about 90.8% of total European output.[2]

Note 7: Estimating the Regional Distribution of U. S. Long Term Capital Flows, 1927-1933.

The aggregate long term capital flow data were revised by Hal B. Lary and published in 1943.[3] Lary made few estimates of the regional distribution of any of the items. In conversations with Mr. Lary and Mr. Walter Lederer of the Balance of Payments Division of the Department of Commerce, I learned that the worksheets and other raw data for the balances of payments of the interwar years have been destroyed.

Still available, however, are estimates of the regional distribution of various capital account items contained in the unrevised annual

---

[1]League of Nations Statistical Yearbook 1930/1931, p. 250.

[2]Calculated from data in appendix II, note 2.

[3]H. Lary, op. cit., passim.

balances of payments published as Trade Information Bulletins by the Department of Commerce. Except where otherwise specified, we have estimated the regional distributions of capital items by treating the unrevised geographical distributions as a sample to obtain the regional shares of the revised totals.

a/ Portfolio Investment

Sources: Revised estimates of total U. S. portfolio investment were obtained from H. Lary's "The U. S. in the World Economy"[1], table III. Unrevised estimates of U. S. portfolio investment, together with regional breakdowns of this investment, were taken from the official annual balances of payments for the years 1927 to 1933[2] and from C. Lewis, America's Stake in International Investment.[3]

Lary has no estimate of the regional destination of the new portfolio investment of the United States. Estimates of the regional destination of these investments were made by Lewis and by the compilers of the unrevised balances of payments. However, estimates of total new investment given by Lewis and the unrevised balances of payments are different from Lary's figures. These figures are compared in table 1. Since the sums of both the absolute and squared differences between Lary's series and Lewis's series are least, the

---

[1]ibid, passim.

[2]U. S. Department of Commerce, Trade Information Bulletin, nos. 552, 625, 698, 761, 803, 814 and 819.

[3]C. Lewis, America's Stake in International Investment, pp. 628-629.

regional composition of Lewis's series (table 2) has been used to estimate the regional composition of Lary's series (table 3).

Table 1

U. S. New Issues for Foreign Account

($000,000)

	27	28	29	30	31	32	33
a. Lary[1]	1114	1019	415	775	190	51	83
b. Sample[2]	1344	1244	658	896	223	29	11
a-b	- 230	- 225	- 243	-121	- 33	22	72
a. Lary	1114	1019	415	775	190	51	83
b. Lewis[3]	1370	1186	396	963	240	96	60
a-b	- 256	- 167	19	-188	- 50	- 45	23

Note: (-) indicates outflow of funds from the U. S.

Source: (1) Lary, op. cit., table III.
(2) Sample data for 1927-1933 taken from Trade Information Bulletin, Nos. 552, 625, 698, 761, 803, 814 and 819.
(3) Lewis, op. cit., p. 629.

Table 2

Percentage Share of U. S.
New Portfolio Investment
by Region, 1927-1933

	1927	1928	1929	1930	1931	1932	1933
Europe	47	44	22	28	24	23	____
N. Am.	17	13	57	32	66	77	100
S. Am.	25	30	17	29	10	____	____
A-O-A	11	13	4	10	____	____	____
Int'l	____	____	____	1	____	____	____
Total	100	100	100	100	100	100	100

Source: Calculated from data in Cleona Lewis, *op. cit.*, pp. 628, 629.

Table 3

Estimated Regional Share of Annual
U. S. New Investment

($000,000)

	1927	1928	1929	1930	1931	1932	1933
Europe	524	448	91	217	46	12	____
N. Am.	189	133	236	248	125	39	83
S. Am.	278	306	71	225	19	____	____
A-O-A	123	132	17	77	____	____	____
Int'l	____	____	____	8	____	____	____
Total	1114	1019	415	775	190	51	83

Source: Revised estimates of total U. S. new portfolio investment were obtained from Lary, *op. cit.*, table III. The regional distribution was obtained by using the percentage shares by region shown in table 2 to estimate the distribution of Lary's revised totals.

b/ Direct Investment

Source: Revised estimates of United States' direct investment are from Lary, Table III and pp. 100-105. Unrevised estimates, allocated by region, were taken from the balances of payments for each year, (as noted in Section 1), and from American Underwriting of Foreign Securities.

Lary's revised estimates of total U. S. direct investment include separately enumerated estimates of "Public Offerings of Domestic and Semi-Domestic Corporations for Foreign Purposes"[1]. The unrevised estimates of direct investment are smaller than Lary's estimates for each year except 1932. It is possible, although not necessary, that public offerings were incompletely included in the unrevised estimates. Each series is shown in table 4.

The regional distribution of the unrevised estimates of direct investment are shown in table 4. Lary's revised estimates of direct investment excluding public offerings for the years 1927 to 1930 were distributed according to the shares of this sample. For the years 1931-to-1933 Lary's estimate of direct investment including public offerings was distributed according to this sample.

For the years 1927 to 1930 an unrevised estimate of the regional distribution of public offerings was available.[2] The aggregate

---

[1]H. Lary, op. cit., table III, note 7.

[2]"American Underwriting of Foreign Securities", Trade Information Bulletin number 746, p. 19.

unrevised estimates conform fairly well to Lary's revised estimates, except for the year 1927 (table 5). No information about the regional composition of this series could be found for the years 1931 to 1933. For these years, public offerings are distributed in the same proportions as the unrevised estimates of other direct investment.

Table 4

Estimates of Direct Investment

($000,000)

(-) indicates outflow of funds	1927	1928	1929	1930	1931	1932	1933
Europe	- 99	-159	-160	-124	- 90	- 17	30
N. Am.	- 51	- 91	- 70	- 63	- 35	- 6	———
S. Am.	- 77	-124	- 95	- 43	- 42	- 8	2
A-O-A	- 30	- 4	- 10	- 23	- 29	- 5	———
Total[1]	-257	-378	-335	-253	-196	- 36	32
Lary	-351	-558	-602	-294	-222	- 16	32

Source: (1) Estimates of the regional distribution of direct investment were found in the annual balances of payments of the U.S., 1927-1933 (Trade Information Bulletin, nos. 552, 625, 698, 716, 803, 814 819.)

(2) H. Lary, op. cit., table III.

Table 5

Public Offerings of Securities of American and Semi-American Corporations for Foreign Purposes

($000,000)

	1927	1928	1929	1930	1931	1932	1933
Europe	- 88	- 43	- 26	- 12	n/a	n/a	n/a
N. Am.	- 57	- 28	- 69	- 32			
S. Am.	- 48	- 84	- 109	- 16			
A-O-A	- 24	- 1	- 56	____			
Int'l				- 92			
Total, Unrevised	-217	-156	-260	-152	n/a	n/a	n/a
Lary	-148	-154	-252	-142	- 92	____	- 1

Note: (-) indicates outflow of funds from the U.S.

Source: Unrevised regional estimate from "American Underwriting of Foreign Securities" Trade Information Bulletin Number 746, p. 19. The revised estimate of total direct investment was taken from H. Lary, op. cit., table III.

The final estimate of the regional distribution of United States' direct investment is shown in Table 6.

Table 6

Estimated Regional Distribution of U. S.
Direct Investment Overseas
1927 - 1929 ($000,000)

	1927	1928	1929	1930	1931	1932	1933
Europe	-135	-212	-192	- 86	-102	- 7	30
N. Am.	- 70	-125	-140	- 68	- 40	- 3	____
S. Am.	-105	-216	-205	- 41	- 47	- 4	2
A-O-A	- 41	- 5	- 65	- 14	- 33	- 2	____
Total	-351	-558	-602	-294	-222	- 16	32

Note: (-) indicates outflow of funds from the U. S.

Source: Estimating procedures explained in text.

c/ Transactions in Outstanding Securities

This series, encompassing the sale and purchase of outstanding foreign and domestic securities, presents one of the most intractable estimating provlems encountered in this work. The aggregate series, revised by Lary[1], was thought by earlier compilers of the balance of payments to be the main source of errors and omissions.[2]

There are no systematic geographic breakdowns of the origin and destination of these flows[3], and while some inferences can be made from

---

[1]H. Lary, op. cit., p. 107

[2]The compiler of the 1929 Balance of Payments wrote that 60% of errors and omission were attributable to error in the estimation of the transactions in outstanding securities (Trade Information Bulletin 698, pp. 54-55).

[3]Some of the early balances of payments give a regional breakdown of transactions in outstanding securities. However, by the wording it seems that these are the compiler's estimate rather than actual samples and judging by the questionaire used, geographical distribution was not ascertained. Thus, these estimates are not useful in verifying the calculations made below since the haunting possibility always exists that the compiler may have made his estimates under the same assumptions used below, invalidating the significance of any correspondence of regional distributions between my estimates and his. For an example of the compilers methodology, see Trade Information Bulletin 698, pp. 52-55.

the estimates of the distribution of U. S. longterm assets abroad and foreign long term assets in the U. S., any strict calculation of the regional compositions of transactions in outstanding securities from the stock estimates is precluded by various statistical problems which will be discussed below.

Nonetheless, the composition of this series is of great interest since it reflects both foreign participation in the U. S. stock market boom and foreign repatriation of securities. Since both these activities are important in many explanations of the world depression, some attempt at regional decomposition is worthwhile. While these estimates fall considerably short of a formal ideal, there is merit in making the most reasonable statement one can about the data.

C-1/ Transactions in outstanding foreign securities, 1927-1929

Estimates of aggregate transactions in outstanding foreign securities were taken from Lary.[1] There are no data for the regional distribution of these transactions. We have stock estimates of U. S. foreign assets as of December 1929 based on a compilation of all foreign bonds floated in the United States and still outstanding.[2] Such a compilation takes no account of bonds floated in the United States but immediately transferred to foreign investors, of transactions in outstanding securities, or of repatriations. It serves, however, as one guide to the portfolio preferences of U. S. investors (table 1). The difficulty in using the portfolio composition as a guide to the composition of net transactions in outstanding securities is that the conditions which determined the composition of the portfolio may no longer exist, implying quite different marginal shares.

---

[1] H. Lary, *op. cit.*, p. 107.

[2] C. Lewis, *op. cit.*, pp. 652-655.

Another guide to the portfolio preferences of American investors is the regional distribution of new issues (table 2). It is not immediately obvious which is the best guide to net changes in the portfolio which are attributable to transactions in outstanding securities. It is tempting to use the known distribution of marginal portfolio preferences reflected in the distribution of new issues. However, the regional distribution of new issues depends a great deal on the borrower's willingness to borrow; conceivably, a switch from the foreign to the domestic capital market, reducing the supply of new issues of that region, could result in larger purchases of the outstanding securities of that region.

Estimates of the regional composition of transactions in outstanding securities for the years 1927 to 1929 have been calculated in accord with both of these estimation methods.

Transactions in outstanding securities are made either for the purpose of increasing or decreasing holdings of the securities of some region or for changing the composition of portfolio assets in that region. We are assuming that the latter is in a roughly constant relation to the former. That is, when the United States increases its net investment in a region by 100 and in another region by 10, the accompanying compositional changes will be ten times greater for the former region than the latter, i.e., ten times the number of transactions will be devoted to making changes in the composition of the securities held.

Arithmetically, the above is equivalent to apportioning both purchases and sales of outstanding foreign securities according to the percentage regional distribution of the portfolio and new issues. We obtain two estimates of the geographical distribution of transactions in outstanding foreign securities.

Table 1

Percentage Distribution of U. S. Portfolio Assets by Region

December 1929

	Billion $	Percentage Share
Europe	3.5	43%
N. Am.	2.0	25%
S. Am.	1.7	21%
A-O-A	.9	11%
Total	8.1	100%

Source: Calculated from Cleona Lewis, op. cit., pp. 652-655.

Table 2
Percentage
Distribution of U. S.
New Issues by Region

	1927	1928	1929
Europe	40	39	37
N. Am.	14	15	15
S. Am.	21	21	22
A-O-A	25	25	26
Total	100%	100%	100%

Source: Calculated from distribution of new issues; see section a of this note.

Table 3 gives the estimates obtained from the use of the distribution of the portfolio and the distribution of new issues to estimate the distribution of transactions in outstanding foreign securities.

Table 3

Estimate of Regional Distribution of Transactions in Outstanding Foreign Securities, 1927-1929

($000,000)

Purchases	1927		1928		1929	
	low	high	low	high	low	high
Europe	- 56	- 61	-188	-208	-120	-132
N. Am.	- 21	- 36	- 73	-121	- 46	- 77
S. Am.	- 30	- 30	-101	-101	- 64	- 64
A-O-A	- 16	- 36	- 53	-121	- 34	- 77
Total	-143	-143	-483	-483	-307	-307
Sales						
Europe	131	144	152	167	160	177
N. Am.	50	84	58	97	62	103
S. Am.	71	71	82	82	87	87
A-O-A	37	84	43	97	45	103

(The underlined items are estimates obtained by applying the regional share of the outstanding portfolio to transactions in outstanding securities; those items not underlined are calculated by applying the regional share of new issues.)

Note: (-) indicates outflow of funds from the United States

Source: Derived from table 1, table 2, and data for total transactions in outstanding foreign securities given in Lary, *op. cit.*, p. 107. Estimating procedure is described in the text.

C-2 Transactions in outstanding foreign securities, 1930-1933

C-2.1/ Purchases of outstanding foreign securities

Between 1930 and 1933 the U. S. purchased $1.5 billion in securities from the rest of the world.[1] Substantial qualitative evidence indicates large purchases of gold bloc bonds by the United States. The only other relatively safe foreign bonds during this period, (where safety is determined by the soundness of the government and expectations of devaluation) were post-devaluation British bonds. There is some evidence to indicate purchase of British bonds.[2]

There is little qualitative evidence to indicate that the U. S. purchased significant quantities of the securities of any other region in the world. Reports of such purchases are absent from the financial press of the period, in contrast to frequent reports of substantial purchases of gold bloc bonds. Furthermore, the prices of bonds of the debtor regions of Europe and of the other regions of the world were falling precipitously. Since U. S. citizens held a large portion of these bonds already, it seems unlikely that they were attempting to purchase more of them. Finally, even if U. S. citizens had purchased additional quantities of these bonds, the market price had fallen a small percentage of par value and they could have purchased the remainder of the issue for a relatively small cash outlay. For these reasons, all outflows of funds due to purchases of outstanding foreign securities are attributed to Europe for the years 1930-1933.

---

[1]The sum of U. S. purchases of outstanding foreign securities for the years 1930 to 1933 (Lary, op. cit., p. 107).

[2]See, for example, Trade Information Bulletin no. 819, pp. 84-89.

C-2.2/ Sales of Outstanding Foreign Securities, 1930-1933

There are four possible trends which may have dominated this account (and, of course, any combinations of these trends):

a/ The United States may have been selling foreign bonds back to the debtor countries repatriation).

b/ The United States may have been selling gold bloc or United Kingdom bonds to the debtor and deficit countries (capital flight from the debtor and deficit countries).

c/ The United States may have been selling the bonds of the rest of the world to the gold bloc and the United Kingdom

d/ The United States may have been re-selling gold bloc and United Kingdom bonds to Europe.

Possibility b/: Capital flight statistics are difficult to obtain. However, it is noteworthy that in the period 1934-1937. foreign investment by the non-European world in the United States did not increase appreciably (table 4). Using gold imports as a criterion, the dollar was probably the strongest currency in the world during this period. If residents of the non-European world did not purchase outstanding securities for capital flight purposes in the period 1934-1937, why would they have so employed it in the period 1930-1933? There is almost no qualitative evidence to this effect. This does not preclude capital flight from these countries on the short term capital accounts. There is, though, no evidence to lend us to believe that there was any particularly substantial purchase by the non-European world of Gold Bloc or British securities in the period

1930-1933.[1]

Table 4

Foreign Investment in the United States

($000,000)

	12/1934	12/1939
Europe	2,819	4,818
N. Am.	1,007	1,060
S. Am.	40	120
A-O-A	491	192
Total	4,357	6,290

Source: Foreign investment data for 1934 were taken from the U. S. Department of Commerce, Bureau of Foreign and Domestic Commerce <u>Foreign Investment in the United States</u>, (Washington, D.C.: Government Printing Office, 1937). Data for 1939 were taken from <u>Banking and Monetary Statistics</u>, p. 637.

Possibility c/: There is no qualitative evidence to indicate that the United States was selling non-European bonds to European investors. Large portions of these bonds were in default in the early thirties, the prospects of renewal of payment were not bright, and, in fact, renewal was not begun for many years. All of this makes the lack of qualitative evidence of European purchases of these bonds quite understandable. Furthermore, U.S. investment bankers dominated committees which attempted to make the debtors pay, indicating a lack of European interest which one might expect were

[1]While the spectacle of officials and entrepreneurs in underdeveloped countries cultivating investments in Europe and the U.S. as a hedge against economic or political insecurity in their own countries has become well-fixed as an element of life in these regions, it is not unreasonable that these amounts, while large fortunes for the individuals involved, are extremely small compared with the funds which can be mobilized in industrial Europe, generally believed to be the source of most of the flight capital in the period 1934-1937. It is also possible that such operations would be conducted through United States and European agents. In this case they would appear as, and should be treated as, transactions by Europeans or U. S. nationals.

Europe a large or increasing holder of bonds of these areas.

This leaves us with possibilities a/ and d/: sales comprised repatriations by the debtor regions and resale of gold bloc and United Kingdom bonds to Europe. There is substantial qualitative evidence for both types of transactions.

Repatriations were first estimated in 1937. The size and geographic distribution of repatriated and outstanding bonds are given in table 5. These tend to be underestimates because of the cancellation of some of the repatriated issues prior to December 1937.

Table 5

Repatriations 12/1937

($000,000)

Europe	$717
N. Am.	20
S. Am.	155
A-O-A	337
Total	$1,229

Source: U. S. Department of Commerce, Economic Series Number 3, p. 60.

The par value of the American portfolio dropped from $7.2 billion in December 1930[1] to $4.2 billion in December 1937[2]. Thus, of a $3 billion decline in par value of the U. S. foreign portfolio investments, at least $1.2 billion is due to repatriation. The remaining $1.8 billion is due to

---

[1] Trade Information Bulletin no. 767, passim.

[2] Economic Series no. 3, p. 57.

unknown repatriation or the sale of foreign bonds to third parties.

We have estimates of the American portfolio investments, for December 1930 and December 1937, in terms of par value, distributed geographically, and taking account of transactions in outstanding securities by region. For the intervening years we can interpolate with the regional distribution of new issues and amortization payments, which would give us stock estimates for the intervening years which did not take account of transactions in outstanding securities. These, naturally, are not of great use in making statements about the regional composition of transactions in outstanding securities.

It is not possible to use the two stock estimates of American portfolio investments to estimate the composition of transactions in outstanding securities for the years 1930-1933. The main obstacle is the divergence between market value and par value of the securities traded. Speaking generally, in the period 1930-1933 British consels sold at between 55% and 75% of par value, Swiss bonds close to par, and French bonds between 75% of par value and 100% of par value.[1] Transactions in outstanding securities are measured in market value, not in par value. Hence, depending on the country of purchase or sale, a very large variety of flow estimates are consistent with the regional composition of stock estimates.

An example will clarify the difficulty. The stock figures show a net decline in American holdings of European securities of $1.5 billion

---

[1]Calculated from the table showing coupon and actual percentage yield of bonds (League of Nations Statistical Yearbook, 1937, pp. 222-224).

between December 1930 and December 1937.[1] Of these, it is estimated that $700 million were repatriations. Hence, $800 million of the decline is attributable to transactions in outstanding securities. It is not necessary however for the United States to reduce the net capital flow to Europe in order to reduce the par value of its investment in Europe. Suppose that United States citizens, in the face of British devaluation, sell $1 billion (par value) of British bonds. With the British bonds selling at 55, this represents an inflow of funds of about $550 million. Then suppose that, anticipating the U. S. devaluation, U. S. citizens use the proceeds of the sale of British bonds to purchase Gold Bloc bonds. These are selling close to par, so $550 million obtains $550 million in bonds (par value). The net capital flow to Europe during this period is zero, but the par value of American long term assets in Europe has fallen by $450 million.

Because of this problem, we proceed as follows: we will allocate repatriations (par value) by the annual volume of American sales of foreign securities in the period 1930 to 1937. These repatriations, allocated in this way, will then be adjusted to market value. The remainder of sales of foreign securities will be allocated to Europe; no additional adjustment for repatriation will be made.

The grounds for this procedure are as follows: market value of repatriated bonds had fallen so low by the early thirties, that the United States could have sold its entire portfolio of these bonds and one could

---

[1]December 1930 data were obtained from Trade Information Bulletin no. 767, passim; December 1937 data were taken from Economic Series no. 3, p. 57.

still not explain the reported volume of sales of outstanding foreign securities. Therefore, a large part of sales must have been the higher value European bonds. In light of the qualitatively well established purchases of European gold bloc bonds by the United States after the British devaluation, it is most satisfactory to construct the following picture of sales of outstanding foreign securities. Therefore, a large part of sales must have been the higher value European bonds. In light of the qualitatively well established purchases of European gold bloc bonds by the United States after the British devaluation, it is most satisfactory to construct the following picture of sales of outstanding foreign securities: substantial sales of British bonds prior to the British devaluation, sales of gold bloc bonds after the British devaluation, and sales of gold bloc and British bonds after the American devaluation. The details of the estimating procedure are contained in the following steps.

a/ Repatriations

1. Par Value of Securities Repatriated from the U. S., December 1937 ($000,000)

Europe	$717
N. Am.	$ 20
S. Am.	$155
A-O-A	$337
Total	$1,229

Source: U. S. Department of Commerce, Economic Series no. 3, p. 60.

b/ What portion of these bonds were repatriated in the period between December 1929 and December 1933?

1. We assume that no significant repatriations took place prior to

December 1929. There was some German and Canadian repatriation prior to that date but the financial journals indicate that it was tiny in contrast to that which followed.

2. Assume that repatriations occurred in proportion to the sales of all foreign securities. Total sales of foreign securities between December 1929 and December 1937 were $4,442 million; sales between December 1929 and December 1933 were $2,276 million.[1] Thus, 51.2% of foreign security sales during this period took place between December 1929 and December 1933; we will assume that 51.2% of the repatriations took place in the same period. This probably tends to understate the extent of repatriations. We have already noted that some of the repatriated securities which had expired were not included in the list of repatriations. Furthermore, 1932 and 1933 represented the period of lowest prices for many foreign issues. During this period the maximum incentive for repatriation was present.

Table 6 shows repatriations distributed for each region by the percentage of sales of outstanding foreign securities for that year. For example, total European repatriations were $717 million (par); of all sales of foreign securities, between December 1929 and December 1937, 16.46% were sold during 1930; therefore, ($717) (.1646) = $118 million in repatriations are ascribed to Europe in 1930.

---

[1]H. Lary, op. cit., p. 107.

Table 6

Repatriations by Region and Year

($000,000 in par value)

	1930	1931	1932	1933
Europe	118	97	57	91
N. Am.	3	3	1	3
S. Am.	26	21	12	20
A-O-A	55	45	27	42

Source: Estimation procedure is described in the text.

c/ Finding the market value of repatriated securities. Price series of the bonds of each region are available for government bonds, sub-national government units, government-guaranteed corporate bonds, and private corporate bonds.[1] The composition of the American foreign portfolio by region and by type of borrower within the region for December 1930 is also available.[2]

We will use the frequency of occurrence of the various classes of bonds within each region to weight the prices of these bonds to obtain the weighted average annual market price, in terms of percentage of par, of the bonds of each region held by the United States.

For example, of European bonds held by the United States, 58.67% were national government bonds, 15.60% were sub-national government bonds, and 25.72% were private corporate bonds. The average price of European national government bonds in 1931 was 93, of sub-national bonds was 78, and

---

[1] New York Stock Exchange Monthly Bulletin, Vol. I #1-Vol. IV #12, passim.

[2] Trade Information Bulletin no. 767, passim.

the bonds of private corporations averaged 73. The weighted average price in 1931 of European bonds held by the United States is 85.5 (compared with the arithmetic average price of 81.3).

Since the weighted average price so obtained is expressed in terms of market price as a percentage of par value, multiplying that price by the estimate of par value repatriation will yield the annual market value of repatriations by region. For example, the weighted average market price of European bonds in 1931, as a percentage of par value, was 85.5; we estimated earlier that the par value of European repatriations in 1931 was $97 million (table 6); hence, the market value of European repatriations in 1931 was equal to (.855) ($97 million) or $83 million. Table 7 shows this calculation carried out for the repatriations of all regions.

Table 7

Estimated Annual Market Value of Repatriations

($ million)

	1930	1931	1932	1933
Europe	114	83	36	68
N. Am.	2	1	2	2
S. Am.	22	11	3	5
A-O-A	48	32	16	31
Total	186	127	57	106

Source: Estimation procedure described in text.

d/ We assume that aside from repatriations, remaining American sales of foreign securities were entirely to Europe. This assumption seems plausible for several reasons. While there probably was additional repatriation of bonds, these are probably unimportant in estimating transactions in outstanding securities for South America and Asia-Oceania-Africa because of the low prices of South American bonds (an unrecorded $100 million in repatriation would mean only a $25 million unrecorded flow on average for 1932 and 1933) and the comparatively small unrepatriated total investment in Asia-Oceania-Africa ($900 million par, amounting to 11% of U. S. investment portfolio in December 1930, of which $332 million par was reported repatriated; this leaves $568 million par which may have been sold or repatriated. This sum had an average market value of (568) (.935) = 528 in 1930, falling to an average market value of (568) (.690) = 392 in 1933.

Any underestimation of repatriations by Europe will be attributed to Europe, since all remaining sales are attributed to Europe. Thus, the only important exclusion may be repatriations by Canada. Unfortunately, I can think of no way to correct this. Qualitatively, however, attention focused on the sizeable German repatriations, while relatively little was said about Canadian repatriations.

Finally, the belief that most of the transactions in outstanding foreign securities took place between Europe and the United States is consistent with both the general proposition that the majority of these transactions had to take place among regions with large pools of fairly liquid capital and with the specific observation that it is consistent with risk averse liquidation of foreign holdings. That pattern, recall, was that American investors would sell British securities and purchase gold bloc securities prior to the British devaluation, sell gold bloc securities and purchase British securities after the British devaluation, and sell all European securities after the American devaluation.

Table 8 is the summary table of transactions in outstanding foreign securities.

Table 8

Purchases of Outstanding
Foreign Securities

($ millions)

	1927	1928	1929	1930	1931	1932	1933
Europe	- 59	-198	-126	-326	-316	-205	-685
N. Am.	- 28	- 97	- 62	____	____	____	____
S. Am.	- 30	-101	- 64	____	____	____	____
A-O-A	- 26	- 87	- 55	____	____	____	____
Total	-143	-483	-307	-326	-316	-205	-685

Table 9

Sales of Outstanding
Foreign Securities

	1927	1928	1929	1930	1931	1932	1933
Europe	138	160	169	659	555	331	527
N. Am.	28	97	62	2	1	1	2
S. Am.	71	82	87	22	11	3	5
A-O-A	60	70	74	48	32	16	31
Total	336	389	412	731	599	351	565

Note: (-) indicates outflow of funds

Source: Estimates for 1927-1929 are averages of the range estimates of table 3. Estimating procedure is described in text.

C-3/ Transactions in Outstanding Domestic Securities.

Transactions in outstanding domestic securities represent efforts by foreigners to change the size and composition of their portfolio assets in the United States. There are no estimates of the regional breakdown of these transactions for which either the methodology or sample is identified.[1]

There are three survey estimates of foreign investment in the United States by market value and by investing region. We avoid the problem of the difference between par value and market value which we faced in the estimation of the regional composition of transactions in outstanding foreign securities, since foreign holdings of American assets tended to be in equities. However, we now face the problem that changes in the stock estimates of foreign investment in the U. S. are due not only to transactions in outstanding domestic securities, but also to increases and decreases in capital value, a significant problem in the period 1927-1933.

In estimating the regional composition of these transactions, we assume first that all regions investing in the United States were equally subject to capital gains and losses. This enables us to use the estimated changes in stocks as a correct indication of the distribution of net purchases and sales of outstanding domestic securities. This assumption has a number of implications which vary in credibility. If we assume that all regions are equally subject to capital gains and losses, we imply that identical information is available to all investing regions,

---

[1]As with transactions in outstanding foreign securities, estimates of the geographic composition of the net flow is given in the annual balance of payments for the years 1927-1929. The compiler states that these are his estimates but does not say whether they are derived from sample distributions from some theoretically derived distribution. The form of the questionaire distributed by the Bureau of Foreign and Domestic Commerce does not provide for notation of this information. To avoid the risk that the compiler may have used the same estimating technique as that described below, thus rendering spurious any correspondence between his estimates and the following (the significance of) estimates, his estimates will not be used.

that given this information all regions are equally capable of profit maximizing behavior, (i.e. investment acumen is equal and any other constraints are either absent or operate on all parties similarly), that investors in all regions have identical risk-preference behavior, and that any miscellaneous investment criteria are either absent or applied identically.

It is difficult to measure differences in the quality of financial information among financial centers. Certainly the folklore of international finance is filled with stories of Swiss and London bankers learning of policy decisions of foreign countries before their foreign ministries. While international differences in the caliber of information seem likely, their influence on investment decisions seems highly conjectural.[1] Much the same problem exists in comparing international differences in the ability to analyze this information.

The proposition that investor risk-preference is equal among nations has been tested and found to be untrue. In a study cited by Harry Dexter White[2], the portfolios of several different European countries showed distinct differences in risk-aversion. If such differences exist among nations, there is reason to believe that similar differences would exist among the regions discussed in this paper.

Such differences might easily lead investors in different regions to behave quite differently during the speculative boom and subsequent collapse of the American stock market. However, the direction of the bias seems again highly conjectural. Would investors in a "speculatively oriented" region change the composition of their holdings more or less often than investors in a less "speculatively oriented" region?

---

[1] For example, does an investor with good information trade more or less frequently than an investor with bad information?

[2] H. D. White, The French International Accounts 1800-1913, p. 110.

Finally, of the many other influences on investment behavior, it is noteworthy that European investments in the U. S. were more heavily concentrated in extractive industries than the investments of other regions. This preference may be explicable in terms of ties with European manufacturers. However, the relatively large decline in raw materials prices during the depression might mean that European holdings of American equities declined in value more than the equity holdings of other regions.

The second assumption we will make is that trades made to alter the composition of the portfolio are in proportion to trades made for the purpose of changing the absolute size of the portfolio. For example, if one region increases its net holdings of American securities by $100 million, while another increases its net holdings of American securities by $10 million, we would assume that the first region would transact ten times the total number of trades of the second region.

Table 10 shows the three stock estimates of foreign investment in the United States for the period discussed in this paper.

Table 10

Foreign Long Term Assets in the United States

($ 000,000)

	12/1927	12/1929	12/1934
Europe	2,207	3,300	2,819
N. Am.	722	935	1,007
S. Am.	125	163	40
A-O-A	20	115	491
Total	3,074	4,513	4,357

Source: United States Department of Commerce, Bureau of Foreign and Domestic Commerce, "Foreign Investment in the United States" (Government Printing Office, Washington, D. C., 1937). 1927 and 1929 data, p. 27; 1934 data, p. 17.

Estimation: 1928 and 1929

According to the stock estimates, foreigners purchased $1.439 billion worth of American securities between December 1927 and December 1929. However, the sum of the flow estimates of transactions in outstanding domestic securities for 1928 is only $861 million. That is, the change in stock estimates implies foreign investment in the U. S. was almost twice as great as the sum of the flow estimates of this investment. This may be due to capital gain on the foreign portfolio in the U. S., over-reporting of foreign investment in the stock estimate, or under-reporting of foreign investment in the flow estimate.[1]

Since we are assuming that all regions partook equally of capital gains and losses and that any error in reporting is distributed in equal proportion among the holdings of each region, we will first apply the geographic distribution of the change in shares to the net flow on transactions in outstanding securities.

1. Estimating the distribution of net transactions in outstanding securities.

Table 11

Composition of Change in Stock
and Estimated Composition of Net Flow

($ 000,000)

	Change in Stock	Estimate of Composition of Net Flow
Europe	1,093	654
N. Am.	213	127
S. Am.	38	23
A-O-A	95	57

Source: Derived from table 10

[1]The compiler of the balance of payments for this period believed strongly that a large part of errors and omissions were attributable to inaccurate reporting of transactions in outstanding securities. However, for the years 1928 and 1929, were we to increase the absolute size of the inflow on transactions in outstanding securities in order to bring it into line with the change in stock estimates, the size of errors and omissions would increase.

The estimate of the flow composition given in the above table is also our estimate of minimum sales of domestic securities to these regions. That is, if Europe increased its holdings of U. S. securities by $654 million in 1928 and 1929, then minimally Europe must have purchased $654 million in securities during those two years. Of course, Europe might have purchased, say $1,654 million in domestic securities, and resold $1,000 million which would have yielded the same net sale figure of $654 million. Thus, sales of domestic securities to Europe were at least $654 million, and at most $2,06. million (i.e., total recorded sales of domestic securities, less the minimum estimated purchases of non-European regions).

Choosing an estimate between the minimum and maximum is considerably facilitated by the assumption we have made that transactions made to change the composition of the portfolio are proportional to transactions made to change the size of the portfolio. Total sales of domestic securities in 1928 and 1929 amounted to $2,268 million. Minimum sales, or those minimally necessary to attain the desired net increase by foreigners in their holdings of U. S. securities, are $861 million. The difference, $1,407 million were presumably transactions engaged in to change the composition of the foreign portfolio of U. S. investments. These will be allotted to each region according to the size of the net change in the portfolio. These adjusted sales of outstanding domestic securities are given in the first column of table 12. The third column lists the net sales of domestic securities to foreigners, estimated as discussed earlier. The second column may be solved for algebraically.

We can now allot the total purchases by region for 1928 and 1929 to these two years separately by prorating total sales by the proportion of total sales taking place in each of the two years. Thus, of total sales of $2,268 million of domestic securities, $973 million were made in 1927;

hence, (973)/(2268) = .429 of each regions sales will be allotted to 1928.

Table 12

Estimates of Sales of Outstanding Domestic Securities, 1927 and 1928

($ million)

	Sales	Purchases	Net Sales
Europe	1,723	-1,069	654
N. Am.	334	- 207	127
S. Am.	61	- 38	23
A-O-A	150	- 93	57
Total	2,268	1,407	861

Note: (-) indicates outflow of funds

Source: Estimating procedure described in text.

An analogous procedure is followed for estimating transactions in outstanding securities for the years 1930 to 1933, using the stock estimates of December 1929 and December 1934 (table 10). However, for the year 1927, we have used the average share of purchases and sales recorded for 1928 and 1929 because of the absence of a stock estimate of foreign investment in the U. S. for a date close to December 1926. The resulting estimates of transactions in outstanding domestic securities are shown in table 13.

Table 13

Estimated Regional Distribution
of Sales and Purchases
of Outstanding Domestic Securities
($000,000)

Purchases	1927	1928	1929	1930	1931	1932	1933
Europe	-474	-372	-697	-400	-237	-147	-306
N. Am.	- 92	- 72	-135	- 38	- 23	- 14	- 29
S. Am.	- 17	- 13	- 25	-119	- 71	- 43	- 91
A-O-A	- 41	- 33	- 60	-201	-119	- 74	-154
Total	-624	-490	-917	-758	-450	-278	-580

Sales	1927	1928	1929	1930	1931	1932	1933
Europe	451	739	984	307	195	99	277
N. Am.	88	143	191	72	46	23	64
S. Am.	16	26	35	91	58	29	82
A-O-A	39	65	85	374	237	121	337
Total	594	973	1,295	844	536	272	760

Note: (-) indicates outflow of funds.

Source: Total transactions in outstanding domestic securities were taken from H. Lary, _op. cit._, p. 107. Transactions by region were estimated according to the procedure described in the text.

d-1/ Amortization Payments to the United States.

d-1.1/ Private

Unrevised estimates of amortization payments by region, taken from the annual balances of payments, are shown in table 1. The discrepancy between the revised and unrevised estimates is serious only for the year 1931. For this year the estimate of amortization payments from South America has been revised downward to conform more closely with the apparent downward trend of amortization payments from South America. The distribution of the sample was used to estimate the distribution of Lary's revised figures and is shown in table 2.

Table 1

Estimate of Private Amortization Payments to the United States

($ 000,000)

	1927	1928	1929	1930	1931	1932	1933
(-) indicates outflow of funds							
Europe	104	154	157	167	133	115	51
N. Am.	102	134	77	84	81	47	50
S. Am.	89	64	36	39	88	37	19
A-O-A	9	9	6	6	11	17	17
Total, Unrevised	304	361	276	296	313	216	137
Total, Revised	285	361	276	300	257	172	123

Sources: Unrevised regional and aggregate estimates taken from the annual balances of payments <u>Trade Information Bulletin</u>, nos. 552, 625, 698, 761, 803, 814, and 819. Revised estimates of total amortization were taken from Lary, <u>op. cit.</u>, table III.

Table 2

Estimate of the Regional Distribution
Of Amortization Payments to the United States

($000,000)

	1927	1928	1929	1930	1931	1932	1933
Europe	98	154	157	169	133	91	46
N. Am.	96	134	77	85	74	38	45
S. Am.	83	64	36	40	39	29	17
A-O-A	8	9	6	6	11	14	15
Total	285	361	276	300	257	172	123

Source: Total taken from H. Lary, op. cit., table III. The procedure used to estimate regional shares is discussed in the text.

d-1.2/ Inter-Allied Debts

All payments of inter-allied debts and activities of the Alien Property Custodian represent flows between the United States and Europe (table 3).

Table 3

Amortization of Inter-Allied Debt,
Government Aid and Settlement

($000,000)

	1927	1928	1929	1930	1931	1932	1933
Europe	53	41	26	51	- 7	23	- 5
N. Am.	____	____	____	____	____	____	____
S. Am.	____	____	____	____	____	____	____
A-O-A	____	____	____	____	____	____	____
Total	53	41	26	51	- 7	23	- 5

Note: (-) indicates outflow from the U. S.

Source: Annual balance of payments, Trade Information Bulletin, nos. 552, 625, 698, 761, 803, 814, and 819. See text for estimating procedure.

d-2/ Amortization Payments by the United States.

Outward amortizqtion payments are a series of minor importance largely because foreign portfolio investment in the United States was primarily in equities. However, the apparent constancy of this series is probably largely due to the rather vague ideas of the Department of Commerce about the size of amortization payments by the United States.

American amortization payments have been allotted according to the estimated regional share of foreign investment in the United States. The only estimates, apparently, are those for December of 1927, 1929 and 1934.[1] The estimates for the period 1930 to 1933 are based on the assumption that the change in the composition of the foreign portfolio of American assets was linear between 1929 and 1934. A similar procedure, using the estimates of regional distribution of foreign assets for 1927 and 1929, was used to estimate the regional composition of amortization payments in 1928. The final estimate of the regional allocation of amortization payments is shown in table 4.

---

[1]U. S. Department of Commerce, "Foreign Investment in the United States," pp. 17, 27.

Table 4

Estimate of the Regional Distribution of Amortization Payments by the United States

($000,000)

	1927	1928	1929	1930	1931	1932	1933
Europe	- 15	- 15	- 15	- 14	- 14	- 14	- 10
N. Am.	- 4	- 4	- 4	- 4	- 4	- 4	- 3
S. Am.	- 1	- 1	- 1	- 1	- 1	- 1	___
A-O-A	___	___	___	- 1	- 1	- 1	- 2
Total	- 20	- 20	- 20	- 20	- 20	- 20	- 15

Note: (-) indicates outflow of funds from the U. S.

Source: Regional composition estimated according to procedure described in text; totals taken from Lary, op. cit., table III.

1
Note 8: Estimating the Regional Distribution of Receipts and Payments of Interest and Dividends on Long Term Capital Assets

a. Receipts of Interest Payments from American Portfolio Investment Overseas.

During the years 1927 to 1930 the Department of Commerce apparently estimated total and regional interest payments on the basis of the average yield of outstanding dollar bonds applied to the outstanding loans to that region. These estimates of regional shares and total interest receipts are shown in table 1. For these years we have used the percentage shares of the sample data to estimate the regional composition of Lary's revised estimates of total interest receipts. Finally we have adjusted the regional shares to reflect the tendency during this period for the average yield on Canadian bonds to be about one percent less than the average for all foreign bonds and for South American bonds to yield about one percent more than the average for all foreign bonds [1] (table 2).

---

[1] H. Lary, op. cit., pp. 205-206.

The Department of Commerce instituted a more complicated estimating technique in 1930 which attempted to account for inter-regional differences in yields on outstanding dollar bonds. However, there is systematic disparity of about ten percent between the original estimates of interest receipts and Lary's revised estimates which were based on an issue-by-issue compilation of outstanding bonds [1] (table 1). We cannot explain this disparity and have used the regional shares of the unrevised estimate to estimate the regional shares of the revised estimate, essentially distributing any error among the regions in proportion to their weight (table 2).

Table 1

Sample Estimate of the Regional
Distribution of Interest Receipts
from U. S. Foreign Portfolio Investment

($000,000)

	1927	1928	1929	1930	1931	1932	1933
Europe	124	145	199	210	213	150	135
N. Am.	72	97	68	84	89	91	86
S. Am.	87	67	104	96	80	47	37
A-O-A	18	27	28	43	49	48	48
Total Unrevised	301	336	399	433	431	336	306
Total Lary	311	364	399	429	383	311	267

Source: Unrevised totals and Regional distributions were taken from *Trade Information Bulletin* nos. 552, 625, 698, 761, 803, 814, and 819. Revised estimates of total interest payments were taken from Lary pp. 80, 82-83.

---

[1] H. Lary, *op. cit.*, p. 212

Table 2

Estimated Regional Distribution of Interest Receipts by the U. S. on Long Term Portfolio Investment

($000,000)

	1927	1928	1929	1930	1931	1932	1933
Europe	127	156	199	212	188	140	117
N. Am.	60	58	53	88	81	84	75
S. Am.	105	121	119	80	72	44	32
A-O-A	19	29	28	49	42	43	43
Total	311	364	399	429	383	311	267

Source: Revised estimates of total interest receipts were taken from H. Lary, op. cit., pp. 80, 82-83. The regional distribution of these payments was estimated according to the procedure described in the text.

b. Interest on War Debts

Virtually all of these transactions took place between the United States and Europe. Interest payments on interallied debts came solely from Europe and are shown in table 3.

Table 3

Receipts of Interest Payments on Inter-Allied War Debts by the U. S.

($000,000)

	1927	1928	1929	1930	1931	1932	1933
Europe	160	157	145	164	92	67	20
N. Am.	___	___	___	___	___	___	___
S. Am.	___	___	___	___	___	___	___
A-O-A	___	___	___	___	___	___	___
Total	160	157	145	164	92	67	20

Source: Annual balances of payments 1927 to 1933, Trade Information Bulletin nos. 552, 625, 698, 761, 803, 814, and 819. H. Lary shows only the sum of interest payments, amortization payments, and transactions by the Alien Property Custodian (H. Lary, op. cit., pp. 83-84 and table I).

c. Dividends and Remissions from Overseas American Investments

Lary's estimate of total returns from direct investment were taken from a chart; there is no accompanying table. These totals appear identical with the total returns taken from the annual balances of payments. Therefore, no adjustment was made. The final estimate of the regional distribution is shown in table 4.

Table 4

Estimated Regional Distribution of Dividends and Remissions from U. S. Direct Investments Overseas

($000,000)

	1927	1928	1929	1930	1931	1932	1933
Europe	66	82	86	101	70	25	25
N. Am.	124	135	134	114	50	20	25
S. Am.	208	221	214	113	48	30	40
A-O-A	44	43	43	42	12	10	15
Total	442	481	477	370	180	85	105

Source: Totals were taken from H. Lary, op. cit., p. 80; totals and regional distribution were taken from annual balances of payments cited in source of table 3. Estimating procedure is described in the text.

d. Payment of Interest and Dividends by the U. S.

Lary does not separate total interest payments by the United States into payments on short and long term funds in the United States. However, since his estimate of short term balances in the United States is virtually identical with the data from the annual balances of payments for the years 1927 to 1933, and since he makes no explicit reference to any adjustment of interest from short term investment, I presume he is retaining the old estimates of interest paid on short term funds. Interest and dividend payments on long term funds may then be calculated by subtracting U. S. payments of interest on short term funds from total interest payments. This calculation is shown in table 4.

Table 4

Estimating Total Interest and Dividend Payments by the U. S. on Foreign Long Term Funds

($000,000)

	1927	1928	1929	1930	1931	1932	1933
Short	- 78	-107	-144	- 73	- 26	- 8	- 3
Long	-162	-168	-186	-222	-194	-127	-112
Interest Payments	-240	-275	-330	-295	-220	-135	-115

Note: (-) indicates outflow of funds from the U. S.

Sources: Total payments are from Lary, op. cit., table I. Interest payments on short term funds are taken from the annual balances of payments, 1927 to 1933, Trade Information Bulletin nos. 552, 625, 698, 761, 803, 814, and 819.

Interest payments on long term foreign assets in the United States were distributed among regions according to the shares of each region in total foreign investment in the United States. Estimates of the regional composition of foreign assets in the United States were taken from Foreign Investments in the United States for December of 1927, 1929, and 1934.[1] For the years 1928 and 1930 to 1933 it was assumed that the composition of the foreign portfolio changed linearly with respect to time. The final estimate of the regional distribution of interest payments to foreigners on long term investment in the United States is shown in table 5.

[1] U. S. Department of Commerce, Foreign Investments in the United States (1937) pp. 17, 27.

Table 5

Estimated Regional Distribution of U.S. Payments of Interest and Dividends on (Long Term) Foreign Investment

	1927	1928	1929	1930	1931	1932	1933
Europe	-119	-123	-136	-159	-136	- 86	- 74
N. Am.	- 33	- 35	- 39	- 47	- 42	- 28	- 25
S. Am.	- 6	- 6	- 7	- 7	- 5	- 3	- 2
A-O-A	- 4	- 4	- 4	- 9	- 11	- 10	- 11
Total	-162	-168	-186	-222	-194	-127	-112

Note: (-) indicates outflow of funds from the U. S.

Source: Total payments of interest and dividends on long term funds were taken from table 4. The method of estimating the regional distribution is discussed in the text.

Appendix 2: Notes to chapter 3, "The Decline in Net American Long Term Capital Exports: Its Causes and its Effects on the World Economy, 1927-1933."

Note 1: Estimating the Net Outflow of Capital from the U.S. During the Periods January 1927-June 1928 and July 1928-September 1929.

Long term capital flows have three components: portfolio investment, direct investment, and transaction in outstanding securities. We have discussed[1] the method of estimating the total and regional flows of capital on a calendar-year basis. We deal here with the question of whether the use of a calendar-year time period masks any important economic characteristic of the flows.

a/ Portfolio investment

The total outflow of funds from the U. S. due to portfolio investment for the years 1927-1929 is shown in table 1.

Table 1

Portfolio Investment

($000,000)

1927	1928	1929
-1114	-1019	- 415

Note: (-) indicates outflow of funds from the U. S.

Source: Lary, *op. cit.*, table III.

New issues, however, are not floated at a uniform rate during the year; table 2 shows the percentage distribution of new issues by quarter. Table 3 shows the absolute amount of new issues by quarter and clearly indicates that the sharp decline in new lending began with the third quarter of 1928 rather than in 1929.

---

[1]See appendix 1, note 7.

Table 2

Percentage Quarterly Distribution
of Long-Term Foreign Loans, 1927-1929

	I	II	III	IV
1927	21.4	23.4	19.8	34.4
1928	29.9	44.7	10.3	15.1
1929	43.0	32.0	8.4	16.7

Source: Calculated from Survey of Current Business, Annual Supplement 1932, pp. 92-93.

Table 3

Quarterly Distribution of
Long-Term Foreign Loans, 1927-1929

($000,000)

	I	II	III	IV
1927	238.4	260.7	220.6	383.2
1928	304.7	455.5	105.0	153.9
1929	178.0	132.8	34.9	69.3

Source: Calculated from table 1 and table 2.

During the six quarters from January 1927 to June 1928 new American lending was $1,874.2 million; during the six quarters from June 1928 to December 1929 total U. S. new lending amounted to $673.9 million. This represented a decline in new lending of about $1.2 billion.

Since we have no direct data on the quarterly distribution of direct investment, we have assumed that these investments take place at a uniform rate during the year. Thus, direct investment was $351 million or $87.75 million per quarter in 1927; $558 million or $139.5 million per quarter in 1928; and $602 million or $150.5 million per quarter in 1929.[1]

[1]Estimates of total direct investment taken from appendix 1, note 7.

c/ Transactions in Outstanding Securities

The four types of transactions in outstanding securities are the purchases and sales of outstanding foreign and domestic securities. Total transactions by calendar year are shown in Table 4. There are no data concerning the distribution of these transactions within the year.

Transactions in outstanding securities are undertaken by investors who wish to change the composition or net holdings of their foreign assets. Under these circumstances, we can estimate the flows due to transactions in outstanding securities under various assumptions.

Table 4

Transactions in Outstanding Securities, 1927-1929

($000,000)

	1927	1928	1929
Purchases			
-foreign securities	-143	-483	-307
-domestic securities	-624	-490	-917
subtotal	-767	-973	-1224
Sales			
-foreign securities	336	389	412
-domestic securities	594	973	1295
subtotal	930	1362	1707
TOTAL	163	389	483

Note: (-) indicates outflow of funds

Source: H. Lary, op. cit., p. 107

1. Assume that all transactions are undertaken at a uniform rate throughout the year.

Under this assumption, the net inflow of funds to the United States would have been $357.5 million during the period from January 1927 to June 1928, and $677.5 million during the period from June 1928 to December 1929. This assumption yields a minimum estimate of the inflow during the period June 1928 to October 1929. To reduce the inflow below this would require the dubious assumption that foreigners sold American securities during the boom and purchased them during stagnant or declining phases of the market.

2. Assume that foreigners and Americans sold each others securities during stagnant or declining markets but purchased each others securities during periods when the market was rising.

The major American bull market (rounding to the nearest quarter of a year) lasted from June 1928 to September 1929 (chart 1). Under assumption 2, all sales during 1928 would have been made prior to June 1928 while all purchases in 1928 would have been made after June 1928. Similarly, all purchases of securities in 1929 would have been made during the boom, prior to September 1929, while all 1929 sales would have occurred during the last quarter of 1929. The results, given these assumptions, are shown in table 5.

Under this assumption, there would have been three distinct phases of activity in outstanding securities transactions. During 1927 and the first half of 1929, transactions in outstanding securities would lead to a net inflow of $62 million to the U.S. From June 1928 to September 1929 there would have been a net inflow of $1,377 million. In the last quarter of 1929 there would have been a net outflow of funds from

Chart 1

Quarterly Stock Price Indices
January 1927-December 1929
as a Ratio of the Index Value for December 1926

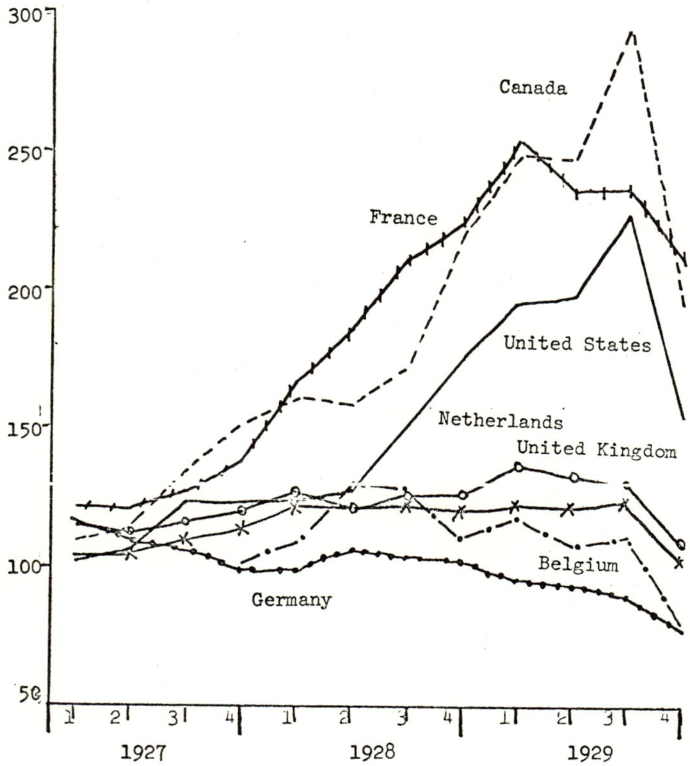

Source: U.S. data (Dow Jones Industrial) from the U.S. Department of Commerce, Survey of Current Business Annual Supplement, 1932, p. 103.

Foreign data from the League of Nations Statistical Yearbook 1930-1931, p. 255.

the U. S. of $505 million. Of course, if assumption 2 correctly describes investor behavior, then the estimates of table 5 would tend to overstate the true flows since we would expect to have some transactions devoted to compositional changes whatever the investor's desire concerning his net position. So, for example, even if foreign investors did increase their holdings of American stocks during the bull swing, it is unlikely that they sold some stocks while purchasing more of others in order to change the composition of their portfolios.

Table 5

Estimate 2: Distribution of Transactions in Outstanding Securities During the Years 1928 and 1929

($000,000)

Purchases	1927	1/28-6/28	7/28-12/28	1/29-9/29	9/29-12/29
Foreign	-143	____	- 483	- 307	____
Domestic	-624	-490	____	____	- 917
Subtotal	-767	-490	- 483	- 307	- 917
Sales					
Foreign	336	389	____	____	412
Domestic	594	____	973	1295	____
Subtotal	930	389	973	1295	412
TOTAL	163	-101	490	988	-505

Note: (-) indicates outflow of funds from the U. S.

Source: Estimating procedure described in text.

3. Assume finally that during periods when the American stock market was steady or declining that foreigners reduced their holdings of American securities while Americans increased their holdings of foreign securities; conversely, during periods when the American stock market was rising, assume that Americans reduced their holdings of foreign securities while foreigners increased their holdings of American securities.

Under this assumption all foreign sales of American securities and all American purchases of foreign securities in 1928 would take place prior to June while all foreign purchases of American securities and American sales of foreign securities would take place between June and December of 1928. On the other hand, all foreign purchases of American securities and all American sales of foreign securities in 1929 would take place prior to September 1929 while all American purchases of foreign securities and all foreign sales of American securities would take place between September and December of that year. Table 6 shows the results of these assumptions.

Table 6
($000,000)

Estimate 3: Distribution of Transactions in Outstanding Securities During the Years 1928 and 1929

Purchases	1927	1/28-6/28	6/28-12/28	1/29-9/29	9/29-12/29
Foreign	-143	-483	___	___	-307
Domestic	-624	-490	___	___	-917
Subtotal	-767	-973	___	___	-1224
Sales					
Foreign	336	___	389	412	___
Domestic	594	___	973	1295	___
Subtotal	930	___	1362	1707	___
TOTAL	163	-973	1362	1707	-1224

Note: (-) indicates outflow of funds from the U.S.

Source: See text for estimating procedure.

Under assumption 3 transactions in outstanding securities would also represent three distinct phases of movement; however, this assumption yields a maximum estimate of the inflow of capital to the United States during the stock market boom. The net outflow of funds during 1927 and the first half of 1928 would have amounted to $810 million. There would have been an inflow of funds to the United States between June 1928 and September 1929 of about $3,069 million. Finally, in the last quarter of 1929, there would have been an outflow of funds of about $1,224 million.

We can treat this as a maximum estimate of the inflow of funds on account of transactions in outstanding securities for two reasons: first, as we mentioned earlier, it is unlikely that sharp changes in net positions would occur without changes in the composition of portfolios which would tend to reduce the net flow of funds; second, this represents the most extreme assumption about investor behavior--there is no other assumption which could produce a larger net inflow of funds during the period June 1928 to September 1929.

Table 7 summarizes the estimates based on assumptions 1, 2, and 3. Our estimate of the reduction in outflow of long term funds from the United States from June 1928 to September 1929 because of outstanding security transactions ranges from a minimum of $149 million, through $1,315 million, to a maximum of $3,879 million.[1]

Table 7*

Estimated Distribution of Net Transactions in Outstanding securities, 1927-1929

($000,000)

	1/27-6/28	7/28-9/29	10/29-12/29
Est. 1	357	557	121
Est. 2	62	1478	-505
Est. 3	-810	3069	-1224

Note: (-) indicates outflow from U. S.

Source: See tables 4, 5, 6 and text for estimating procedure.
*Revised, 1975

---

[1]The reader should note that the period January 1927 to June 1928 contains six quarters, while the period July 1928 to September 1929 contains only five quarters. This tends to bias the case in favor of someone, such as myself, who is pointing to the sharp decline from the first to the second period. Comparisons of flows should always be over the same time interval.

However, it would be extremely difficult to make this adjustment without erecting a large number of additional assumptions which would rather confuse the argument and would most likely be inaccurate. That is, with the bull market swing of 1928 and 1929 we have a dramatic event which is relatively easy to tie with the three assumptions which have been made. No such dramatic move exists in 1927. In any case, such a correction is unlikely to change the nature of the reversal of the flow of funds we have been discussing and it is the qualitative nature of this shift rather than its precise magnitude which is of greatest interest.

Table 8*

Change in Net Inflow on Transactions in Outstanding Securities, 1927-1929

($000,000)

	July 1928 to September 1929 compared with January 1927 to June 1928	October 1929 to December 1929 compared with July 1928 to September 1929
Est. 1	+ 200	- 436
Est. 2	+1416	-1983
Est. 3	+3879	-4293

Note: (+) indicates decline in outflow.

Source: Table 7.
*Revised, 1975

Summary

Table 9 summarizes the estimates of all types of long term lending during the periods January 1927 to June 1928 and July 1928 to September 1929.

Table 9*

Intra-Calendar Year Estimates of American Foreign Investment 1927-1929

($000,000)

	January 1927 to June 1928	July 1928 to September 1929	October 1929 to December 1929
I Portfolio Investment	-1874	- 605	- 69
II Direct Investment	- 630	- 730	- 151
I+II	-2504	-1335	- 220
III Transactions in Outstanding Securities			
Est. 1	357	557	121
Est. 2	62	1478	- 505
Est. 3	- 810	3069	-1224
I+II+III (Est. 1)	-2147	- 778	- 99
I+II+III (Est. 2)	-2442	+ 143	- 725
I+II+III (Est. 3)	-3314	+1734	-1444

Note: (-) indicates outflow of funds from the U. S.

Source: See table 3, table 7 and section b/; estimating procedure described in text.

*Revised, 1975

Note 2: Estimating European Net Domestic Capital Formation in 1928

We observe in 1928 and 1929 in Europe all of the symptoms of a sudden tightening in the European money markets: rising interest rates, declining flotations of new issues, and official policies to tighten the money markets. However, we are also interested in determining the size of the decline in American long term lending relative to long term domestic net investment in Europe to see if it is plausible that the decline in American lending could have had such an effect in European capital markets. To make such a comparison, we will first estimate European gross domestic product and then European net domestic capital formation.

We will attempt first to arrive at a maximum estimate of European Gross Domestic Product (GDP). This estimate will involve the following steps: 1) Convert Maizel's estimate of GDP for selected European countries from 1955 dollars to 1929 dollars; 2) Convert United Nations national income estimates for other European countries in 1929 dollars; 3) Estimate the GDP of the remaining European countries.

Alfred Maizels has estimated the GDP for certain European countries in 1929 in dollars at 1955 prices.[1] Assuming that prices in these European countries rose in the same proportion as prices in the United States, we could deflate the estimates in 1955 dollars by the same factor needed to reduce the estimate of American GDP in 1955 dollars in 1929 to American GDP in 1929 dollars to 1929. Thus, in 1955 dollars, American GDP in 1929 was $168 billion[2] while in terms of 1929 prices, U.S. GDP was $103.6 billion.

---

[1] A. Maizels, Industrial Growth and World Trade, p. 531

[2] Maizels, op. cit., p. 531

[3] Historical Statistics of the United States, p. 140.

Thus, to take account of price changes in the United States, we would have to reduce the estimate of GDP in 1955 prices by a factor of (10_.6/168) or .6190.

Multiplying the estimates of the GDP of selected European countries in terms of 1955 prices by this factor of .6190 would give us an estimate of European GDP in 1929 prices only if we assume that European prices changed by the same amount as American prices. However, for those countries for which we have data, both wholesale prices and the consumer price index rose more in Europe between 1929 and 1955 than either of these indexes in the United States.[1] Therefore, valuing 1929 European output in terms of 1955 prices would give a higher estimate of the value of European output relative to American output in 1929 than would an estimate in terms of 1929 prices. Therefore, reducing these estimates by a constant (.6190) will give us a maximum estimate of European GDP in 1929 prices.

This procedure for converting the GDP estimates to dollars ignores the problems arising from different price levels in the non-trade sectors. Thus while the exchange rates tend to determine the value of currencies through trade and factor flows, the currency value determined in that way may not give a clear idea of the amount of non-traded goods and services which a unit of foreign currency commands in two countries. For example, with the dollar exchanged for 25 francs, a dollar would buy roughly the same value of American or French export products (in equilibrium, precisely the same value). However, a dollar might reasonably be expected to purchase more non-traded goods and services in France than it would in the United States. Therefore, we could not use the market exchange

---

[1] United Nations Statistical Yearbook 1956, pp. 450-469.

rate to determine the dollar value of French output in 1929.

Maizels has attempted to take this problem into account by calculating purchasing power parity exchange rates for those countries whose GDP he has estimated. To the extent that the relative price levels in traded and non-traded sectors remained unchanged during the period between 1929 and 1955, we would still be able to use the estimating procedure described in the preceding paragraph to arrive at a maximum estimate of European GDP. There is, of course, little reason to believe that these relative price remained unchanged and therefore we might ask about the likely direction of movement.

Services probably comprise the largest single element of the non-trade sector. Development in the United States indicates that productivity increases are greater in manufacturing and industry than they are in the service sector and that therefore price increases tend to occur more rapidly in the service sector. If we compare Europe and the United States in 1929 we observe that the European population is larger, the industrial sector is smaller, and the agricultural sector more primitive. It is reasonable to expect that Europe experienced a more substantial shift into industry during the period 1929-1955 than did the United States. Such relative shifts would imply that prices in the European service sector rose at a more rapid rate than they did in the United States. If this is so, valuing those services at 1955 prices and then reducing them by the constant factor (.6190) would tend to overestimate European Gross Domestic Product. Maizels estimates of European GDP for selected countries in 1929 at 1955 prices and the conversion to 1929 prices is shown in table 1.

Table 1

Estimates of European Gross Domestic Product, 1929

($000,000,000)

	GDP (1955 prices)[1]	GDP (1929 prices)[2]	National Income (1929 prices)[3]	NI ('29) / GDP ('29)
Austria	2.56	1.58	1.02	.646
Belgium/Luxembourg	6.05	3.74	n.a.	____
Denmark	2.55	1.58	n.a.	____
Finland	1.18	.73	.54	.739
France	25.00	15.47	9.60	.621
Germany	40.50	25.07	18.07	.721
Ireland	1.00	.62	.78	1.258
Italy	11.10	6.87	n.a.	____
Netherlands	4.37	2.71	2.45	.904
Norwav	1.77	1.10	n.a.	
Sweden	4.00	2.48	2.20	.887
Switzerland	2.87	1.78	1.82	1.022
United Kingdom	42.00	26.00	20.29	.780
Yugoslavia	2.53	1.57	n.a.	____

Notes: [1]Taken from A. Maizels, Industrial Growth and World Trade, (New York: Cambridge University Press, 1965), p. 531.

[2]Calculated from column 1; estimating procedure is described in text.

[3]National Income in national currency are taken from the United Nations Statistical Yearbook, 1948, pp. 371-372 and converted to dollars at the annual average market exchange rates given on pages 373-375.

The countries listed in table 1 account for approximately 250 million of the 350 million persons living in Europe in 1929. We have estimates for national income (NI) in 1929 for several other European countries. The problem arises in converting these estimates to dollars and thence to gross domestic product estimates. We have converted NI to dollars at the prevailing average market exchange rate in 1929 (table 1). The difference between the dollar estimate of NI and the dollar estimate of GDP lies in the failure to account for price differences in the non-traded sector, indirect business taxes, depreciation, and income originating in foreign countries. For those countries for which we have data, national income varies between 60% and 130% of gross domestic product. The reason for this discrepancy would lie in international differences in the factors mentioned above together with statistical error and conceptual variations in national income accounting. However, as far as we can tell from our sample, an assumption that NI was equivalent to 60% of gross domestic product would give us a maximum estimate of GDP.

We will assume that NI was equivalent to .6 of GDP in those countries for which we have NI estimates but lack GDP estimates. These estimates are shown in table 2.

Table 2

National Income and Estimated Gross Domestic Product
for Selected European Countries, 1929

($000,000,000)

	National Income[1]	Gross Domestic Product[2]
Poland	3.18	4.92
Rumania	1.17	1.81
Hungary	.88	1.36
Bulgaria	.41	.63
Czechoslovakia	2.00	3.09
Greece	.53	.82
Iceland	.02	.03

Notes: [1]National income estimates were taken from the United Nations Statistical Yearbook, 1948, pp. 371-372 and converted to dollars at the annual average exchange rate for 1929 given on pp. 373-375.

[2]Gross domestic product estimates were derived under the assumption that NI represents a minimum of .6 of GDP; therefore, these GDP estimates are maximum estimates based on the information contained in table 1.

Finally, we must estimate GDP for those countries for which we have no output data. This estimate has been made on the basis of the separation of "unknown" Europe into two blocs: Central Europe and Mediterranean Europe. We are assuming that per capita gross domestic product in these blocs is equal. These calculations are shown in table 3. The summary estimate of European GDP in 1929 is shown in table 4.

Table 3

Estimates of Gross Domestic Product for
Remaining European Countries, 1929

Central Europe Known		Population (000)	GDP ($000,000,000)
Bulgaria		5,950	.63
Hungary		8,784	1.36
Poland		32,638	4.92
Rumania		18,540	1.81
Yugoslavia		13,931	1.57
	subtotal	79,843	10.29
Unknown			
Albania		1,050	______
Danzig		410	______
Estonia		1,124	______
Latvia		1,931	______
Liechtenstein		12	______
Lithuania		2,422	______
	subtotal	6,949	.89
Total population and estimated total GDP		86,792	11.18
Southern Europe Known			
Greece		6,548	.82
Unknown			
Spain		24,012	______
Portugal		7,000	______
San Marino		13	
	subtotal	31,025	
Total Population and estimated total GDP		37,573	4.71

Source: GDP estimates of "known" Europe taken from table 1 and table 2. GDP of unknown Europe estimated by assuming equality of per capita output with "known" Europe.

Table 4

Summary of European GDP Estimates, 1929

($000,000,000)

Northern and Western Europe	GDP	
Austria[3]	1.58	
Belgium/Luxembourg[3]	3.74	
Denmark[3]	1.58	
Finland[3]	.73	
France[3]	15.47	
Germany[3]	25.07	
Iceland[1]	.03	
Netherlands[3]	2.71	
Norway[3]	1.10	
Sweden[3]	2.48	
Switzerland[3]	1.78	
United Kingdom[3]	26.00	
subtotal		82.89
Central Europe		
Yugoslavia[3]	1.81	
Bulgaria[1]	.63	
Hungary[1]	1.36	
Poland[1]	4.92	
Rumania[1]	1.81	
Czechoslovakia[1]	3.09	
Other Central Europe[2]	.89	
subtotal		14.51
Southern Europe		
Greece[1]	.82	
Italy[3]	6.87	
Other Southern Europe[2]	3.89	
subtotal		11.58
TOTAL EUROPE		108.98

Notes on table 4:

[1]Estimates taken from table 2.

[2]Estimates taken from table 3.

[3]Estimates taken from table 1.

For six European countries for which we have data, the average ratio of net domestic capital formation to net domestic product, weighted by their estimated gross domestic products, is 7.2% (table 5). Since NDP is always less than GDP, NDCF/GDP would be less than NDCF/NDP or less than 7.2%. Hence, 7.2% of our estimated European GDP of $109 billion in 1929 would give us a maximum estimate of 1929 European net domestic capital formation of $7.8 billion.

Table 5

Estimating European Net National Capital Information, 1929

Country	(1) NDCF[1]/NDP	(2) GDP est.	(3) Weight of GDP	(4) = (3)(1) Weighted NDCF/NDP (3)(1)
United Kingdom	3.3	26.0	.417	1.36
Germany[2]	10.0	25.1	.397	3.97
Italy	10.3	6.9	.109	1.12
Denmark	6.5	1.6	.025	.16
Norway	10.1	1.1	.017	.17
Sweden[2]	9.9	2.5	.040	.40
TOTAL	- -	63.2	.999	7.18

Notes: 1/ NDCF = Net Domestic Capital Information
NDP = Net Domestic Product

Sources: NDCF/NDP taken from Simon Kuznets "Long Term Trends in Capital Information Proportions," Economic Development and Cultural Change, Vol. IX, No. 4, Part II, July 1961. The British entry (ibid, p. 58) is an average for 1921-1929; the German entry (ibid, p. 65) is an estimate for 1928; the Italian entry (ibid, p. 69) is an average for 1921-1930; the Danish entry (ibid, p. 74) is an average for 1921-1930; the Norwegian entry (ibid, p. 80) is an average for 1920-1929; and the Swedish entry (ibid, p. 87) is an average for 1921-1930.

Gross domestic product estimates in current dollars are taken from table 4 above.

Note 3: Estimating the Net Outflow of Capital from the U.S. to Europe During the Periods January 1927-June 1928 and July 1928-September 1929.

Summary Tables:

Table 1

United States Investment in Europe
January 1927 to June 1928 and July 1928 to September 1929

($000,000)

Direct	1927	1/28-6/28	7/28-12/28	1/29-9/29
I Direct[a]	-135	- 106	- 106	- 144
II Portfolio[b]	-524	- 334	- 114	- 76
Subtotal: I+II	-659	- 440	- 220	- 220
III Transactions in Outstanding Securities[c]				
Est. 1	+ 56	+ 165	+ 165	+ 248
Est. 2	+ 56	- 212	+ 541	+ 858
Est. 3	+ 56	- 570	+ 899	+1153
Total: I+II+III (Est. 1)	-603	- 275	- 55	+ 28
I+II+III (Est. 2)	-603	- 652	+ 321	+ 638
I+II+III (Est. 3)	-603	-1010	+ 679	+ 933

Source: a/ Calendar-year regional estimate taken from appendix 1, note 7/b, table 4; quarterly estimate obtained by prorating annual estimate by month.

b/ Calendar-year regional estimate taken from appendix 1, note 7/a, table 3; quarterly estimate based on quarterly distribution of all foreign new issues from Survey of Current Business, Annual Supplement, 1932, pp. 92-93.

c/ Calendar-year regional estimate taken from appendix 1, note 7/c. table 8, table 9, and table 13; the procedure for estimating quarterly investment is discussed below.

Table 2

U.S. Net Capital Exports to Europe
(January 1927 to June 1928) and (July 1928 to September 1929)
($000,000)

	January 1927 to June 1928[1]	July 1928 to September 1929[1]	Change[2]
I Direct	- 241	- 250	- 9
II Portfolio	- 858	- 190	+ 668
I+II	-1099	- 440	+ 659
III Transactions in Outstanding Securities			
Est. 1	+ 221	+ 413	+ 192
Est. 2	- 156	+1399	+1555
Est. 3	- 514	+2052	+2397
Total:			
I+II+III (Est. 1)	- 878	- 27	+ 851
I+II+III (Est. 2)	-1255	+ 959	+2214
I+II+III (Est. 3)	-1613	+1612	+3225

Notes: 1. (-) indicates an outflow of capital from the U.S.
2. (+) indicates decline in the outflow of funds from the U.S.

Source: Calculated from table 1.

Estimating the Distribution of Transactions in Outstanding Securities During the Periods January 1927 to June 1928 and July 1928 to September 1929.

Estimate 1.

Assume: All purchases and sales of outstanding securities occurred at a uniform rate over time (table 3).

Table 3

Estimate 1: Intra-Calendar Year Transactions in Outstanding Securities between the United States and Europe, 1927-1929

($000,000)

1927	January 1928 to June 1928	July 1928 to December 1929	January 1929 to September 1929
+56	+165	+165	+248

Note: (+) indicates capital import by the U.S.

Source: Annual totals by region are taken from appendix I, note 7, tables 8, 9 and 13; for estimating procedure, see text.

Estimate 2.

Assume: Foreigners sold American securities and Americans sold foreign securities when the U. S. stock market was steady to declining (January 1927 to June 1928 and October 1929 to December 1929); foreigners purchased American securities and Americans purchased foreign securities when the American stock market was rising July 1928 to September 1929 (table 4).

Table 4

Estimate 2: Intra-Calendar Year
Transactions in Outstanding Securities
between the United States and Europe, 1927-1929

($000,000)

	1927	January 1928 to June 1928	July 1928 to December 1928	January 1929 to December 1929
Sales				
foreign	+138	+160	———	———
domestic	+451	———	+739	+984
subtotal	+589	+160	+739	+984
Purchases				
foreign	- 59	———	-198	-126
domestic	-474	-372	———	———
subtotal	-533	-372	-198	-126
TOTAL	+ 56	-212	+541	+858

Note: (+) indicates capital import by the United States.

Source: Annual totals by region are taken from appendix 1, note 7, tables 8, 9, and 13; for estimating procedure, see text.

Estimate 3.

Assume: Foreigners sold American securities and Americans purchased foreign securities when the U.S. stock market was steady or declining; foreigners purchased American securities and Americans sold foreign securities when the U.S. stock market was rising (table 5).

Table 5

Estimate 3: Intra-Calendar Year Transactions in Outstanding Securities Between the United States and Europe, 1927-1929

($000,000)

	1927	January 1928 to June 1928	July 1928 to December 1928	January 1929 to September 1929
Sales				
foreign	138	——	+160	+169
domestic	451	——	+739	+984
subtotal	589		+899	+1153
Purchases				
foreign	- 59	-198	——	——
domestic	-474	-372	——	——
subtotal	-533	-570		
TOTAL	+ 56	-570	+899	+1153

Note: (+) indicates capital import by the U.S.

Source: Annual totals by region are taken from appendix 1, note 7, tables 8, 9, and 13; for estimating procedure, see text.

Note 4: Estimating the Relative Magnitude of the Change in U.S. Net Lending and European Net Domestic Capital Formation.

The decline in U.S. net lending to Europe between the periods January 1927-June 1928 and July 1928-September 1929 ranged between $.9-$3.2 billion.[1] Prorating the European annual rate of net domestic capital formation of $7.8 billion in 1928,[2] European investment would be $11.70 billion during the period from January 1927 to June 1928; the decline in U.S. lending represents 8%-27% of investment in this period. By the same method, European net domestic capital formation would have been

[1]Appendix 2, note 3, table 2.

[2]Appendix 2, note 2.

about $9.76 billion during the period from July 1928 to September 1929; the decline in U.S. lending represents 9%-33% of investment during this period.

Note 5: "Potential" British Exports in 1929 and 1930.

British exports to five major trading partners in 1928 and 1929 declined while British exports to other countries increased through 1929.[1] American lending to these five countries also declined.[2] We are calculating "potential" U.K. exports in 1929 under the assumption that exports to these five countries would have increased at the same rate as exports to the remaining British export customers, had American capital exports been maintained.

1. Total British exports to Germany, Argentina, Brazil, Australia and Japan are shown in the following table.

Table 1

U.K. Exports to Five Trading Partners, 1927-1930

($000,000)

1927	1928	1929	1930
$777	$771	$716	$487

Source: See table 6, p. 43, ch. 3.

2. The percentage change per year in British exports to all other countries is shown in table 2.

---

[1]See chapter 3, table 6, p. 43.

[2]See chapter 3, pp. 35, 42.

Table 2

Percentage Change per Year in U.K.
Exports to All Other Countries, 1928-1930

1927	1928	1929	1930
----	+1.9%	+ .9%	-19.4%

Source: See table 6, p. 43, ch. 3

3. Assuming that with the continuation of U.S. capital exports to the five countries mentioned, U.K. exports to other countries, we estimate U.K. exports to these five countries in table 3.

Table 3

Estimated U.K. Exports to
Five Trading Partners, 1927-1930

($000,000)

1927	1928	1929	1930
$777	$791.4	$798.8	$643.8

Source: Calculated from table 1 and table 2.

4. Table 4 shows the sum of British exports to other countries plus the above estimate of potential exports to the five trading partners, and the percentage difference such a performance by the five countries would make in total U.K. exports.

Table 4

Potential British Exports

($000,000)

	1927	1928	1929	1930
a/ Actual U.K. exports	$4049.1	$4106.7	$4083.2	$3200.2
b/ Estimated difference in exports to five trading partners	$ 0	+$ 20.8	+$ 82.9	+$ 157.4
c/ c = a+b	$4049.1	$4127.5	$4166.1	$3357.6
d/ Change in exports to five countries as a percentage of actual total U.K. exports [(a+b/a) - 1]	(0)	(.5%)	(2.0%)	(4.9%)

Source: a/ see Ch. 3, table 6, p. 43
b/ see table 1 and table 3, this note.

Appendix 3: Notes to Chapter 4, "Alternative and Complementary Explanations of the Depression."

Note 1. Estimating Foreign Liquidation of U. S. Equities.

1/ Foreign assets in the United States amounted to $4.5 billion in December 1929.[1] Since $900 million of U.S. securities were sold by foreigners during 1929,[2] foreign assets at most were $5.4 billion during 1929. Assuming all foreign liquidation took place after September 1929, foreign liquidation amounted to about 17% of their total U.S. assets.

This procedure tends to give a maximum estimate of the percentage of foreign liquidation, except that the $5.4 billion estimate of foreign holdings of U.S. equities is probably too great. This estimate includes all foreign assets in the U.S., of which equities are only part. However, foreign net purchases of equities between 1926 and 1929 alone amounted to $1.8 billion[3] (assuming the $900 million in sales in 1929 represent foreign liquidation during the crash) and it is likely that there were foreign holdings of U.S. equities prior to 1926.

Note 2. Estimating the Value of Sales on the New York Exchange from October 1929 to December 1929.

No data on the value of sales appear to have been systematically gathered until after the Securities and Exchange Commission was formed. Therefore, we must estimate the value of sales in October, November and December 1929.

1/ Round lot trading on the New York Stock Exchange in shown in table 1.

---

[1]Appendix 1, note 7, table 10.

[2]H. Lary, op. cit., p. 107

[3]H. Lary, op. cit., p. 107. Unfortunately data on transactions in outstanding domestic securities are not available for the years 1922-1925, making the data for 1919-1922 worth little. There are no data prior to 1919.

Table 1

Round Lot Trading on the New York Stock Exchange

(000,000 shares)

October	November	December
142	72	84

Source: Banking and Monetary Statistics, 1943 ed., p. 485.

2/ The volume shown in table 1 must be corrected for the failure to include odd lot and stopped-stock transactions, estimated to be about 30% of round lot transaction.[1] This is likely to be an underestimated figure because of the unusually large number of executions of stop orders during the 1929 decline.

Table 2

Estimated Total Volume

(000,000 shares)

October	November	December
185	94	109

Source: Estimating procedure described in text.

3/ In April 1935, with Standard and Poor's index of common stocks at 71.3[2] 30 million shares (including round lot and stopped sale) exchanged with a total value of $747 million. Table 3 shows the estimated value of the volume of transactions in 1929 at 1935 prices (assuming the composition of transactions was about the same in 1929 and 1935).

---

[1] Banking and Monetary Statistics, p. 431.

[2] Banking and Monetary Statistics, p. 481.

Table 3

Estimated Total Value of Stocks Traded in October to December 1929

at April 1935 Prices

($000,000,000)

October	November	December	TOTAL
4.6	2.3	2.7	9.6

Source: Estimating procedure described in text.

4/ Finally, assuming that the stock index moves in rough proportion to the total value of stocks, we can adjust the estimates of table 3 to 1929 values (table 4).

Table 4

Estimated Total Value of Stocks Traded

at 1929 Prices

($000,000,000)

	October	November	December	TOTAL
a/ April 1935 stock index	(71.3)	(71.3)	(71.3)	____
b/ Value at above prices	4.6	2.3	2.7	9.6
c/ Stock index	(213.0)	(159.6)	(162.4)	____
d/ Value at 1929[1] prices	13.7	5.1	6.1	24.9

Note: [1]d = (c/a) (b)

Source: Stock indices from Banking and Monetary Statistics, p. 481; estimating procedure described in text.

5/ Hence, the total value of sales during October to December 1929 amounted to \$9.6 billion to \$24.9 billion. Since the total value of stocks listed in early October was \$87 billion,[1] sales were between 11% and 29% of the total value of the stock.

---

[1]G. Soule, Prosperity Decade, pp. 70-72.

Note 3. Some Observations about the size and direction of the flow of short term funds from Germany, January 1931 through July 1931.

I have not found any systematic presentations of the size or direction of either the gross or the net withdrawals of short funds from Germany between January and July 1931. We may estimate this, very roughly, from either changes in stocks of foreign exchange and gold or from the balance of payments' estimates of the total size of the annual short term flows. We may draw inferences about the direction of the short term flows from the direction of regional distribution of changes in the gold stock. All this, may it be explicit, is extremely crude.

a/ Changes in the stock of foreign exchange and gold.

A "run" on a country's currency must involve either a reduction in its holdings of foreign exchange or gold, or a reduction in its exchange rate. Unless there is a net conversion to gold or a hard currency, then the ultimate step in liquidating the currency in question has not been taken. Thus, a 100% increase in the rate of liquidation of that countries short term loans from foreign countries will only lead to pressure on the currency if it is not matched by a commensurate increase in new loans by foreign countries. In the case in question, we are interested not only in the heavy liquidation of foreign assets in Germany but also in whether new lending on short term to Germany failed to increase.[1]

---

[1]This does not mean that changes in gross flows are unimportant. Heavy liquidation of German commercial paper, hypothetically, might be offset in the exchange market by heavy purchases of short term official paper and yet seriously damage the German economy.

Between January and the end of July 1931, the Reichsbank's holdings of gold and foreign exchange declined by 1075 million marks, or about \$255.8 million.[1] This decline, of course, represents the algebraic sum of all elements of the balance of payments. By estimating the new flow of other elements of the balance of payments in the first half of 1931, the residual will give us the net flow on the short term capital account.

The German current account improved sharply during 1931, with a net balance for the year of 1,115 marks or \$265.4 million.[2] Inasmuch as this was due to the more rapid decline in payments than in receipts, and inasmuch as prices and incomes were everywhere falling, it is likely that the German current account was more active in the second half of 1931 than in the first. By linearly allotting the annual surplus [(7/12) (\$265.4 million) = \$154.8 million] we will tend to overestimate the inflow of funds during that period attributable to current transactions and over-estimate the outflow of funds due to other elements.

There was a net inflow of long term capital during 1931 of 180 million marks or \$42.8 million, the sum of an inflow of \$270.1 million and an outflow of \$227.3 million.[3] Inasmuch as we have no data on the distribution of these flows within the year, we will use the values of the gross flows to get the extreme values of our estimate of the net short term capital flow between January and July 1931. We maximize our estimate of the short term outflow if we assume that the entire long term inflow took place early in the year (table 1, cols. 1 and 2) and minimize our

---

[1] Banking and Monetary Statistics, 1943 ed., p. 646.

[2] League of Nations, Balance of Payments Yearbook 1933, pp. 88-90.

[3] ibid.

estimate of the short term outflow if we assume that the long term outflow took place early in the year (table 1, cols. 3 and 4).

Errors and omissions amounted to an outflow of $797.3 million. If we assume that these lay with long term capital, then we minimize our estimate of the short term capital outflow by assuming that these errors occurred in the early part of the year (table 1, col. 4) and maximize our estimate of the short term outflow if we assume the errors took part in the latter part of the year (table 1, col. 1). If these errors lay with the current account, then we should allot them in the same linear manner [(7/12) (-$797.3 million) = -$465.1 million] as we allotted the rest of the current account (table 1, cols. 2, 3).

Table 1 shows the range of estimates of net short term capital outflow from Germany during the period in question under the foregoing assumptions.

Table 1

Estimate 1: Outflow of Short Term Funds from Germany, January 1931 through July 1931 ($000,000)

	1	2	3	4
1. Change in gold and foreign exchange assets	-255.9	-255.9	-255.9	-255.9
2. Flow on current account	+154.8	+154.8	+154.8	+154.8
3. Flow on long term capital	+270.1	+270.1	-227.3	-227.3
4. Errors and omissions	____	-465.1	-465.1	-797.3
5. Estimate 1 of net outflow (-) on short term capital [(1)-(2+3+4) = 5]	-680.8	-215.7	+281.7	+613.9

Source: Change in gold and foreign exchange holdings of the Reichsbank were taken from <u>Banking and Monetary Statistics</u>, p. 646. German balance of payments data was taken from the League of Nations, <u>Balance of Payments Yearbook 1933</u>, pp. 87-89.

b/ The outflow of short term capital based on balance of payments estimates.

The German balance of payments contains estimates of the annual gross and net flows of short term capital, together with errors and omissions, which the compilers apparently felt largely reflected unreported short term capital transactions.[1] In the absence of any information about movements of short term capital within the year, a maximum estimate of the outflow for the period from January through July 1931 may be obtained by assuming that there were no gross inflows of short term funds during this period and that all of errors and omissions reflect unreported short term capital items; a minimum estimate may be obtained by assuming the converse. These estimates are shown in table 2.

Table 2

Estimate 2: Outflow of Short Term Funds from Germany, January 1931 through July 1931. ($000,000)

	High		Low
1/ Outflows of short term capital	-524.8		+739.9
2/ Errors and omissions	-797.3		______
3/ Estimate 2 [(1+2 = 3)]	-1,322.1		+739.9
4/ Mean estimate 2		-291.1	

Source: See notes to table 1.

---

[1] League of Nations, Balance of Payments Yearbook 1933, pp. 89-90.

Total Short Term Capital Exports

While these estimating procedures do serve to give us a rough idea of the minimum and maximum estimates of the size of the short term capital flight from Germany in early 1931, an estimate ranging between an outflow of $1.3 billion and an inflow of $.7 billion is not terribly useful in determining the relationship of short term capital flows to other flows in ordering the factors which contributed to the collapse of the German economy, nor is it very useful to an attempt to determine the effects of short term capital outflows of the German economy. By making further simplifying assumptions and using additional information we can construct a more precise estimate of the outflow, although we increase the already great chance of error.

If we assume that our earlier estimate of the current account balance through July 1931 is correct, that all errors and omissions are attributable to short term capital, and that all inflows and outflows of long term capital occurred at a uniform rate during the year, then the current [+(7/12) (265.4) = $154.8 million] and the long term capital [+(7/12) (42.8) = $25.0 million] accounts imply that holdings of gold and exchange should have risen by $179.8 million. Instead, gold and exchange holdings declined by $255.9 million, implying that there was a net outflow of short term funds amounting to $435.7 million.[1]

Alternatively we might assume that the same factors which led to a liquidation of short term assets would lead to a liquidation of long term assets,[2]

---

[1]See table 1 for source of data.

[2]Fear of devaluation or capital embargo would reduce the attractiveness of German equities and securities denominated in marks; it would increase the attractiveness of repatriating and otherwise purchasing bonds denominated in dollars or sterling.

but otherwise retain our previous assumptions. In this case the current account ($154.8 million) and the long term capital account (-$227.3 million) together imply that the stock of gold and foreign exchange should have declined by $72.5 million. Since these assets actually declined by $225.9 million, net short term capital movements amounted to $153.4 million.[1]

Regional Composition of the Withdrawal of Short Term Funds

The assumption that gold exports by Germany were closely related to the withdrawal of short term funds is confirmed by the sudden drop in German gold reserves during June and July,[2] when qualitative evidence indicates that the withdrawal of short term funds was at its peak.

If this is the case, it is reasonable to assume that the regional composition of German gold exports will give us some clue about the identity of those withdrawing funds. The heaviest withdrawals of gold from Germany were by France, the United States, the United Kingdom and the Netherlands (see table 3). Not surprisingly, these countries, together with Belgium and Switzerland were probably Germany's largest short term creditors.[3]

---

[1]See table 1 for source of data.

[2]Banking and Monetary Statistics, 1943 ed., p. 646. Contrast this with the steady increase in Reichsbank gold and foreign exchange reserves from February through May.

[3]See League of Nations, Balance of Payments Yearbook 1933, p. 92. The nations of origin of German short term credit outstanding on September 30, 1933 are shown.

Table 3

Regional Composition of the
Outflow of Gold from Germany
January 1931 to July 1931

($000,000)

Exports of Gold by Germany to:	[1] 1/31-7/31	[2] 6/31-7/31
United States	36.9	36.9
United Kingdom	36.6	42.0
France	96.4	97.6
Netherlands	22.9	24.0
Switzerland	5.9	6.1
U.S.S.R.	-53.8	-10.4
Other	14.6	15.6
Total[1]	159.4	211.9

Note: [1]Because of rounding, separate items do not add to total.

Source: Calculated from data contained in the Federal Reserve Bulletin, May 1932, p. 320.

Note 4. Some Observations about British Short Term Capital Imports and Exports Between January and September 1931.

In our discussion of Germany we were able to discuss liquidation aided by the knowledge that short term capital exports were likely to be liquidation of existing assets and not new short term lending by Germany. This could not be reasonably assumed in the case of Great Britain. Furthermore, British balance of payments estimates are much less complete than German balance of payments estimates, and in particular, there is no official estimate of the British capital account. However, we may still draw some inferences from the available data.

Britain had a current account deficit amounting to about $471.6 million dollars during 1931;[1] assuming this occurred at a uniform rate during the year, the deficit as of the end of September would have been about $353.7 million.[2] We have incomplete data for long term capital movements, but it appears that £46.1 million in new issues were floated in 1931[3] while £26.8 million in amortization was received[4] leaving a deficit on known long term capital items of £19.3 million or $93.6 million. Assuming that these movements took place at a uniform rate during the year, the net outflow on long term capital prior to the end of September would have been about $70.2 million.

Thus, the total deficit on current and known capital account items by September would have amounted to about $423.9 million under these assumptions. During this period Great Britain exported $321.8 million in monetary gold.[5] The excess of current account and known capital account

---

[1]League of Nations Balance of Payments Yearbook 1933, p. 13; £ = $4.86 throughout.

[2]This is likely to be an overestimate of the deficit for the first nine months of 1931 since the current account deficit appears to have been increasing. In addition, given the large proportion of primary products in British imports, the British balance of payments probably had a seasonal deficit toward the end of the year when most of the world's food crops tend to be harvested and shipped.

[3]League of Nations, Balance of Payments Yearbook 1933, p. 170.

[4]op. cit., p. 173.

[5]Calculated from data contained in the Federal Reserve Bulletin, March 1933, p. 155. Since the merchandise balance includes imports of gold bullion we have subtracted gold imports shown for Straits Settlements, Australia, South Africa, Rhodesia, and West Africa.

items over gold exports indicates that there was during this period a net inflow of either (or both) unknown long term capital items or short term capital amounting to about $100 million. This is little help in estimating the extent of the run, since even a net positive inflow might be the combination of a large inflow at the beginning of the year offset by a large outflow around September; there is, in the absence of other information, an infinite number of pairs of numbers which would suit our requirements.

Another Approach

Great Britain appears to have had merchandise deficits in her relations with the United States, France, Belgium, Netherlands and Switzerland.[1] Unfortunately, this tells us nothing about the service account. However, we do know that Great Britain was in deficit on her overall current account in 1931, so let us assume that she was in deficit with respect to these countries. Let us further assume long term capital account and interest and dividend payments would bring the British balance of payments to zero with respect to these countries.[2]

[1] Commerce Yearbook 1933, p. 350.

[2] This assumption is probably generous, tending to maximize our estimate of the withdrawal of short term capital from Britain by these countries.

British long term assets were concentrated in the Commonwealth areas. If total interest and amortization payments were insufficient to cover the overall British merchandise deficit, then payments from the six countries mentioned earlier were surely not large enough to cover the British deficits with respect to them. Moreover, the British advantage in shipping, and hence, net shipping revenues, would probably tend to be least with respect to countries possessing their own merchant marines or lacking harbors (Switzerland). Therefore, the British probably tended to be in surplus against the Commonwealth and in deficit against Europe and the United States on current account.

(Continued on page 258).

If this is the case, the net outflow of short capital would have equalled the outflow of gold. Since the outflow of gold during the first nine months of 1931 to the major creditors of Britain amounted to about $388.8 million, so by our measure did their net liquidation of short term assets. Of this withdrawal, $386.5 million went to France, Belgium, Netherlands, and Switzerland,[1] and $2.3 million went to the United States.

We can combine this bit of information with others which are available to get an idea of the composition and source of British short term capital movements (table 1). Prior to September 1931 we know of two major inflows of capital amounting to $650 million. Exchange reserves of France, Netherlands, Switzerland, Belgium declined by about $448 million. Inasmuch as these reserves probably also included dollars, $448 million would represent a maximum estimate of official liquidation of sterling reserves during this period by these countries.[2]

(Continued from page 257)

While we can safely neglect the chance of long term investment among these countries during 1931, the great imponderable is transactions in outstanding securities. No-one seems to have very good information about the magnitude of these transactions. Nonetheless, it might reasonably be argued that the same factors which led to foreign liquidation of their short term assets in Britain would have led as well to the liquidation of their long term assets. If this is so, the British balance of payments, excluding short term capital movements, would have been passive with respect to these countries.

[1]Federal Reserve Bulletin, March 1933, p. 155. France, $223.8 million; Belgium, $36.7 million; Netherlands, $96.0 million, Switzerland, $30.0 million. We have no gold flow data by region for Italy. However, Italian foreign exchange reserves declined by $114.3 million during 1931 (calculated from League of Nations Statistical Yearbook 1933-1934, pp. 210-212). It is likely that a good part of this represented sterling liquidation.

[2]World exchange reserves declined by $1,094 million during 1931. Of (Continued on page 260).

Table 1

British Short Term Capital Flows
January 1931 to September 1931

($000,000)

(1) Imports		
	+250	Joint loan by Federal Reserve and Bank of France[a]
	+400	Private loan (joint French and American)[b]
(2) Exports		
	-448	Total decline in exchange reserve holdings of Gold Bloc (excluding Italy)[c]
(3) Net known Imports (-) [1+2=3]	+202	
(4) Net flows of gold to lending creditors	-389	
(5) "Other" flows [4-3=5]	-591	

[a]Federal Reserve Bank of New York Annual Report 1931, p. 12.

[b]ibid.

[c]Calculated from the League of Nations Statistical Yearbook 1933-1934, pp. 210-212.

Table 2

British Short Term Capital Flows
by Source of Transaction
January 1931 to September 1931

($000,000)

	Imports	Exports	Net
Private	+400	-591	-191
Public	+250	-448	-198
Total	+650	-1039	-389

Source: see table 1; see text for description.

The combination of these known flows yields a net inflow of short term funds to Britain of $202 million. However, we estimated earlier that the actual net outflow of funds from Britain to her major creditors was $389 million. Therefore, by implication we missed capital exports of net value of $591 million which presumably were private.

We can show the relative impact of private and official short term transactions by recombining this information (table 2). It appears, on net, that the outflow of capital from Britain was evenly divided between official liquidation of assets held in Britain and private liquidation. This is subject to the qualification that our estimate of official liquidation by these countries was a maximum estimate, leading therefore to a minimum estimate of net private liquidation by these countries. The upper bound to gross private liquidation is $2.1 billion; this represents total British liabilities at the end of 1930, a figure given without reference by Hodson.[1] If we eliminate the $250 million loan by the Federal Reserve and the Bank of France which was aimed at supporting the pound the net outflow of short term capital on other accounts from Britain is estimated at $639 million. Again, we cannot determine precisely the division between private and public official liquidation.

(Continued from page 258.)
this decline, $1,030 million represented the reduction in foreign exchange assets of European central banks. The Gold Bloc, including Italy, accounted for $562 million of this decline. (Calculated from League of Nations Statistical Yearbook 1933-1934, pp. 210-212.)

[1]Hodson, Slump and Recovery, p. 84.

BIBLIOGRAPHY

American Acceptance Council. Acceptance Bulletin. Vol. 10, Nos. 1-12 (January-December 1928).

_________________________. Vol. 11, Nos. 1-12 (January-December 1929).

_________________________. Vol. 12, Nos. 1-12 (January-December 1930).

_________________________. Vol. 13, Nos. 1-12 (January-December 1931).

_________________________. Vol. 16, No. 2 (February 1934).

Ando, Albert and Modigliani, Franco, "The 'Life Cycle' Hypothesis of Saving: Aggregate Implications and Tests," American Economic Review, Vol. LIII, No. 1, part I (March 1963), pp. 55-84.

Angell, James W., Financial Foreign Policy of the United States. New York: Council on Foreign Relations, 1933.

Arena, John J., "The Wealth Effect and Consumption: A Statistical Inquiry," Yale Economic Essays. Vol. 3, No. 2 (Fall 1963), pp. 251-303.

Arndt, H. W., The Economic Lessons of the Nineteen Thirties. Issued under the auspices of the Royal Institute of International Affairs. London, New York: Oxford University Press, 1944.

Balogh, T., "International Reserves and Liquidity," Economic Journal. Vol. LXX, No. 278 (June 1960), pp. 357-377.

Baster, A. S. J., "The International Acceptance Market," American Economic Review. Vol. XXVII, No. 2 (June 1937), pp. 294-304.

Bloomfield, Arthur I., Capital Imports and the American Balance of Payments, 1934-39. Chicago: University of Chicago Press, 1950.

___________________., Monetary Policy Under the International Gold Standard, 1880-1914. New York: Federal Reserve Bank of New York, 1959.

___________________., Short Term Capital Movements under the Pre-1914 Gold Standard. Princeton: International Finance Section, Princeton University, 1963.

Board of Governors of the Federal System. Banking and Monetary Statistics. Washington, D. C., 1943.

______________________________________. Federal Reserve Policy, by Karl R. Bopp, Robert V. Rosa, Carl E. Parry, Woodlief Thomas and Ralph A. Young. Postwar Economic Studies, No. 8. Washington, 1947.

Board of Governors of the Federal Reserve System. *Sixteenth Annual Report of the Federal Reserve Board Covering Operations for the Year 1929*. Washington: Government Printing Office, 1930.

__________. *Twentieth Annual Report of the Federal Reserve Board Covering Operations for the Year 1933*. Washington: Government Printing Office, 1934.

Brems, Hans, "The Foreign Trade Accelerator and the International Transmission of Growth," *Econometrica*. Vol. 24. Mp/ 3 (July 1956), pp. 223-238.

Brown, William Adams. *The International Gold Standard Reinterpreted*. New York: National Bureau of Economic Research, 1940, Vols. I and II.

Burgess, W. Randolph. *Interpretations of Federal Reserve Policy in the Speeches and Writings of Benjamin Strong*. New York: Harper and Brothers Publishers, 1930.

__________. "The Money Market in 1928," *Review of Economic Statistics*, Vol. II, No. 1 (February 1929), pp. 19-25.

Cairnes, J. E. *Some Leading Principles of Political Economy* (1874 Ed.). New York: Harper, 1874.

Carr, E. H., *The Twenty Years' Crisis, 1919-1939*. London: Macmillan and Co., Ltd., 1958.

Chandler, Lester V., *Benjamin Strong, Central Banker*. Washington: Brookings Institute, 1958.

Chase-National Bank, *Report of the Chairman of the Board of Directors*, (1926-1932).

Clarke, Stephen. *Central Bank Cooperation, 1924-1931*. New York: Federal Reserve Bank of New York, 1967.

Clay, Sir Henry. *Lord Norman*. London: Macmillan and Co., Ltd., 1957.

Dakin, Allin W., "Foreign Securities in the American Money Market, 1914-30," *Harvard Business Review*. Vol. X, No. 2 (January 1932), pp. 227-40.

Domar, Evsey D., "The Effect of Foreign Investment on the Balance of Payments," *American Economic Review*. Vol. XL, No. 5, part I (December 1950), pp. 805-26.

Dulles, Eleanor Lansing. *The French Franc, 1914-1928*. New York: The Macmillan Company, 1929.

Einzig, Paul. *A Dynamic Theory of Foreign Exchange*. London: Macmillan Co., 1961.

__________. *Behind the Scenes of International Finance.* London: Macmillan and Co., Ltd., 1932.

__________. *The Theory of Forward Exchange*. London: Macmillan and Co., Ltd., 1937.

European Economic and Political Survey. Issued by Reference Service on International Affairs. American Library in Paris, 1926, Vol. II, Nos. 2, 3, 5, 7, 8, 9, 10, 11, 15.

Federal Reserve Bank of New York. Annual Report. (December 1928).

__________. Annual Report. (December 1929).

__________. Annual Report. (December 1930).

__________. Annual Report. (December 1931).

__________. Annual Report. (December 1932).

__________. Annual Report. (December 1933).

__________. Annual Report. (December 1934).

__________. Monthly Review of Credit and Business Conditions (February 1, 1928 and July 1, 1928).

Feiler, Arthur, "International Movements of Capital," American Economic Review, Vol. 25 (May 1935), pp. 63-73.

Firestone, John M., Federal Receipts and Expenditures During Business Cycles, 1879-1958. National Bureau of Economic Research. Princeton: Princeton University Press, 1960.

Friedman, Milton and Schwartz, Anna. Monetary History of the United States, 1867-1960. National Bureau of Economic Research Study. Princeton: Princeton University Press, 1963.

Furth, J. Herbert, "Unbalanced International Accounts: Diagnosis and Therapy," American Economic Review/s, Vol. LI, No. 2 (April 1961), pp. 430-38.

Gordon, R. A., Business Fluctuations, 2nd ed. New York: Harper and Brothers, 1961.

Harberger, Arnold C., ed., The Demand for Durable Goods. Chicago: University of Chicago Press, 1960.

Hardy, Charles O. The Warren-Pearson Price Theory. Washington, D. C.: Brookings Institute, 1935.

Hart, A. G. and Keumen, P. B., Money, Debt, and Economic Activity. Englewood Cliffs, N. J.: Prentice-Hall, 1961.

Harvard Economic Service, Weekly Letters, Vol. VI (1927).

Hinshaw, Randall, "International Investment, Foreign Investment, and American Employment," American Economic Review/s, Vol. 36, No. 2 (May 1946), pp. 66-71.

Hodson, H. V., Slump and Recovery. New York: Oxford University Press, 1938

Holmes, Alan R., *The New York Foreign Exchange Market*. New York: Federal Reserve Bank of New York, 1960.

Institute of International Finance, *Institute of International Finance Bulletin*, No. 51 (April 14, 1932).

Iversen, Carl. *Aspects of the Theory of International Capital Movements*. London: Oxford University Press, 1935.

Johnson, Harry. "Equilibrium Growth in an International Economy," *Canadian Journal of Economics*, Vol. 19: 478-500 (November 1953).

Keynes, John Maynard. *A Treatise on Money*. London: Macmillan & Co., Ltd., 1930.

__________________. *Essays in Persuasion*, 1932 ed. New York: Harcourt, Brace, and Company, 1932.

Kindleberger, C. P., *Economic Growth in France and Britain, 1851-1950*. Cambridge, Massachusetts: Harvard U. Press, 1964.

__________________. *International Economics*, Revised edition. Homewood, Illinois: Richard D. Irwin, Inc., 1958. 1968 Edition.

__________________. *International Short-Term Capital Movements*. New York: Columbia University Press, 1937.

__________________. "Industrial Europe's Terms of Trade on Current Account, 1870-1953," *Economic Journal*, Vol. 65, No. 257 (March 1955), pp. 19-35.

Knapp, John. "The Theory of International Capital Movements and Its Verification," Review of Economic Studies, Vol. X, No. 2 (Summer, 1943) pp. 115-121.

Kuznets, Simon. *Capital in the American Economy*. A National Bureau of Economic Research Study. Princeton: Princeton University Press, 1961.

__________________. "Long Term Trends in Capital Information Proportions," *Economic Development and Cultural Change*, Vol. IX, No. 4, Part II, July 1961.

__________________. "Quantitative Aspects of the Economic Growth of Nations: VI. Long Term Trends in Capital Formation Proportions," *Economic Development and Cultural Change*, Vol. IX, No. 4, Part II (July 1961).

Lary, Hal B., "Disturbance and Adjustment in Recent U. S. Balance of Payments Experience," *American Economic Review/s*, Vol. LI, No. 2 (April 1961), pp. 417-29.

League of Nations. *Balance of Payments Yearbook*, Series II, Economic and Financial, 1927-29, No. 54.

__________________. Balance of Payments Yearbook, Series II, Economic and Financial, 1928, No. 16 (1929).

League of Nations. Balance of Payments Yearbook, Series II, Economic and Financial, 1931-32, No. 26 (1933).

________. Balance of Payments Yearbook, Series II, Economic and Financial, 1933, No. 19 (1934).

________. Balance of Payments Yearbook, Series II, Economic and Financial, 1934, No. 20 (1935).

________. Course and Phases of the World Economic Depression, by Bertil Ohlin. Geneva: Secretariat of the League of Nations, 1931.

________. Industrialization and Foreign Trade. Series II. A League of Nations Publications, Economic and Financial, No. 20 (1945).

________. Monthly Bulletin of Statistics, Vol. XV, No. 1 (January 1934).

________. Monthly Bulletin of Statistics, Vol. II, 1930

________. Statistical Yearbook of the League of Nations, for 1930-31, Series II. A., No. 16. Geneva: League of Nations, 1931.

________. Statistical Yearbook of the League of Nations, for 1933-34, Series II. A., No. 6. Geneva: League of Nations, 1934.

________. Statistical Yearbook of the League of Nations, for 1934-35, Series II. A., No. 3. Geneva: League of Nations, 1935.

________. World Production and Prices, 1925-1934. Geneva: League of Nations, 1935.

Leuchtenberg, William E. The Perils of Prosperity. Chicago: University of Chicago Press, 1962 [paperback]

Machlup, Fritz. "The Liquidity of Short-Term Capital," Economica, Vol. XI, No. 33 (August 1932), pp. 271-84.

________. "Three Concepts of the Balance of Payments and the So-Called Dollar Shortage," Economic Journal, Vol. LX, No. 237 (March 1950), pp. 46-68.

Maizels, A. Industrial Growth and World Trade. New York: Cambridge University Press, 1965.

Mitchell, Broadus. Depression Decade. New York: Holt, Rhinehart and Winston, 1966.

Moreau, Emile. Souvenirs d'un Gouverneur de La Banque de France. Paris: M. - T. Génin, 1954.

Morgenstern, Oskar. International Financial Transactions and Business Cycles. National Bureau of Economic Research Study in Business Cycles. Princeton: Princeton University Press, 1959.

Morgenstern, Oskar. The Validity of International Gold Movement Statistics. Princeton: International Finance Section, Princeton University, 1955.

Moulton, Harold G. and Pasvolsky, Leo. War Debts and World Prosperity. Published for the Brookings Institution, New York: The Century Co., 1932.

______________________________. World War Debt Settlements. New York: The Macmillan Company, 1926.

Nevins, Allan. The Emergence of Lincoln, Vol. II. New York: Scribner, 1950.

New York Stock Exchange, New York Stock Exchange Bulletin, Vols. I through V, (April 1930-December 1934).

Polak, J. J., "The Repercussions of Economic Fluctuation in the U. S. on Other Parts of the World," International Monetary Fund Special Papers, Vol. V. No. 2 (August 1956), pp. 279-83.

Preston, H. H., "Europe's Return to Gold". Harvard Business Review, Vol. IX, No. 3 (March 1931), pp. 319-29.

Royal Institute of International Affairs. The International Gold Problem; Collected Papers. London: Oxford University Press, H. Milford, 1931.

______________________________. The Problem of International Investment, 1937. New York: Oxford University Press, 1937.

Samuelson, Paul A. Newsweek, March 18, 1968, p. 89.

Schacht, Hjalwar. "The Money Markets Fore and After the War," Harvard Business Review, Vol. IX, No. 2 (January 1931), pp. 129-39.

Seers, Dudley. "A Model of Comparative Rates of Growth in the World Economy," Economic Journal, Vol. 72 (March 1962), pp. 45-78.

Silverstein, Nathan. "Effects of the American Devaluation on Prices and Export Trade," American Economic Review, Vol. XXVII, No. 2 (June 1937), pp. 279-93.

Soule, George. Prosperity Decade. New York: Holt, Rhinehart and Winston, 1964.

Spraos, John. "The Theory of Forward Exchange and Recent Practice," Manchester School, Vol. XXI, No. 2 (May 1953), pp. 87-117.

Stolper, et al. The German Economy: 1870 to the Present. New York: Harcourt, Brace and World, Inc., 1967.

Stolper, Gustav. "Where Do We Stand?", Harvard Business Review, Vol. IX, No. 3 (March 1931), pp. 289-98.

Triffin, Robert. The Evolution of the International Monetary System: Historical Reappraisal and Future Perspectives. Princeton: International Finance Section, Princeton University, 1964.

Triffin, Robert. Gold and the Dollar Crisis. New Haven: Yale University Press, 1960.

United Nations. Department of Economic Affairs. International Capital Movements During the Inter-War Period. Lake Success, New York, October 1949.

____________. Statistical Yearbook, 1956.

____________. Statistical Yearbook, 1948.

United States Department of Commerce. Commerce Yearbook, Vol. II, 1931.

____________. Commerce Yearbook, Vol. II, 1929 (1927 data).

____________. Commerce Yearbook, Vol. II, 1923 (1923 data).

____________. Commerce Yearbook, Vol. II, 1924 (1924 data).

____________. Commerce Yearbook, Vol. II, 1926 (1925 data).

____________. Commerce Yearbook, Vol. II, 1928 (1926-27 data).

____________. Commerce Yearbook, Vol. II, 1932 (1928-30 data).

____________. Commerce Yearbook, Vol. II, 1933.

United States Department of Commerce, Bureau of the Census. Historical Statistics of the United States, Colonial Times to 1957. Washington, 1960.

____________. Statistical Abstract of the U. S. for 1930. Washington: U. S. Government Printing Office, 1930.

United States Department of Commerce, Office of Business Economics. Survey of Current Business, Vol. 12 (1932).

____________. Survey of Current Business, Vol. 16 (1936).

____________. Survey of Current Business, Vol. 45, No. 9 (September 1965).

____________. "American Direct Investments in Foreign Countries," Trade Information Bulletin, No. 731.

____________. "American Underwriting of Foreign Securities in 1930," Trade Information Bulletin, No. 746.

____________. "A New Estimate of American Investments Abroad," Trade Information Bulletin, No. 767.

United States Department of Commerce, Office of Business Economics. "The Balance of International Payments," (1927-1935), Trade Information Bulletin, Nos. 552, 625, 698, 761, 803, 814, 819, 826, 833.

__________________________________. "The Balance of Payments of the U. S. in 1937," Economic Series, No. 3.

__________________________________. "Banking System and Practices in France," Trade Information Bulletin, No. 740.

__________________________________. "Foreign Trade of the U.S., 1927," Trade Information Bulletin, No. 537.

__________________________________. "Foreign Trade of the U. S., 1929," Trade Information Bulletin, No. 684.

__________________________________. "Foreign Trade of the U.S., 1930," Trade Information Bulletin, No. 749.

__________________________________. "Overseas Travel and Travel Expenditures," Economic Series, No. 4, by August Maffry.

__________________________________. "The United States in the World Economy," Economic Series, No. 23, by Hal B. Lary.

__________________________________. Foreign Investments in the United States. Washington: U. S. Government Printing Office, 1937.

Viner, Jacob. Canada'a Balance of International Indebtedness, 1900-1913. Cambridge: Harvard University Press, 1924.

Warburg, James P., The Money Muddle. Alfred A. Knopf: New York, 1934.

Whale, P. Barrett. "International Short-Term Capital Movements," Economica, Vol. VI, No. 21 (February 1939), pp. 30-39.

White, Harry Dexter. The French International Accounts, 1800-1913. Cambridge: Harvard University Press, 1933.

Wicker, Elmus. Federal Reserve Monetary Policy, 1917-1933. New York: Random House, 1966.

Williams, David. "London and the 1931 Financial Crisis," Economic History Review, Vol. XV, No. 3 (April 1963).

______________. "The 1931 Financial Crisis," Yorkshire Bulletin of Economics and Social Research, Vol. 15, No. 2 (November 1963).

Williams, John H., Argentine International Trade Under Inconvertible Paper, 1880-1900. Cambridge: Harvard University Press, 1920.

Wright, Carl Major. "Convertibility and Triangular Trade as Safeguards Against Economic Depression," Economic Journal, Vol. 65, No. 259 (September 1955), pp. 422-35.

Youngson, A. J., The British Economy, 1920-1957. London: George Allen and Unwin Ltd., 1960.

Dissertations in American Economic History

An Arno Press Collection

Adams, Donald R., Jr. **Wage Rates in Philadelphia, 1790-1830.** (Doctoral Dissertation, University of Pennsylvania, 1967). 1975

Aldrich, Terry Mark. **Rates of Return on Investment in Technical Education in the Ante-Bellum American Economy.** (Doctoral Dissertation, The University of Texas at Austin, 1969). 1975

Anderson, Terry Lee. **The Economic Growth of Seventeenth Century New England:** A Measurement of Regional Income. (Doctoral Dissertation, University of Washington, 1972). 1975

Bean, Richard Nelson. **The British Trans-Atlantic Slave Trade, 1650-1775.** (Doctoral Dissertation, University of Washington, 1971). 1975

Brock, Leslie V. **The Currency of the American Colonies, 1700-1764:** A Study in Colonial Finance and Imperial Relations. (Doctoral Dissertation, University of Michigan, 1941). 1975

Ellsworth, Lucius F. **Craft to National Industry in the Nineteenth Century:** A Case Study of the Transformation of the New York State Tanning Industry. (Doctoral Dissertation, University of Delaware, 1971). 1975

Fleisig, Heywood W. **Long Term Capital Flows and the Great Depression:** The Role of the United States, 1927-1933. (Doctoral Dissertation, Yale University, 1969). 1975

Foust, James D. **The Yeoman Farmer and Westward Expansion of U. S. Cotton Production.** (Doctoral Dissertation, University of North Carolina at Chapel Hill, 1968). 1975

Golden, James Reed. **Investment Behavior By United States Railroads, 1870-1914.** (Doctoral Thesis, Harvard University, 1971). 1975

Hill, Peter Jensen. **The Economic Impact of Immigration into the United States.** (Doctoral Dissertation, The University of Chicago, 1970). 1975

Klingaman, David C. **Colonial Virginia's Coastwise and Grain Trade.** (Doctoral Dissertation, University of Virginia, 1967). 1975

Lang, Edith Mae. **The Effects of Net Interregional Migration on Agricultural Income Growth:** The United States, 1850-1860. (Doctoral Thesis, The University of Rochester, 1971). 1975

Lindley, Lester G. **The Constitution Faces Technology:** The Relationship of the National Government to the Telegraph, 1866-1884. (Doctoral Thesis, Rice University, 1971). 1975

Lorant, John H[erman]. **The Role of Capital-Improving Innovations in American Manufacturing During the 1920's.** (Doctoral Thesis, Columbia University, 1966). 1975

Mishkin, David Joel. **The American Colonial Wine Industry:** An Economic Interpretation, Volumes I and II. (Doctoral Thesis, University of Illinois, 1966). 1975

Oates, Mary J. **The Role of the Cotton Textile Industry in the Economic Development of the American Southeast:** 1900-1940. (Doctoral Dissertation, Yale University, 1969). 1975

Passell, Peter. **Essays in the Economics of Nineteenth Century American Land Policy.** (Doctoral Dissertation, Yale University, 1970). 1975

Pope, Clayne L. **The Impact of the Ante-Bellum Tariff on Income Distribution.** (Doctoral Dissertation, The University of Chicago, 1972). 1975

Poulson, Barry Warren. **Value Added in Manufacturing, Mining, and Agriculture in the American Economy From 1809 To 1839.** (Doctoral Dissertation, The Ohio State University, 1965). 1975

Rockoff, Hugh. **The Free Banking Era: A Re-Examination.** (Doctoral Dissertation, The University of Chicago, 1972). 1975

Schumacher, Max George. **The Northern Farmer and His Markets During the Late Colonial Period.** (Doctoral Dissertation, University of California at Berkeley, 1948). 1975

Seagrave, Charles Edwin. **The Southern Negro Agricultural Worker:** 1850-1870. (Doctoral Dissertation, Stanford University, 1971). 1975

Solmon, Lewis C. **Capital Formation by Expenditures on Formal Education, 1880 and 1890.** (Doctoral Dissertation, The University of Chicago, 1968). 1975

Swan, Dale Evans. **The Structure and Profitability of the Antebellum Rice Industry:** 1859. (Doctoral Dissertation, University of North Carolina at Chapel Hill, 1972). 1975

Sylla, Richard Eugene. **The American Capital Market, 1846-1914:** A Study of the Effects of Public Policy on Economic Development. (Doctoral Thesis, Harvard University, 1968) 1975

Uselding, Paul John. **Studies in the Technological Development of the American Economy During the First Half of the Nineteenth Century.** (Doctoral Dissertation, Northwestern University, 1970) 1975

Walsh, William D[avid]. **The Diffusion of Technological Change in the Pennsylvania Pig Iron Industry, 1850-1870.** (Doctoral Dissertation, Yale University, 1967). 1975

Weiss, Thomas Joseph. **The Service Sector in the United States, 1839 Through 1899.** (Doctoral Thesis, University of North Carolina at Chapel Hill, 1967). 1975

Zevin, Robert Brooke. **The Growth of Manufacturing in Early Nineteenth Century New England.** 1975

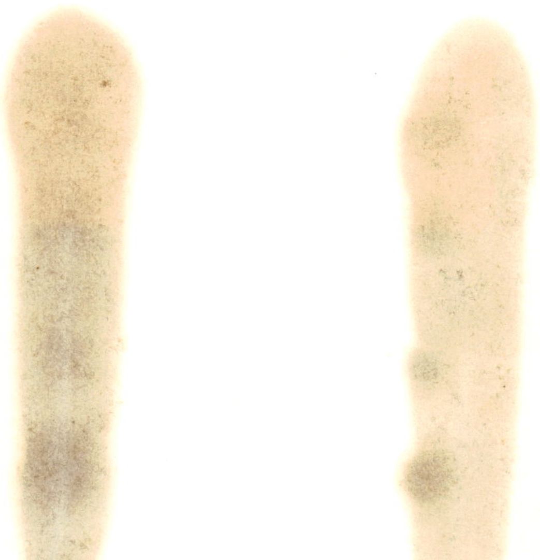